Beltane

Beltane: A Guide, Workbook and Journal

Robin Ginther Venneri

KIPS Publishing LLC
Rochester, PA

LEGAL DISCLAIMER

We, KIPS Publishing, and the author Robin Ginther-Venneri are not herbal experts by any means and are not medical professionals. The products available, along with statements, opinions, views expressed, ideas, notes, procedures, and suggestions in this book, on the blog, on the website, in e-Books, on Facebook, Pinterest, and/or Twitter pages, and any follow-up comments on-site or by email, are opinions and are meant for informational purposes only. They are not meant to be used to diagnose, treat, prescribe, prevent, or cure any disease or to administer in any manner to any physical ailments and are not intended as a substitute for the medical advice of a trained health professional. We cannot be held liable for your decisions and choices and/or the outcome of those decisions and choices. You are encouraged to do your own research and consult your healthcare professional before treating yourself or anyone else.

The information in this book, on the blog, on the website, in e-Books, on Facebook, Pinterest, and/or Twitter pages, and any follow-up comments on-site or by email is general and not specific to individuals and their circumstances. You must study herbs thoroughly and talk with a healthcare practitioner before you treat yourself or anyone else. All matters regarding your health require medical supervision. Please consult your health care professional before adopting the statements, opinions, views expressed, ideas, notes, procedures, and suggestions in this book, on the website, in e-Books, on Facebook, Pinterest, and/or Twitter pages, and any follow-up comments on-site or by email, as well as about any condition that may require diagnosis or medical attention.

Herbs are very powerful, and if they are misused, they can be harmful. Herbs can also cause allergic reactions and interfere with traditional medications by blocking their effectiveness, increasing their effectiveness, or reacting with them in a harmful way. Always check with your health care professional before using herbs or herbal products!

Do not use herbal products of any kind if you are nursing, pregnant, taking medications, or undergoing treatment for any medical condition without consulting your health care professional.

Any plant substance, whether used as food or medicine, externally or internally, can cause an allergic reaction in some people. Neither KIPS Publishing nor the author Robin Ginther-Venneri can be held responsible for claims arising from the mistaken identity of any herbs or from the use of any remedy or healing regime or because you did not first seek the advice of a trained healthcare professional as recommended. Do not try self-diagnosis or self-treatment for serious or long-term problems without consulting a healthcare professional. Do not undertake self-treatment while undergoing a prescribed course of medical treatment without seeking professional advice. Always seek medical advice if symptoms persist.

In addition, the statements made by the author regarding any products and/or services represent opinions alone. They do not constitute a recommendation or endorsement of any product or service by KIPS Publishing or the author. We, KIPS Publishing, and Robin Ginther-Venneri disclaim any liability arising directly or indirectly from the use of this book, on the website, on the blog, in e-Books, a class, class notes, follow-up email contacts, or of any products available or mentioned herein.

Additionally, the statements on the website, on the blog, in e-Books, on Facebook, Pinterest, and/or Twitter pages, and any follow-up comments on these sites or by email, have not been evaluated by the FDA. The information on this site is not intended to diagnose, treat, or cure any disease.

Thank you,
KIPS Publishing

Print ISBN: 979-8-9875591-3-0
SECOND EDITION, 2023
KIPS Publishing LLC
Rochester, PA
www.kipspublishingllc.com

Everyone's approach to their craft is totally unique and awesome, and it doesn't matter what others do as long as you're happy with what you're doing. The only thing that counts is what speaks to you and what moves your soul. Different things work for other people-like the photo of the dress that went viral on Facebook in 2015, for example. Did you see it as white-gold or blue-black? The practice of Witchcraft works the same way. I think it is subjective to your own interpretation of what you see, hear, and feel. In my books, I write about the basics with the intention of giving you a starting point for your own research or something new entirely. I'm not perfect, and I don't know everything (if we're being honest), I don't know anything. But I do think that every journey should always be about learning and growing your knowledge. And as I research some of these things, I'm learning right alongside you. So I guess I'm saying that everyone is on their own enlightenment path, and that you are not alone!

As always,
Blessings to You and Yours

Contents

Acknowledgments

Amber and Moji ~ Carpe Diem Holistic Wellness. I'm so blessed to have you in my life. Your friendship, support, and encouragement mean the world to me - from our chats over wine at your shop to being welcomed into a circle of amazing girls – thank you for making me feel part of something special.

Colby Chance Parrish ~ The Wondering Fool, You have been my rock throughout this journey. I am so thankful for all the beautiful gifts you have given me: your wise guidance, valuable support, meaningful contributions, and, most importantly - a friendship I will always treasure. With deep love and appreciation- thank you!

Jamie ~ Lightworker Path. Without your help and companionship, I would have never been able to unlock the power of meditation—something that has brought me so much joy. Thank you for supporting my journey!

Melissa ~ Melusina, Astrology Oracle. Words cannot express how grateful I am for your help. Your kind and generous gestures were essential in leading me down a better path. You have been not only my guide but also my friend, lighting the way with sincere advice that will continue to remain close to my heart. Thank you so much!

Suzanne ~ Whimsical Cauldron and Crafts. I'm so lucky to have a friend like you! Your generosity, compassion, and willingness to share your knowledge of crystals have been invaluable gifts for which I am forever grateful.

Teresa ~ Odie's Curiosities. I'm beyond blessed to have you in my life; the memories we share are truly precious. Every time I see your beaming face, I feel so cherished that I am part of your world!

Lylah ~ I deeply appreciate your profound impact on my life. Your presence has brought me unfathomable joy and restored hope to every corner of my being, making these books possible. I can never express in words how much I love you; it surpasses all measure!

Jeff ~ I'm so lucky to have my husband by my side, empowering me with patience and support throughout this journey, something I could not have achieved on my own five years ago.

Readers ~ I am so grateful to everyone who has supported me throughout my growth as a writer. Your encouragement helps fuel the creative process, allowing me to craft books that I hope will bring joy and inspiration for years to come!

WHEEL OF THE YEAR

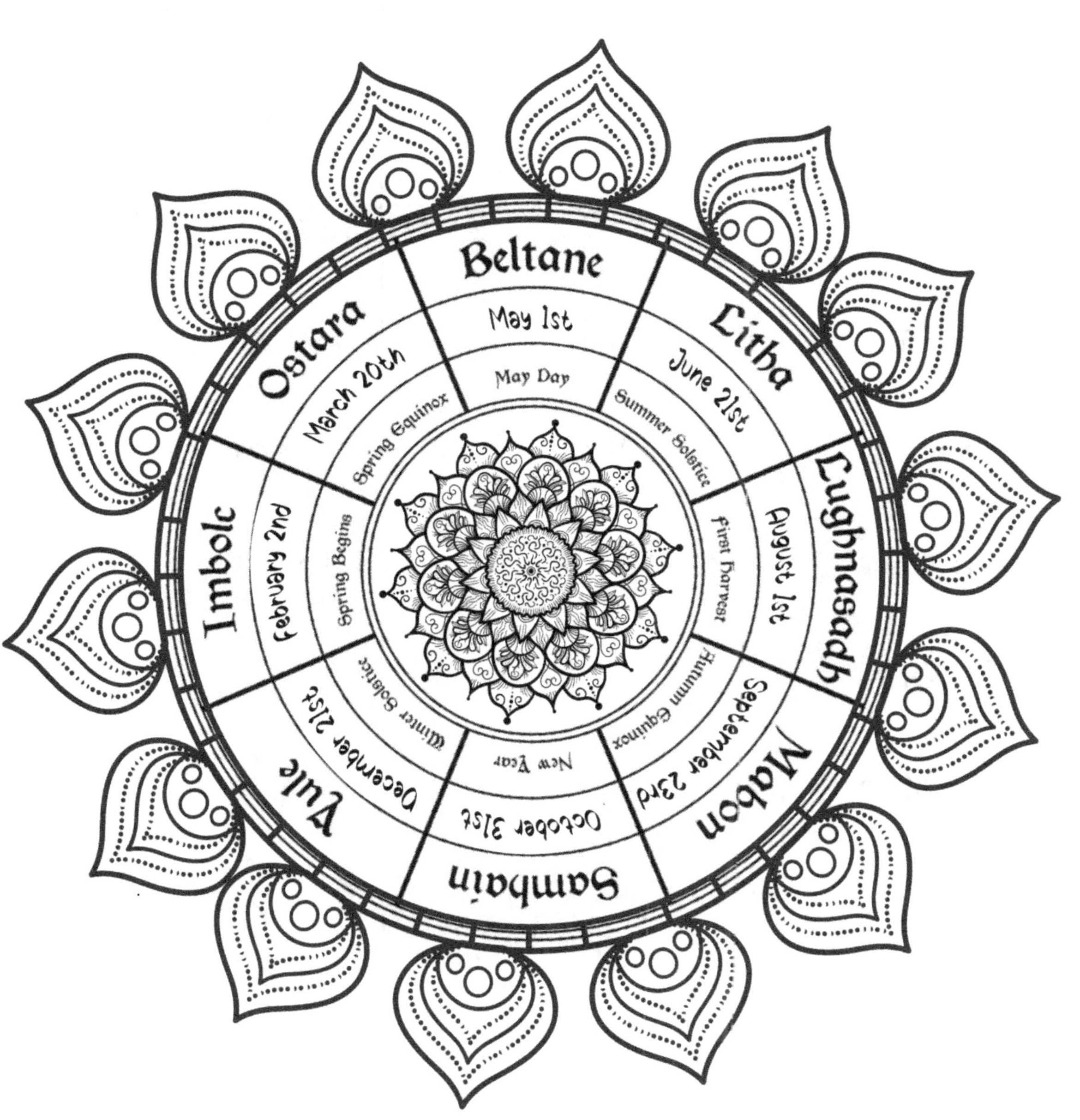

Sabbat Dates

Sabbat	**Northern Hemisphere Date**	**Southern Hemisphere Date**
Imbolic	February 1-2	August 1-2
Ostara	March 19-21	September 20-23
Beltane	May 1	October 31
Litha	June 20-22	December 20-23
Lammas	August 1-2	February 1-2
Mabon	September 21-24	March 20-22
Samhain	October 31	April 30
Yule	December 20-23	June 20-22

Beltane at a Glance

Beltane - May 1st or November 1st in the Southern Hemisphere

Also called: Lá Bealtaine (Irish), Latha Bealltainn (Scottish Gaelic), Laa Boaltinn/Boaldyn (Manx), Beltain; Beltine; Beltany

Beltane, also spelled Beltine, Irish Beltaine, or Belltaine, also known as Cétamain

Commonly observed on the first of May, the festival falls midway between the spring equinox and summer solstice in the northern hemisphere. The festival name is synonymous with the month marking the start of summer in Ireland, May being Mí na Bealtaine. Historically, it was widely observed throughout Ireland, Scotland, and the Isle of Man. In Irish, the name for the festival day is Lá Bealtaine ([l̪ˠaː ˈbʲal̪ˠt̪ˠənʲə]), in Scottish Gaelic Latha Bealltainn ([l̪ˠaː ˈpjaul̪ˠt̪ɪɲ]), and in Manx Gaelic Laa Boaltinn/Boaldyn. Beltane is one of the principal four Gaelic seasonal festivals—along with Samhain, Imbolc, and Lughnasadh—and is similar to the Welsh Calan Mai.

See Also:
May Day, Calan Mai, Walpurgis Night

There is no right or wrong way to celebrate any of the Sabbats. Pagans base their celebrations on cultural traditions, historical practices, and inclinations.

So live and let live!

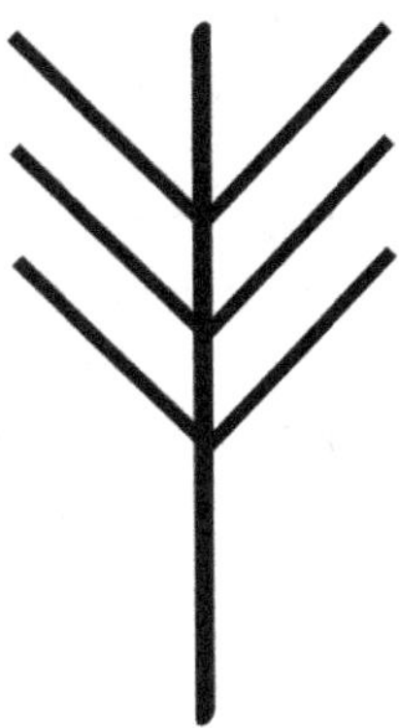

Beltane

Beltane, also spelled Beltine, Irish Beltaine, or Belltaine, also known as Cétamain, is a festival held on the first day of May in Ireland and Scotland, celebrating the beginning of summer and open pasturing. Beltane has a recorded history dating back to ninth-century Ireland. According to texts, cattle were driven through two bonfires on Beltane as part of a ritualistic way to prevent them from getting ill before they entered their summer pastures. Customs like this were still happening in the nineteenth century, along with other traditional activities such as Maypole dances and picking green boughs and flowers.

In early Irish lore, Beltane was the focus of several important customs and beliefs. As with other pre-Christian Celtic societies, the Irish recognized two periods in their annual calendar: winter and the start of the year on November 1 (Samain) and midsummer and summer on May 1 (Beltaine). During these crossroads between worlds, it was believed that certain restrictions between humans and supernatural forces were temporarily lifted – fairies and witches could roam freely. Accordingly, precautions would have to be taken to protect against their influence.

The term Beltaine has been traced to its roots in the name of a god, "Bel" or "Bil," and the Old Irish word for fire, "Tene." Despite disputes concerning its origin, some scholars in the 20th century proposed an etymological link between the first element of the word and Belenos, an ancient Gaulish deity.

Beltane is a special time to celebrate the fertility and abundance of the earth. On this day, ancient communities would observe rituals to honor the union between Earth's Mother and Fertility God, bringing new life into being.

Today, there are still many ways to mark Beltane. From small group gatherings and individual practitioners alike, people have access to numerous rites and ceremonies that focus on the celebration of fertility. Examples include circle casting, crafting wreaths with ribbons or flowers, creating maypole poles with greenery, and festive baking cakes stuffed with luck tokens and fertility symbols like rabbits or eggs. Alternatively, you could also build a bonfire for purification purposes or offer prayers for newly sowed seeds in your garden. No matter how you decide to celebrate it—on your own or with a group—with observance of these traditions come hopes for abundance in our lives!

Set Up Your Beltane Altar
Beltane Prayers
Celebrate Beltane With a Maypole Dance
Honor the Sacred Feminine with a Goddess Ritual
Beltane Bonfire
Handfasting Ceremonies

Celtic Reconstructionists

Celtic Reconstructionists aim to practice early Celtic religion as accurately to history as possible. They often time their Beltane celebrations by observing visible signs in Nature. When the local hawthorn trees begin to flower, it can be interpreted as a signal that Beltane's time has arrived. Alternatively, Beltane may be celebrated on the first full moon following the blossoming of the hawthorns or timed to coincide with the date when the sun is at fifteen degrees Taurus. Many Celtic Reconstructionists refer to Beltane by its Gaelic name, Lá Bealtaine. Like the Celts themselves, Celtic Reconstructionists typically mark Beltane with ritual bonfires. Two bonfires are lit, and live-stock pets and people are passed between them to ensure blessings and protection. Afterward, candles might be lit from the main fire and brought home, a reflection of the original Celtic tradition of relighting the hearth fires from the sacred Beltane flames. Modern practitioners may substitute torches or candles in urban areas where bonfires aren't possible.

Feasting and general merrymaking are also popular traditions, and traditional Celtic foods and beverages are sometimes prepared. Flowering tree branches might be brought inside the home, and rowan crosses are often hung on the wall to gain magickal protection. Once widely known and commonly praised throughout the British Isles as a protective charm, a rowan cross is an equal-armed cross made from two pieces of rowan wood, which is often tied in the middle with a piece of red thread. May bushes may also be used, and deities are honored. Celtic Reconstructionists might also celebrate Beltane by visiting wells, where prayers or praises to the spirit of the well may be uttered, and offerings are left behind.

Druids

Unlike Celtic Reconstructionists, who strive to follow the historical religion of the ancient Celts as closely as is feasible, modern Druids are more of the Celtic Revivalist style, picking and choosing from ancient Celtic beliefs and adapting these for current times. Contemporary Druids are often eclectic, merging various traditions and new inventions with the time-honored practices of the ancient Celts. Modern Druids may mark Beltane with a ritual in honor of the goddess Danu, the earth mother, and the god Belenos, the sun king. Beltane is seen as a time to celebrate fertility, union, and sexuality. It's a time of protection and purification, and it's a time to honor the dead. Faeries are believed to make extra mischief on Belt-ane, the veil between the worlds thinning at this time just as it does on Samhain. Some modern Druids may wear bells to help keep the naughty faeries at bay. Prayers for health, prosperity, protection, and love may be made, and offerings of bread, beer, or mead are left for the gods and the dead.

Heathen

Heathenry encompasses Asatru and other Neopagan paths that practice the pre-Christian religious traditions of Germany, Scandinavia, and other places in northern Europe. While May Day celebrations aren't among the most important holidays of the Heathen year, many modern Heathens do mark the occasion, celebrating the Germanic holiday of Walburg, or Walpurgis Night, on April 30 and celebrating May Day on May 1. It's a time when magick is believed to be afoot, a time when spirits wander. So Heathens today may mark the occasion with a great bonfire, a simple feast, and liberal toasts made to the god Wotan (aka Odin) and the magick goddesses.

Traditional

Traditional Witchcraft is the religion of non-Wiccan witches who base their practices on pre-Christian animism, traditional folk magick, and an often polytheistic belief system. Traditional Witchcraft varies from place to place, and specific practices are based on the local culture and the environment in which one lives. Some Traditional witches celebrate the solstices and equinoxes, and some celebrate the four cross-quarter days, but most do not celebrate both. Traditionally, either the solstices and equinoxes were honored, or the cross-quarter days were honored according to local lifestyles and the needs of the land.

Traditions that were mostly agricultural tended to celebrate the solstices and equinoxes. In contrast, more pastoral-based traditions with their roots in Celtic lands acknowledge the cross-quarter and systems such as tarot, runes, pendulums, or the I Ching to discern the general outlook for health, wealth, love, and over.

Wicca

Wicca is a Witchcraft tradition introduced near the middle of the twentieth century and based on Pre-Christian religion, animistic belief, and shamanic principles and practices. Most Wiccans revere a male deity known as the Horned God and a female, triple-aspected deity known as the Triple Goddess. Her three aspects are referred to as the Maiden, the Mother, and the Crone. Most Wiccans tend to be eclectic in their practices. While certain traditional methods or guidelines might be adhered to, there is usually plenty of room for personalization, improvisation, and creativity. Wiccan Beltane celebrations typically focus on fertility and sexuality, though themes of abundance, protection, purification, or growth might also be prevalent. Maypole dances often take center stage, and many local groups host large community get-togethers. There's usually a bonfire or two, along with a fair amount of revelry, merrymaking, and mayhem.

Quicky Beltane Correspondences

Deities and Heroes

Goddesses

Aphrodite (Greek)
Artemis (Greek)
Astarte (Greek)
Bona Dea (Roman)
Chin-hua-fu-jen (Chinese)
Danu (Irish)
Diana (Roman)
Flora (Roman)
Freya (Norse)
Horae (Greek)
Maia (Greek)
Prosperina (Roman)
Rauni (Finnish)
Sarasvati (Hindu)
Venus (Roman)

Gods

Apollo (Greek)
Baldur (Norse)
Beal, Bel, or Belenos (Celtic)
Cernunnos (Celtic)
Chung K'uei (Chinese)
Horned God (Celtic)
Odin (Norse)
Pan (Greek)
Pluto (Greek)
Ra (Egyptian)
Wotan (Germanic)

Archaeoastronomical Timing

Astrological Timing and Associated Planets

The astronomical midpoint between the Spring Equinox and Summer Solstice; is the Sun at 15 degrees of Taurus in the Northern Hemisphere and the Sun at 15 degrees of Scorpio in the Southern Hemisphere. Some Pagans celebrate Beltane on the astronomical date, while others stick to May 1 out of tradition. Still, others wait for visible clues in nature. When the hawthorn blossoms, it signals that Beltane has officially arrived.

Archetypes

FEMALE

Earth Goddess
Goddesses associated with water, plants, or animals, the Lover preparing to lie with her Beloved Maiden Goddess, Mother Goddess

MALE

Dying and resurrecting gods
gods associated with fire, plants, or animals
Green Man
Horned God
Lord of the wild wood
the lusty young god getting ready to fertilize the goddess earth with his seed
Sun gods

Flowers
Daisy, ivy, lily of the valley, rose, and violet

Trees
Birch, hawthorn, oak, pine and willow

Crystals
Bloodstone, emerald, rose quartz

Metals
Copper, gold, and silver

Incense
Frankincense, jasmine, lemon, mint, pine, rose, woodruff, and ylang-ylang

Herbs
Lemon, mint, mugwort, and woodruff

Animals, Totems, and Mythical Creatures
Bees, cow, dove, frog, and rabbit

Symbols and Tools
Flowers, maypole, the priapic wand

Food
Honey and light cakes

Drinks
Lemonade and May Wine

Colors
Brown, green, pink, white, and yellow

Activities and Traditions of Practice
Bringing in the May (collecting foliage the night before and placing it in and on the home in time for the May Day sunrise), decorating a May Bush distributing May baskets, divination, feasting, fertility magick, handfastings, and other romantic partnerships, lighting bonfires, making offerings to deities, ancestors, and faeries, Maypole dancing, nature walks, purification ceremonies, protection rituals, sacred sex, singing, and visiting wells

Acts of Service
Beautifying a neighbor's living quarters with fresh flowers and herbs planting a tree, rehabilitating the banks of a stream, removing litter from an outdoor area, and working on a community garden

Alternate Names for Beltane in Other Pagan Traditions

Cetsamhain (Celtic, meaning Opposite Samhain)
Lá Bealtaine (Celtic, meaning Day of Beltane)
May Day (widespread usage)
Walpurgisnacht (Germanic, meaning Walpurgis Night)

Holidays or Traditions Occurring During Beltane in the Northern Hemisphere:
RELIGIOUS

Rowan Witch Day (Finnish, May 1)
Sacred Thorn Tree Day (Irish, May 4)
Festival of Shashti (Hindu, May 12)

SECULAR

Earth Day (April 22)
Walpurgis Night (Germanic, April 30)
May Day (European, May 1)
Mother's Day (most of Europe, North America, and many other countries around the world celebrate sometime in May)
Holidays or Traditions Occurring During Beltane in the Southern Hemisphere

Holidays or Traditions Occurring During Beltane in the Southern Hemisphere:
RELIGIOUS

All Soul's Day (Christian Catholic, some Protestant denominations)
Diwali (Hindu)
Hollantide (Welsh)
Martinmass (Christian Catholic)

SECULAR

Guy Fawkes Day (UK)
Halloween
Recreation Day (northern Tasmania)

Aphrodite / Venus (Greco-Roman)

Aphrodite: Greek goddess of love and war. Daughter of the sea, Aphrodite is the goddess of beauty, love, and pleasure. Though she rules marriages and the love within them, she is also the goddess of illicit affairs. Thought to have originated from the Mesopotamian goddesses Astarte and Ishtar, Aphrodite has been associated with war and battles. She teaches dedication and love of the self and is known for her quick and sometimes unscrupulous responses to petitions. Her symbols are the ocean, doves, apples, roses, and the mirror.

Artemis (Greek)

Artemis is the Greek goddess of hunting, wilderness, and wild animals. She is also a goddess of childbirth and the protector of young girls. As the Virgin Huntress, she is the personification of independence, self-reliance, and strength. Artemis is usually depicted as a young woman holding a bow and arrow. The deer, bear, and cypress tree are sacred to her.

Astarte/Ishtar (Babylonian/Greek)

As the Mesopotamian goddess of love and war, Astarte was similar to the goddess Ishtar and was worshipped throughout ancient Mesopotamia. Her name literally means "star," and she was seen as the power behind the moon. The queen of both the morning and evening stars, she was all-encompassing power over the heavens and all of creation. She ruled the spirits of the dead and was the mother of the astral bodies throughout the universe. As a love goddess, she ruled passion, marriage, and sexual encounters, personifying the sensuality of a woman's body and the power of feminine independence. She was also the Warrior Queen in her dark aspect, her passion channeled into war and battle victories. Her symbols include the sphinx, the dove, and the star.

Bona Dea (Roman)

Bona Dea is the Roman goddess of fertility, chastity, and healing. She was worshiped by Roman women as a fertility goddess and as the spirit of chastity. Her festivals on December 4th and May 1st were only accessible to women, and representations of men and beasts were forbidden inside her temple walls. Her powers of healing and restoration led the sick and disabled to be tended to in the gardens of her temples. Snakes are sacred to Bona Dea, and she was often invoked by slaves seeking freedom from bondage.

Chin-hua-fu-jen (Chinese)

I was confused by this one so instead of getting it incorrect will leave it up to you to research.

Danu (Irish)

Dana, also Danu, Anu: Earth-mother goddess of Ireland. Dana is the queen and mother of the Tuatha Dé Danann, a tribe of deities. Her name translates as "knowledge," and her influence spread throughout all Celtic lands. She is the power and magick of fertile soil, rivers, and vegetation. Dana is thought to be the Irish equivalent of the Welsh goddess Don.

Please note that in my previous books, I mentioned the Goddess Danu. There are two goddesses with this name. I will make the corrections in my previous books but for clarity, I will include both goddesses in this one.

Danu (Hindu)

Danu: Hindu goddess of water. Danu is the primordial force of water. She is the personification of the ocean, from which all creation in the universe springs. She produces streams and rivers to purify the earth and bestows luck on those seeking treasure within her depths.

Please note that in my previous books, I mentioned the Goddess Danu. There are two goddesses with this name. I will make the corrections in my previous books but for clarity, I will include both goddesses in this one.

Diana (Etruscan / Roman)

Diana: Roman queen of Witches. Diana is the independent huntress, the virgin of woodlands and forests, and the guardian of all that is wild and free. A moon deity, she is known for her great beauty, magickal skills, and protection of women who practice magickal arts. In addition, she is the keeper of wild and domesticated animals and the patroness of slaves and the poor. Often depicted carrying a bow and arrow and surrounded by animals, Diana is quick to anger when slighted. Her annual festival is held on August 13th; she is said to protect the harvests from the coming storms. Artemis is the Greek equivalent of Diana.

also known as
Jana, Tana (Italian)
Debena, Devana (Czech)
Diiwica (Serbian)
Dziewona (Polish)

Flora (Roman)

Flora is the Roman goddess of flowers and springtime. She's celebrated throughout April and early May with singing, dancing, and lots of drinking. Not only does she rule over flowering plants and fruits, but she also protects vegetation from disease and rot. Plus, she's considered a handmaiden of Ceres and is responsible for blossoming plants and girls into womanhood.

Freya (Norse)

Freya is the Norse goddess of love and war. She's incredibly beautiful, and no man or god can resist her. She's invoked for happiness in love and sex, as well as familial relations. As the Queen of the Valkyries, she gathers the souls of dead warriors and escorts them to the afterlife. Freya is also the mistress of cats and is thought to have inspired all poetry. Her sacred day is Friday, and her number is thirteen.

Horae (Greek)

The Horae are Greco-Roman goddesses of the seasons and natural order. They are the children of Zeus and Themis, and their names indicate their role in human life: Good Order, Justice, and Peace. In Athens, there were three Horae: Thallo, Auxo, and Carpo. They had a yearly festival called the Horaea. In Homer's Iliad, they are the gatekeepers of Olympus. In the Homeric Hymn to Aphrodite, they greet Aphrodite at her birth and accompany her to Olympus. In the Hellenistic and Roman periods, the Horae became the four seasons. Conventional attributes represented them, and each took the name of Hora. The daughters of the sun god Helios and the moon goddess Selene personified aspects of time that were divided into 12 parts.

Maia (Greek)

Maia is the Greek goddess of spring. She's the eldest of the Pleiades and the mother of Hermes. As a solitary goddess, she lives alone in a cave and is associated with spring magick and midwifery. She helps vegetation and flowers grow and makes the land more fertile.

Persephone/Proserpina (Greek/Roman)

Persephone is the Greek goddess of spring, agriculture, and growth. She's the daughter of Demeter, making her the spring maiden. As the queen of the underworld, she's also the keeper of souls. She embodies the wisdom of life and death and is skilled in magick and divination.

Rauni (Finnish)

Rauni, the goddess of rowan trees, embodies all of the powers of this sacred tree. The rowan tree is an important part of Northern magical and spiritual traditions. It is a small, tough tree that can grow in very poor soil. Rowan trees are thought to have metaphysical properties, such as providing spiritual protection. According to one Finnish creation myth, the rowan tree was the first tree on Earth. In the beginning, Rauni came to Earth and saw that there were no plants. She transformed into a rowan tree. Her husband, thunder spirit Ukko, struck her with lightning, and she became pregnant. Rauni and Ukko are the parents of all plants. Rauni presides over fertility and childbirth. She is invoked to heal pain and minimize suffering.

Sarasvati (Hindu)

Sarasvati is the Hindu goddess of knowledge, wisdom, music, and the arts. She is the inventor of Sanskrit and the patron goddess of learning and scholarship. She is often depicted as a beautiful woman with white skin and a peacock feather. Hindus revere Sarasvati for her role in promoting creativity, learning, and knowledge.

Venus (Roman)

Venus is the Roman goddess of love, sex, and beauty. She is the equivalent of the Greek Aphrodite. Venus is known as the morning and evening star and is the daughter of the sea. Venus dispels troubles and turmoil and brings happiness and joy to her devotees. She is also the patroness of prostitutes and heals sexual issues on both mental and physical levels.

Apollo (Greek/Roman)

Apollo was a deity with many functions and meanings in Greco-Roman mythology. He was one of the most revered and influential gods of all time. Apollo was known as the god of divine distance, who sent or threatened from afar. He was also the god who made men aware of their own guilt and purified them of it. Apollo presided over religious law and the constitutions of cities. He also communicated with mortals through prophets and oracles, informing them of the future and the will of his father Zeus. Even the gods feared Apollo, with only his father and mother, Leto being able to endure his presence easily. Additionally, Apollo was a god of crops and herds. He was primarily a divine bulwark against wild animals and disease. His Greek epithet Alexikakos (Averter of Evil) indicates this function. Additionally, the view became current that he was connected with the Sun, owing to his forename Phoebus meaning "bright" or "pure."

Balder/Baldur (Norse)

In Norse mythology, Balder is the son of Odin and Frigg. He is beautiful and just and the favorite of the gods. Most of the legends about him concern his death. In Icelandic stories, the gods amused themselves by throwing objects at him, knowing that he was immune from harm. The blind god Höd killed Balder by hurling mistletoe at him. After Balder's funeral, the giantess Thökk refused to weep the tears that would release Balder from death. Some scholars believe that the passive, suffering figure of Balder was influenced by Christ.

Cernunnos/Cernunnus/Kernunnos (Celtic)

The Gaelic god Cernunnos presides over all beasts, nature, and the wild. The Horned One, or even the Celtic horn god, was the go-between between humanity and the natural world. While his identity remains unknown, he may have been one of several Celtic mythology's horned gods. In Celtic mythology, Cernunnos, sometimes the Horned Man, is the god of animals and the wilderness. Unfortunately, we don't know anything much about him. That could be because some myths need to be included in the collections or because Celtic mythology features roughly 50 gods with horns. He is typically shown as an elderly or middle-aged guy in artwork, wearing antlers and a beard and sitting cross-legged.

This horned woodland deity was the supreme ruler of the planet's wildlife. In other stories, he even served as a de facto head of the natural and animal worlds he governed. Moreover, he possessed an uncanny ability to maintain harmony. He was the go-to guy to negotiate when conflicts arose between beings and nonhuman animals. A fertility deity, a guardian god, or a god on the hunt are all possible roles he may have had in his people's religion. He shared characteristics with other nature deities, suggesting he was a creator deity. Since there is no comprehensive mythology about him and many accounts exist, it needs to be clarified what exactly his characteristics were. His primary focus, however, as befitting a god for nature, was outside.

This ancient Gaelic name translates to "horned" or "horned one." The Indo-European root cern is used worldwide to describe a horn or antler, and it's a close relative of the Greek word "corn," from which we get the English word "corn," as in the horned unicorn. Like Cailleach, Cernunnos is a generic name for a deity with horns. Scholars use his name as a catch-all for all the horned gods in world mythology because he lacks a distinct mythology and may be a composite of several other deities.

Horned god

Symbol of power, virility, and the hunt

The horned god symbol has roots in Europe. It dates back to Paleolithic times. One of the first sightings was on a cave wall in France from around 13,000 BC. The image is called the Sorcerer and is believed to depict the Great Spirit or master of animals. In Greek mythology, Osiris was the horned god of fertility, rebirth, and the underworld. In Celtic paganism, the god Cernunnos is depicted with horns. He was the god of fertility, the underworld, animals, life, and wealth.

These gods are all a part of the Wiccan religion, which uses the horned god symbol to represent the masculine polarity of the universe. The Horned God is an equal opposite of the Goddess in the Wiccan religion.

In newer Wiccan traditions, there is more emphasis on the Goddess. The Horned God impregnates the Goddess in the winter months, dies in autumn, and is reborn in winter. The Horned God is a mediator between the people and a larger unknown deity. The Horned God's main function is to impregnate the goddess

Today the symbol represents Wicca and is found in fantasy and science fiction novels.

One representation of the horned god is a curve above a circle. The horns symbolize male virility and spiritual power. It also represents the crescent moon which is associated with goddesses.

Chung K'uei (Chinese)

ZHONG KUI
Chinese Protection God
Also known as Chung-K'uei, Chung-Kwei, Zhong Guei, Zhongkui

Zhong was a promising young student who failed the Imperial exams because the Emperor didn't like his face. In old China, this was a death sentence for any hope of a career. Zhong was so ashamed that he committed suicide outside the Imperial palace. Sent to the hell of Diyu for his crime, he was noticed by Yanluo Wang, who was impressed by his scholarly credentials. "Clever and dead? That's just the person I'm looking for!"

Zhong Kui has been given the title of Chief Ghostly Demon Killer. His mother had hoped for a different career path for him, but Zhong Kui has made the most of his new title. He is now an in-demand figure for protection against evil spirits. His sword is his main weapon, but he is also known for crushing demons beneath his bare feet.

When there are no more demons to quell in China, Zhong Kui heads off to Japan to tackle the demons there under the name Shoki.

Odin/Woden (Norse)

Odin, also called Wodan, Woden, or Wotan, is one of the principal gods in Norse mythology. However, his exact nature and role are difficult to determine because of the complex picture of him given by the wealth of archaeological and literary sources. The Roman historian Tacitus stated that the Teutons worshiped Mercury. Because dies Mercurii ("Mercury's day") was identified with Wednesday ("Woden's day"), there is little doubt that the god Woden (the earlier form of Odin) was meant. Though Woden was worshiped preeminently, there is insufficient evidence of his cult to show whether all the Teutonic tribes practiced it or to enable conclusions to be drawn about the nature of the god. Later literary sources, however, indicate that at the end of the pre-Christian period, Odin was the principal god in Scandinavia.

From earliest times, Odin was a war god and appeared in heroic literature as the protector of heroes; fallen warriors joined him in Valhalla. The wolf and the raven were dedicated to him. His magical horse, Sleipnir, had eight legs, teeth inscribed with runes, and the ability to gallop through the air and over the sea. Odin was the great magician among the gods and was associated with runes. He was also the god of poets. In outward appearance, he was a tall, old man with a flowing beard and only one eye (the other he gave in exchange for wisdom). He was usually depicted wearing a cloak and a wide-brimmed hat and carrying a spear.

Pan (Greek)

Pan, in Greek mythology, is a fertility deity, more or less bestial in form. He was associated by the Romans with Faunus. Originally an Arcadian deity, his name is a Doric contraction of paon ("pasturer") but was commonly supposed in antiquity to be connected with pan ("all"). His father was usually said to be Hermes, but a comic invention held that he was the product of an orgy of Odysseus's wife Penelope with her many suitors. Plutarch wrote that during the reign of Tiberius, the crew of a ship sailing near Greece heard a voice calling out, "The great Pan is dead." Christians took this episode to be simultaneous with the death of Christ.

Pan was generally represented as a vigorous and lustful figure having the horns, legs, and ears of a goat; in later art, the human parts of his form were much more emphasized. He haunted the high hills, and his chief concern was with flocks and herds, not with agriculture; hence he can make humans, like cattle, stampede in "panic" terror. Like a shepherd, he was a piper, and he rested at noon. Besides Hellenistic bucolic, Pan was insignificant in literature, but he was a very common subject in ancient art. His rough figure was antithetical to, for example, that of Apollo, who represented culture and sophistication.

Pluto (Greek)

Pluto was one of five children born to the Roman gods Saturn and Ops. When Saturn died, and the Titans were defeated, Pluto became the ruler of his father's underworld realm; his siblings Jupiter and Neptune divided up the sky and sea, respectively. Despite its dark imagery, the Roman Underworld had many positive representations; it was believed that gold, silver, crops, and various other items rose from it. It is said that Pluto lived in a magnificently regal palace at the entrance to the Elysian Fields - despite being underground, it served as a grand place of respite for him.

Ra (Egyptian)

Ra (also given as Re) is the sun **god** of ancient **Egypt**. He is one of the oldest deities in the **Egyptian pantheon** and was later merged with others such as **Horus**, becoming Ra-Horakhty (the morning sun), **Amun** (as noonday sun), and Atum (the evening sun) associated with primal life-giving energy.
Ra is the Egyptian word for 'sun'. As a solar deity, Ra embodied the power of the sun but was also thought to be the sun itself, envisioned as the great god riding in his barge across the heavens throughout the day and descending into the underworld at sunset. As he made his way through the darkness beneath the earth, he was attacked nightly by the giant serpent **Apophis** (also known as Apep), who tried to prevent the sun from rising and so destroy all life on earth.

Ra was the king of the deities and the father of all creation. He was the patron of the sun, heaven, kingship, power, and light. He was not only the deity who governed the actions of the sun; he could also be the physical sun itself and the day.

Staff of Ra

Symbol of power and divine guidance.

Ra was the most important god in ancient Egypt. Ancient Egyptians believed that Ra created all the animal life on the planet by whispering their secret names. He created man from his tears and sweat. Ra is often pictured with a staff. The staff's top resembles a gazelle, and the bottom resembles a gazelle's foot. It is a symbol of power and divine guidance.

The staff of Ra was also fictionalized and featured in the movie Raiders of Lost Ark. The headpiece to the staff of Ra was supposed to be a guide to the Ark of the Covenant. If someone held the staff correctly, the sun would shine through the headpiece and lead the person to the burial site.

Woden/Odin (Germanic)

Woden (wō'dən; German vō'dĭn), Norse Odin (ō'dĭn), in Germanic religion and mythology, is the supreme god. His cult, although widespread among the Germanic tribes, was sometimes subordinated to that of his son Thor. With his brothers, Woden fashioned the earth and the sky from the dead body of the giant Ymir, and from an ash tree and alder, he created the first man and woman. As chief of the gods of **Asgard**, he established the laws that governed the universe and controlled the destiny of humanity. At his court at **Valhalla**, he was attended by the Valkyries. Woden was widely known as a god of war, but he was also important as a god of learning, poetry, and magic. His wife was Frigg, and his children included Thor, Balder, and Tiw. He was identified with the Roman god Mercury, and among Germanic peoples, Mercury's day became Woden's day (Wednesday). In Richard Wagner's opera cycle, Der Ring des Nibelungen, Woden is called Wotan.

Quicky Guide to Greek and Roman Gods

Greek	**Roman**
Zeus	Jupiter
Hera	Juno
Poseidon	Neptune
Cronus	Saturn
Aphrodite	Venus
Hades	Pluto
Hephaestus	Vulcan
Demeter	Ceres
Apollo	Apollo
Athena	Minerva
Artemis	Diana
Ares	Mars
Hermes	Mercury
Dionysus	Bacchus
Persephone	Proserpine
Eros	Cupid
Gaia	Terra
Hypnos	Somnus
Rhea	Ops
Uranus	Uranus
Nike	Victoria
Eos	Aurora
Pan	Faunus
Selene	Luna
Helios	Sol
Heracles	Hercules
Odysseus	Ulysses

Telling the Bees

There was a time when almost every rural British family who kept bees followed a strange tradition. Whenever there was a death in the family, someone had to go out to the hives and tell the bees of the terrible loss that had befallen the family. Failing to do so often resulted in further losses, such as the bees leaving the hive, not producing enough honey, or even dying. Traditionally, the bees were kept abreast of not only deaths but all important family matters, including births, marriages, and long absences due to journeys. If the bees were not told, all sorts of calamities were thought to happen. This peculiar custom is known as "telling the bees."

Humans have always had a special connection with bees. In medieval Europe, bees were highly prized for their honey and wax. Honey was used as food, to make mead—possibly the world's oldest fermented beverage—and as medicine to treat burns, cough, indigestion, and other ailments. Candles made from beeswax burned brighter, longer, and cleaner than other wax candles. Bees were often kept at monasteries and manor houses, where they were tended to with the greatest respect and considered part of the family or community. It was considered rude, for example, to quarrel in front of bees.

Telling the bees may have origins in Celtic mythology, which held that bees were the link between our world and the spirit world. So if you had any message that you wished to pass to someone who was dead, all you had to do was tell the bees, and they would pass along the message. Telling the bees was widely reported from around England and many places across Europe. Eventually, the tradition made its way across the Atlantic and into North America.

The typical way to tell the bees was for the head of the household, or "goodwife of the house," to go out to the hives, knock gently to get the attention of the bees, and then softly murmur in a doleful tune the solemn news. Little rhymes developed over the centuries specific to a particular region. In Nottinghamshire, the wife of the dead was heard singing quietly in front of the hive—"The master's dead, but don't you go; Your mistress will be a good mistress to you." In Germany, a similar couplet was heard —"Little bee, our lord is dead; Leave me not in my distress".

Telling the bees was common in New England. The 19th-century American poet John Greenleaf Whittier describes this peculiar custom in his 1858 poem "Telling the bees."

Before them, under the garden wall,
Forward and back,
Went drearily singing the chore-girl small,
Draping each hive with a shred of black.

Trembling, I listened: the summer sun
Had the chill of snow;
For I knew she was telling the bees of one
Gone on the journey we all must go!

And the song she was singing ever since
In my ear sounds on:—
"Stay at home, pretty bees, fly not hence!
Mistress Mary is dead and gone!"

In case of death, the beekeeper also wrapped the top of the hive with a piece of black fabric or crepe. If there was a wedding in the family, the hives were decorated, and pieces of cake were left outside so the bees could partake in the festivities. Newly-wed couples introduced themselves to the bees of the house; otherwise, their married life was bound to be miserable.

If the bees were not "put into mourning," terrible misfortunes befell the family and the person who bought the hive. In her book The Honey-Makers (1899), Victorian biologist Margaret Warner Morley cites a case in Norfolk where a man purchased a hive of bees that had belonged to a man who had died. The previous owner had failed to put the bees into mourning when their master died, causing the bees to fall sick. The bees regained their health when the new owner draped the hive with a black cloth. In another tale, an Oxfordshire family had seventeen hives when their keeper died. Because nobody told them about the death, every bee died. There are plenty of such tales in Morley's book.

The intimate relationship between bees and their keepers has led to folklore. According to one, buying or selling hives was bad luck because when you sell one, you sell your luck with your bees. Instead, bees were bartered for or given as gifts. If bees flew into a house, a stranger would soon call. If they rested on a roof, good luck was on its way.

But the relationship between bees and humans goes beyond superstition. It's a fact that bees help humans survive. 70 of the top 100 crop species that feed 90% of the human population rely on bees for pollination. Without them, these plants would cease to exist, and with it, all animals that eat those plants. This can have a cascading effect that would ripple catastrophically up the food chain. Losing a beehive is much worse than losing a supply of honey. The consequences are life-threatening. The act of telling the bees emphasizes humans' deep connection with the insect.

The Adorable Custom of 'Telling The Bees'
KAUSHIK PATOWARY APR 23, 2019

Consequently, in London — As news of the death of Queen Elizabeth II reverberated through the world, a headline over the weekend puzzled many on social media: The Daily Mail's exclusive that the "royal beekeeper has informed the Queen's bees that the Queen has died."

Calan Mai

In Wales, May Day (Calan Mai) is a bit different from the May Day we celebrate at Bryn Mawr. Along with the traditional May Pole dancing, the traditional Welsh Calan Mai included lighting ritual fires that sometimes had animals roasted on them. According to the BBC page, these fires were traditionally made from nine different types of wood collected by participants on May Day and are a purification ritual that can be traced to druidical sacrifice to the god Beltane. It seems that these fires are less common today. However, suppose you happen to head up to Edinburgh for May Day. In that case, the Beltane Fire Society puts on a rather exuberant Beltane festival on Carlton Hill involving these traditional fires, music, and acts that weave their way through the crowds.

Since the first of May is a liminal time zone in Welsh mythology, Calan Mai also involved divination. This divination usually takes the form of divining one's true love rather than divining battle outcomes. Hawthorn was also used to decorate the outside of houses ((but never the inside- hawthorn is unlucky, the last thing you would want to be when welcoming in the spring and the fertility of the ground).

In some areas of Wales, such as Anglesey, straw dolls were made and hung near girls' homes on May Eve. These dolls were hung by young men whose sweethearts had left them for another man and often incited jealousies over the lady's affections that could lead to fights.

Not all the traditions of Calan Mai are different, however. Like at Bryn Mawr's Mayday celebration, dancing around a Maypole was integral to the celebrations. The May Pole is traditionally made of birch, though the way in which the dance is performed varies by region. In the South of Wales, the dancing works much the same at Bryn Mawr, with the dancers weaving their ribbons around the pole through their circling dance.

In the north of Wales, however, the maypole ritual is called "Cangen haf", the summer branch, and requires eighteen young men dressed entirely in white with ribbons attached (rather like the Morris Dancers of May Day look) and two young men to play the Cadi and the Fool. The Cadi carries the "cangen haf" around the town, often decorated with spoons, watches, and other silver borrowed from the people of the village, while the others sing and dance and ask for money from everyone they meet. Calan Mai also has a May Queen, a young woman who presides over the festival. Traditional Welsh dancing also forms a large part of the festival.

Today, amusement park rides and bouncy castles like the ones Bryn Mawr set up this Sunday on Merion and Denbigh Greens also tend to make an appearance, especially since May Day is a bank holiday in the UK, and most people have the day off to join in the festivities.

Walpurgis Night

Walpurgis Night is a traditional holiday celebrated on April 30 in northern Europe and Scandinavia. In Sweden, typical holiday activities include singing traditional spring folk songs and lighting bonfires. In Germany, the holiday is celebrated by dressing in costumes, playing pranks on people, and creating loud noises meant to keep evil at bay. Many people also hang blessed sprigs of foliage from houses and barns to ward off evil spirits, or they leave pieces of bread spread with butter and honey, called ankenschnitt, as offerings for phantom hounds.

In Finland, Walpurgis Night and May Day are effectively merged into a celebration usually referred to as Vappu, among the country's most important holidays. Initially, Walpurgis Night was celebrated by the Finnish upper class. Then, in the late 19th century, students (most notably engineering students) took up its celebration. Today merrymaking begins on the evening of April 30, often augmented with drinking alcoholic beverages, particularly sparkling wine. The carnival-like festivities carry over to the next day, frequently taking on a family dimension. Friends and relatives picnic in parks among balloons and consume sima, a homemade low-alcohol (and sometimes not so low-alcohol) mead.

The origins of the holiday date back to pagan celebrations of fertility rites and the coming of spring. After the Norse were Christianized, the pagan celebration became combined with the legend of St. Walburga. This English-born nun lived at Heidenheim monastery in Germany and later became the abbess there. Walburga was believed to have cured the illnesses of many local residents. Walburga is traditionally associated with May 1 because of a medieval account of her being canonized upon translating her remains from their burial place to a church circa 870. Although the date of her canonization is likely purely coincidental to the date of the pagan celebrations of spring, people were able to celebrate both events under church law without fear of reprisal.

Scotland / Ireland

Beltane - which means 'day of fire' in Celtic - was an ancient Celtic fire festival celebrated in Ireland, Scotland, and the Isle of Man on May 1. Bel was the god of the sun in Celtic tradition, so the festival celebrated the seasonal transition from the dark winter to the beautiful and light summer.

Ancient Celts believed that the sun was taken prisoner during the winter months, so they would light special bonfires on Beltane to welcome the sun back to its rightful place. This tradition has been revived in recent years and still occurs in parts of Scotland today.

In Edinburgh, for example, they light huge bonfires on a hill above the city. Another Scottish legend from Edinburgh says that young women who climb Arthur's Seat (a big hill overlooking the city) at sunrise on May Day and wash their faces in the morning dew will have life-long beauty!

Germany / Scandinavia

Walpurgisnacht, or Hexennacht, is almost like a second Hallowe'en in Germany. Legend has it that witches would meet on this night to celebrate the coming season with bonfires and dancing. Local German people made as much noise as possible to combat the witches and lit huge bonfires to keep the evil witches and spirits at bay. Walpurgisnacht is still celebrated today across Germany and Scandinavia, with big parties, bonfires, and dressing up.

The holiday's name is said to come from St Walburga, an English nun whose feast day is May 1. At that time in Germany, Church authorities banned pagan celebrations and would punish anyone found to be celebrating them. In order to carry on observing Hexennacht, the local people used the excuse of celebrating St Walburga's feast day to appease the Church.

Russia

In Russia and other former Soviet countries, May 1 is still a very important holiday, marking the start of spring/summer and Labor Day. Workers' rights were of hugely important significance in countries under the influence of the Soviet Union countries, and this day continues as a major holiday today. There are often marches or demonstrations on this day, too against capitalist systems or just as a celebration of unions.

England

While the Scots and Irish celebrate with fire festivals, in England, May Day is traditionally celebrated with dancing around the Maypole. Maypoles were traditionally made from young trees, which were cut down and placed in the middle of a village green with multicolored ribbons attached to the top. It was then the job of the young people in the village to each take a ribbon and skip around the outside of the pole to make various patterns with all the ribbons. Maypoles are still a key fixture on Mayday in rural villages and are even making a comeback in more urban parts of England.

Italy

At the ancient festival of Calendimaggio in Assisi, people dress up in traditional dress - including swords and shields for the men - and there are a variety of specific activities to participate in. These include horse riding, crossbow-shooting competitions, and the election of a Madonna Primavera (Queen of Spring). There are also singing competitions, day and night processions, feasts, and flower dances to welcome the new spring and the renewed joy of life.

Hawaii

Lei are traditional Hawaiian flower necklaces worn by practically everyone on the Hawaiian islands on May 1, the official Lei Day! They are a symbol of the aloha spirit in Hawaii. Each island has a different style of Lei. On Lei Day, there are lei-making demonstrations, concerts, food and drink stalls, and lots of celebrations.

Bulgaria

The Bulgarian festival Irminden stems from the legend in Bulgaria that snakes come out of their burrows every year on March 25, but that their king and leader come out on May 1. So, anyone working in the fields is likely to get bitten today! All workers take May Day free in Bulgaria to avoid any such bites. There are bonfires to keep the snakes away and lots of celebrations to welcome in the spring and summer.

France

Demonstrations and parades have been a common Labor Day fixture in France since 1890. However, an older tradition remains alongside them. Giving the Lily of the Valley flower to friends or family is customary. This dates back to 1561 when Charles IX presented Lily of the Valley to all ladies at his court.

The Phases of the Moon

New

Sometimes called the Crescent Moon, when you can see the very first sliver of light in the sky. This phase promotes new beginnings, new endeavors and new relationships. It is the time to make positive changes and plant seeds of ideas that will be harvested later.

Waxing

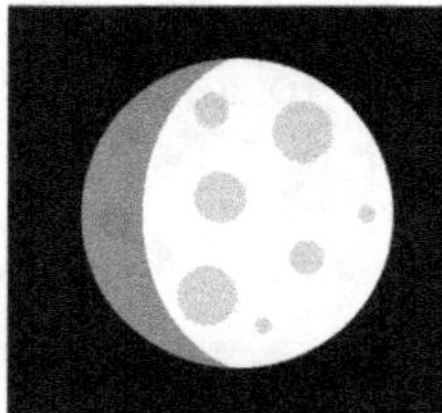

In this phase, the Moon appears to be growing in size, shifting from new to full as though it's gaining strength. It makes sense, then, that this is an excellent time to focus on increasing your knowledge, bank accounts and relationships. This phase promotes healing.

Full

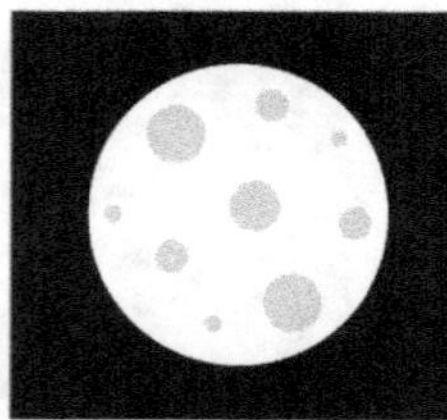

The Moon's most potent phase is when we see her entire illuminated face. This is a time of fulfillment, activity and increased psychic ability; for perfecting ideas, in other words, "getting your act together," celebrations or renewing commitments to people or projects—the best time for spells of any kind.

Waning

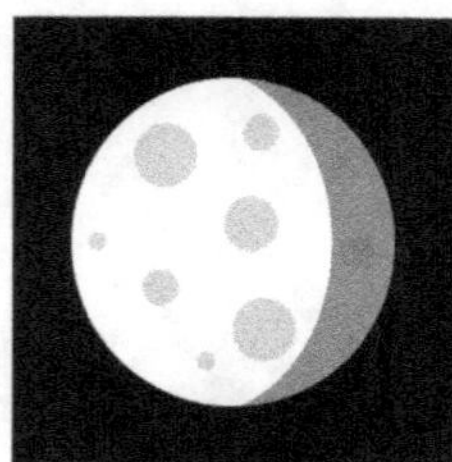

The Moon is decreasing in size as it journeys from full to dark. The waning Moon is a time of decrease, release, letting go and completion. An excellent time to begin dieting, breaking bad habits, breaking off relationships, or dealing with legal matters.

Oh Crap, a Full Moon!

Does the Moon influence our behavior or emotions? There's never been solid proof, but some new evidence suggests that the Moon can affect sleep, and it doesn't matter whether you're in the country or the city!

The Luna-Lunacy Connection

Ancient authorities like Aristotle, Paracelsus and Pliny the Elder, thought some humans were driven crazy by the full Moon. The Latin name for the Moon, "luna," is the root of modern words like "lunacy," "lunatic" and even "loon." (as in crazy as a loon).

Even today, many doctors, nurses, EMTs, police officers and elementary school teachers agree that full Moons will bring out bizarre behavior; 43 percent of healthcare professionals believe in what some call "the lunar influence," as do 81 percent of mental healthcare specialists. But is there a lunar connection to abnormal behavior?

Unless you plan to ask a werewolf (which we don't recommend), it might be time to separate facts from fiction.

The Moon and Sleep

According to one scientific study conducted in 2021, people go to bed later and sleep for a shorter period in the days leading up to a full Moon. Specifically, people would go to bed 30 minutes later than average and sleep almost an hour less per night.

This makes sense because the light from the Moon after sunset is brighter on the days leading up to a full Moon. However, here's the surprising part: Studies found that it didn't matter if you lived in a rural or urban environment (where you might find more light pollution). So if the Moon's brightness isn't a factor, then why do we stay up later and sleep less? One theory goes back to our ancestors and our long history before the industrial age. People paid attention to the Moon and relied on its "night light" for hunting, fishing and other social activities. Think of the "Harvest Moon" in the autumn, so named because it provided several nights of light for farmers to gather their crops at the height of harvest. Every month, the nights leading up to a full Moon bring more light to the evening.

Our natural circadian rhythms control our sleeping patterns; the day and night cycles are driven by Earth orbiting the Sun. But there are also circalunar rhythms, which are tied to lunar cycles. Indeed, some animals will respond to both a circadian rhythm and a lunar clock. Many animal species' behaviors are influenced by the Moon, too. For example, think of birds that rely on the Moon for migration, and will even time their reproduction to coincide with the phases of the lunar cycle. Anecdotally, you have to wonder if less sleep (whether interrupted sleep or going to bed later) for several nights in a row might lead to some crankiness and what you might call moodiness. No, really!

The Moon and Lunacy - That leads us to weird behavior. There have been hundreds of studies about the Moon and lunacy. The few studies that suggest a connection are usually disproved or contradicted by others:

One study says more animal bites (from cats, rats, dogs and horses) occur at the full Moon; another says there's no increase in dog bites.

One shows an increase in crime around the full Moon; others find no increase in arrests, calls for police assistance, prison assaults, batteries or homicides.

Admissions for psychosis are lowest during the Full Moon and psychiatric emergency room visits decline: but calls to suicide prevention hotlines peak at the new Moon, not the full Moon.

We're unsure how you'd prove the connection between the Moon and lunacy. But one explanation might be what psychologists call "confirmation bias." In other words, people are more likely to notice things that confirm a preexisting belief.

If you're working in an emergency room and something weird happens on the full Moon, your older and wiser colleagues nod and say: "Must be a full Moon." They heard likely heard from their elders back when they were new at the job (Psychologists have a name for that, too: "communal reinforcement.").
But if something weird happens at a different lunar cycle phase, nobody says, "Must be the third quarter Moon!" And when nothing unusual happens on the full Moon, nobody says anything.

We call widespread beliefs that are unsupported by fact "folklore." Erika Brady, who teaches folklore at Western Kentucky University, says: "it's a way of imposing order on something that feels frighteningly out of control."

How does a belief that strange things happen on the full Moon help us feel safer? First, the full Moon occurs only once every 29.5 days; that means the other four weeks of the lunar month should be less dangerous and unpredictable.

Therefore, this folk belief implies that our fears about everything from increased bleeding to werewolves may be limited to only 12 or 13 days per year. (Maybe that's why the number 13 worries people!).

What do you think about the Moon? Does it influence behavior or emotions? Or, is it all in our imagination—and our dreams?

Moons of the Year

A rare second Full Moon in a single month is called a "Blue Moon." A rare second New Moon in a month is called a "Black Moon."

Different cultures gave the Moon different titles to express what the Moon means to them in a given month. As a result, some of the moon names make sense, while others may not make any sense.

Full Moon – January
Native American Tribes: Old Moon, Wolf Moon, Ice Moon, Moon after Yule, and Winter Moon
Siouan (Assiniboines) Tribe: Hard Time Moon
Inuit People of Northern Canada: Dwarf Seal Moon
Celtic: Wolf Moon, Stay Home Moon, Moon after Yule
Chinese: Holiday Moon
Fairy: Icicle Moon
And Just for Fun: Airing Cupboard Moon

Full Moon – February
Native American Tribes: Hunger or Starvation Moon, Storm Moon, Trapper's Moon, Moon of Ice, and Tree Moon
Siouan (Assiniboines) Tribe: Long Day Moon
Inuit People of Northern Canada: Seal Pup Moon
Celtic: Storm Moon, Ice Moon, and Snow moon
Chinese: Budding Moon
Fairy: Snowdrop Moon
And Just for Fun: Frozen Paw Moon

Full Moon – March
Native American Tribes: Worm Moon, Crow Moon, Moon of Winds, Sap Moon, Fish Moon, Chaste Moon, and Death Moon
Siouan (Assiniboines) Tribe: Sore Eye Moon
Inuit People of Northern Canada: Snow Bird Moon
Celtic: Plough Moon, Wind Moon, Lenten (lengthening) Moon
Chinese: Sleeping Moon
Fairy: Waking Wood Moon
And Just for Fun: Preparing Claw Moon

Moons of the Year

Full Moon – April
Native American Tribes: Pink Moon, Seed Moon, Frog Moon, Egg Moon, and Awakening Moon
Siouan (Assiniboines) Tribe: Frog's Moon
Inuit People of Northern Canada: Snow Melt Moon
Celtic: Budding Moon, New Shoots Moon, and Seed Moon
Chinese: Peony Moon
Fairy: Birthing Moon
And Just for Fun: Early Mousing Moon

Full Moon – May
Native American Tribes: Flower Moon, Hare Moon, Milk Moon, and Grass Moon
Siouan (Assiniboines) Idle Moon
Inuit People of Northern Canada: Goose Moon
Celtic: Mother's Moon and Bright Moon
Chinese: Dragon Moon
Fairy: Moon of White Petals
And Just for Fun: Small Rabbit Moon

Full Moon – June
Native American Tribes: Strawberry Moon, Planting Moon, and Green Corn Moon
Siouan (Assiniboines) Tribe: Full Leaf Moon
Inuit People of Northern Canada: Hunting Moon
Celtic: Mead Moon, Horse Moon, Dyan Moon, and Rose Moon
Chinese: Lotus Moon
Fairy: Wild Cherry Moon
And Just for Fun: Fence Sitting Moon

Moons of the Year

Full Moon – July
Native American Tribes: Hay Moon, Summer Moon, Thunder Moon, and Buck Moon
Siouan (Assiniboines) Tribe: Red Berries Moon
Inuit People of Northern Canada: Dry Moon
Celtic: Claiming Moon, Wyrt or Herb Moon, and Mead Moon
Chinese: Hungry Ghost Moon
Fairy: Dancing Delight Moon
And Just for Fun: Lazing in Sun Moon

Full Moon – August
Native American Tribes: Sturgeon Moon, Corn Moon, Green Corn Moon, Dog Days Moon, and Lightening Moon
Siouan (Assiniboines) Tribe: Black Cherries Moon
Inuit People of Northern Canada: Swan Flight Moon
Celtic: Dispute Moon, Lynx Moon, and Grain Moon
Chinese: Harvest Moon
Fairy: Blackberry Harvest Moon
And Just for Fun: Fine Bright Fighting Moon

Full Moon – September
Native American Tribes: Singing Moon and Barley Moon
Siouan (Assiniboines) Tribe: Yellow Leaf Moon
Inuit People of Northern Canada: Harpoon Moon
Celtic: Wine Moon, Song Moon, Harvest Moon, and Barley Moon
Chinese: Chrysanthemum Moon
Fairy: Chestnut Moon
And Just for Fun: Late Mousing Moon

Moons of the Year

Full Moon – October
Native American Tribes: Traveller's Moon and Blackberry Moon
Siouan (Assiniboines) Tribe: Gophur Looks Back Moon
Inuit People of Northern Canada: Ice Moon
Celtic: Hunter's Moon, Blood Moon, and Seed Fall Moon
Chinese: Kindly Moon
Fairy: Moon of the Wild Hunt
And Just for Fun: Cushion by Long Fire Moon

Full Moon - November
Native American Tribes: Frosty Moon, Beaver Moon, Dark Moon, Tree Moon, Snow Moon, Freezing Moon, Ice Moon, and Migrating Moon
Siouan (Assiniboines) Frost Moon
Inuit People of Northern Canada: Freezing Mist Moon
Celtic: Mourning Moon and Darkest Depths Moon
Chinese: White Moon
Fairy: Moon of the Wild Hunt
And Just for Fun: Howling Moon

Full Moon – December
Native American Tribes: Cold Moon, Long Night Moon,
Siouan (Assiniboines) Tribe: Younger Hard Time Moon
Inuit People of Northern Canada: Dark Night Moon
Celtic: Oak Moon, Full Cold Moon
Chinese: Bitter Moon
Fairy: Mistletoe Moon
And Just for Fun: Cushion by Long Fire Moon

Book Recommendation

First, I want to talk about
The Voyage and the Return The Path to Self Discovery
by various authors with Inspired Hearts Publishing, and includes my friend, Jamie Wareham, in Chapter 5.

The Voyage and the Return: The Path to Self Discovery is a book for women who have been wondering, "Is this all there is?"
Sharing the voices of women whose lives were turned upside
down--who went through a major upheaval or a life-changing experience. They took that moment as an invitation to find out who they truly are and what is possible for them. Each one of them embarked on a voyage that took them into the unknown. And everyone returned home with an answer to their most important question: What does my heart
most long for?

The Voyage and the Return...
is about taking the first step on your unique path to self-discovery
is about the challenges you might face along the way
is about trust, courage, and celebration
is about truly living these next chapters of your life.
is about believing that you can do this.
is for those of you who are ready to explore your edge
is for those of you who know it's time
is a manual for living an extraordinary life
This book gives you all the tools and stories to help you on your own
journey of self-discovery.

Books

I've compiled a list of books that I found to be both informative and helpful. However, it's ultimately up to you to choose which ones you want to read based on your own goals, taste, and path. But I hope you find this list helpful and a great starting point nonetheless.

The Goddess Guide by Priestess Brandi Auset

Anatomy of a Witch: A Map to the Magical Body
Weave the Liminal: Living Modern Traditional Witchcraft, both by Laura Tempest Zakroff

Llewellyn's Complete Formulary of Magical Oils: Over 1200 Recipes, Potions & Tinctures for Everyday Use (Llewellyn's Complete Book Series 5) by Celeste Rayne Heldstab

Blackthorn's Botanical Brews: Herbal Potions, Magical Teas, and Spirited Libations
Sacred Smoke: Clear Away Negative Energies and Purify Body, Mind, and Spirit
both by Amy Blackthorn

The Four Agreements: A Practical Guide to Personal Freedom (A Toltec Wisdom Book) by Don Miguel Ruiz, Janet Mills

A Lovely 15-Book Series

Llewellyn's Complete Book of Astrology: The Easy Way to Learn Astrology
Llewellyn's Complete Book of Predictive Astrology: The Easy Way to Predict Your Future
Llewellyn's Complete Book of Names: For Pagans, Witches, Wiccans, Druids, Heathens, Mages, Shamans & Independent Thinkers of All Sorts
Llewellyn's Complete Book of Correspondences: A Comprehensive & Cross-Referenced Resource for Pagans & Wiccans
Llewellyn's Complete Dictionary of Dreams: Over 1,000 Dream Symbols and Their Universal Meanings
Llewellyn's Complete Book of Mindful Living: Awareness & Meditation Practices for Living in the Present Moment
Llewellyn's Complete Book of Chakras: Your Definitive Source of Energy Center Knowledge for Health, Happiness, and Spiritual Evolution
Llewellyn's Complete Book of Tarot: A Comprehensive Guide
Llewellyn's Complete Book of Ayurveda: A Comprehensive Resource for the Understanding & Practice of Traditional Indian Medicine
Llewellyn's Complete Book of Lucid Dreaming: A Comprehensive Guide to Promote Creativity, Overcome Sleep Disturbances & Enhance Health and Wellness
Llewellyn's Complete Book of Divination: Your Definitive Source for Learning Predictive & Prophetic Techniques
Llewellyn's Complete Book of the Rider-Waite-Smith Tarot: A Journey Through the History, Meaning, and Use of the World's Most Famous Deck
Llewellyn's Complete Book of Essential Oils: How to Blend, Diffuse, Create Remedies and Use in Everyday Life
Llewellyn's Complete Book of Ceremonial Magick: A Comprehensive Guide to the Western Mystery Tradition
Llewellyn's Complete Book of Reiki: Your Comprehensive Guide to a Holistic Hands-On Healing Technique for Balance and Wellness

A Lovely 7-Book Series

The Witch's Broom: The Craft, Lore & Magick of Broomsticks (The Witch's Tools Series Book 1) by Deborah Blake

The Witch's Wand: The Craft, Lore, and Magick of Wands & Staffs (The Witch's Tools Series Book 2) by Alferian Gwydion MacLir

The Witch's Athame: The Craft, Lore & Magick of Ritual Blades (The Witch's Tools Series Book 3) by Jason Mankey

The Witch's Mirror: The Craft, Lore & Magick of the Looking Glass (The Witch's Tools Series Book 4) by Mickie Mueller

The Witch's Book of Shadows: The Craft, Lore & Magick of the Witch's Grimoire (The Witch's Tools Series 5) by Jason Mankey

The Witch's Cauldron: The Craft, Lore & Magick of Ritual Vessels (The Witch's Tools Series Book 6) by Laura Tempest Zakroff

The Witch's Altar: The Craft, Lore & Magick of Sacred Space (The Witch's Tools Series Book 7) by Jason Mankey, Laura Tempest Zakroff

Research TBR List

Five Little Indians: A Novel by Michelle Good
They Called Me Number One: Secrets and Survival at an Indian Residential School by Bev Sellars
The Four Elements: We Are Earth Mother by Marcus Nobreus, Skyler Kenny
Seasons of a Magical Life: A Pagan Path of Living by H. Byron Ballard
Jesus Through Pagan Eyes: Bridging Neopagan Perspectives with a Progressive Vision of Christ by Mark Townsend, Matthew Fox, Barbara Erskine
Green Witchcraft: Folk Magic, Fairy Lore & Herb Craft by Ann Moura
The Twelve Faces of the Goddess: Transform Your Life with Astrology, Magick, and the Sacred Feminine by Danielle Blackwood
Thirteen Pathways of Occult Herbalism by Daniel A Schulke
The Eclectic Witch's Book of Shadows: Witchy Wisdom at Your Fingertips by Deborah Blake
The Everyday Witch's Coven: Rituals and Magic for Two or More by Deborah Blake
The Daily Spell Journal: A Diary of Enchantments for Every Day of the Year (Volume 6) by Patti Wigington
Medusa: The feminist debut that boldly reclaims her monstrous myth by Rosie Hewlett
The Rape Trial of Medusa by Michael Kasenow

Yet To Come

Inspiring Creativity Through Magick: How to Ritualize Your Art & Attract the Creative Spirit by Astrea Taylor, Michael Herkes (Foreward) coming July 8, 2023

Path of the Moonlit Hedge: Discovering the Magick of Animistic Witchcraft by Nathan M. Hall, Christopher Penczak (Foreword) coming May 8, 2023

Llewellyn's Complete Book of North American Folk Magic: A Landscape of Magic, Mystery, and Tradition (Llewellyn's Complete Book Series 16) by Cory Thomas Hutcheson coming April 8, 2023

TBR List

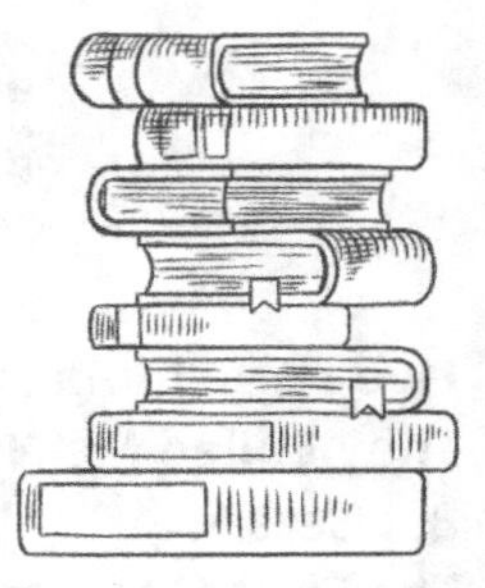

Quicky Correspondence Days

Monday

Best for psychic endeavors, invoking power, creative ideas, divine/inspirational messages, and healing.

Tuesday

Best for protection and building strength of mind, body, and confidence.

Wednesday

Best for career/job issues, intellectual pursuits, travel planning and research.

Thursday

Best for finances, legal matters, spirituality, and development.

Friday

Best for romantic attraction, all relationships, reconciliation, physical makeovers, and beautifying your environment.

Saturday

Best for home-related issues, brainstorming future projects, committing to personal goals, weight loss, releasing bad habits, ending relationships, etc.

Sunday

Best for healing body, mind, soul, management/decision-making, insights into problem-solving, divine intervention/miracles, and unique friendships.

Do what makes you comfortable- there's no need to wait for the "right" day to perform rituals or divination. You do you, Boo!

Monday

Zodiac: Cancer
Solar System: Moon
Rune: Lagu
Numbers: 2, 9
Colors: Blue (pale), Gray, Silver, White
Tarot: High Priestess, Moon
Trees: Birch, Elder, Myrtle, Willow
Misc. Plants: Moonwort, Wormwood
Herb & Garden: Bluebell, Chamomile, Gardenia, Jasmine, Poppy, Rose (white), Violet
Gemstones & Minerals: Emerald, Moonstone, Quartz (clear, white), Sapphire
Metal: Silver
From the Sea: Pearl
Goddesses: Hecate, Selene
Gods: Aegir, Thoth
Angel: Gabriel
Issues, Intentions & Powers: astral realm, clairvoyance, creativity, dream work, emotions, family, fertility, healing, the home, illumination, inspiration, intuition, love, magic (general, moon), prophecy, protection, psychic ability, travel, truth

Tuesday

Zodiac: Aries, Scorpio
Solar System: Mars
Rune: Tyr
Colors: Black, Orange, Red, Scarlet
Tarot: Strength, Wands (5, 6)
Number: 5
Trees: Cedar, Elm, Holly, Palm (dragon's blood)
Herb & Garden: Basil, Garlic, Snapdragon
Misc. Plants: Allspice, Ginger, Patchouli, Thistle
Metal: Iron
Gemstones & Minerals: Bloodstone, Emerald, Garnet, Ruby, Sapphire (star), Topaz
God: Mars
Magical: Elves
Issues, Intentions & Powers: action, aggression, assertiveness, battle/war, challenges, courage, discipline, energy, healing, honor, integrity, justice, passion, purification, strength, truth

Wednesday

Zodiac: Gemini
Solar System: Mercury
Colors: Orange, Purple, Silver, Violet, Yellow
Rune: Odal
Tarot: The Magician, Wheel of Fortune, Pentacles (8)
Number: 3
Trees: Aspen, Hazel, Rowan
Herb er Garden: Dill, Jasmine, Lavender, Lily of the Valley
Misc. Plant: Fern
Gemstones & Minerals: Agate, Amethyst, Aventurine, Lodestone, Opal, Ruby (star), Turquoise
Metal: Mercury
Goddess: Athena
Gods: Hermes, Mercury, Odin
Angel: Raphael
Issues, Intentions & Powers: business, cleverness, communication, creativity, crossroads, divination, fear, improvement (self), insight, intelligence, introspection, knowledge, loss, money, problems, skills, travel, wisdom

Thursday

Zodiac: Capricorn, Pisces
Solar System: Jupiter
Rune: Thorn
Tarot: Pentacles (ace, 9, 10)
Colors: Blue (royal), Green, Indigo, Purple
Numbers: 4, 8
Trees: Laurel, Maple, Oak, Pine
Herb & Garden: Honeysuckle, Sage
Misc. Plants: Cinnamon, Cinquefoil, Grain (wheat), Nutmeg
Gemstones & Minerals: Amethyst, Carnelian, Cat's Eye, Chrysoberyl, Sapphire, Turquoise
Metal: Tin
Goddess: Juno
Gods: Jupiter, Thor, Zeus
Issues, Intentions & Powers: abundance, business, desire, endurance, fidelity, honor, justice (legal matters), leadership, loyalty, luck, money, prosperity, relationships, success, well-being

Friday

Zodiac: Taurus
Solar System: Venus
Rune: Peorth
Colors: Aqua, Blue, Green, Indigo, Pink
Tarot: Empress, Lovers, Cups (2)
Numbers: 6, 9
Trees: Apple, Birch, Myrtle
Misc. Plants: Saffron, Sandalwood
Herb & Garden: Feverfew, Raspberry, Rose, Strawberry, Thyme, Violet
Gemstones & Minerals: Alexandrite, Amber, Cat's Eye, Chrysoberyl, Emerald, Rose Quartz, Ruby
Metal: Copper
Goddesses: Aphrodite, Freya, Frigg, Lakshmi, Venus
God: Eros
Angel: Auriel
Issues, Intentions & Powers: beauty, emotions, fertility, friend/ ship, happiness, love, magic, passion, pleasure, romance, sex, sexuality, wisdom

Saturday

Zodiac: Aquarius
Solar System: Saturn
Colors: Black, Gray (dark), Indigo, Purple (dark)
Rune: Dag
Tarot: Temperance, Swords (knight, 2)
Number: 7
Trees: Alder, Cypress, Hawthorn, Pomegranate
Herb & Garden: Morning Glory, Thyme
Misc. Plants: Mullein, Myrrh
Gemstones & Minerals: Amethyst, Apache Tears, Diamond, Hematite, Jet, Labradorite, Turquoise
Goddess: Hecate
God: Saturn
Magical: Fairies
Issues, Intentions & Powers: banish, bind, business, death, discipline (self), freedom, justice, karma, life, limitations/ boundaries, money, motivation, negativity, obstacles, peace, problems, protection, willpower, wisdom

Sunday

Zodiac: Leo
Solar System: Sun
Rune: Sigel
Number: 1
Colors: Gold, Gray, Orange, Pink, White, Yellow
Tarot: Chariot, Sun, Wands (ace)
Trees: Ash, Birch, Laurel
Misc. Plants: Cinnamon, Frankincense
Herb & Garden: Carnation, Marigold, St. John's Wort, Sunflower
Gemstones & Minerals: Amber, Carnelian, Diamond, Quartz (clear), Sunstone, Tiger's Eye, Topaz
Metal: Gold
From the Sea: Pearl
Goddess: Brigid
God: Helios
Magical: Elves
Issues, Intentions & Powers: accomplishment, action, ambition, attraction, authority, beauty, confidence, creativity, energy (solar), fame, freedom, friend/ship, goals, growth (personal), healing, hope, illumination, justice, leadership, light, money power (personal), pride, prosperity, protection, spirituality, strength, success, visions, warmth, well-being

Quicky Correspondence Times

Magic at Dawn

Dawn is the time when the sun is just beginning to rise in the sky. This is a time of new beginnings and fresh starts. Magic performed at dawn can be used to bring about positive change in your life.

Magic at Midday

Midday is the time when the sun is highest in the sky. This is a time of power and vitality. Magic performed at midday can be used to increase your personal power and manifest your desires.

Magic at Dusk

Dusk is the time when the sun is beginning to set in the sky. This is a time of reflection and introspection. Magic performed at dusk can be used to release negative energy and promote healing.

Do what makes you comfortable- there's no need to wait for the "right" time to perform rituals or divination. So you do you, Boo!

Dawn

Solar System: Venus
Celebration: Ostara
Runes: Beorc, Hagal, Thorn
Element: Air
Direction: East
Tarot: Swords
Gods: Byelobog, Janus, Njord, Surya
Angel: Raphael
Animals: Coyote, Fox, Rabbit
Birds: Chicken (rooster), Dove, Phoenix
Issues, Intentions & Powers: activate/awaken, beginnings, crossroads, fertility, hope, life (vitality), light, nurture, purpose, romance, youth

Midday/Noon

Zodiac: Leo
Solar System: Sun
Celebration: Litha
Runes: Dag, Rad, Sigel
Element: Fire
Direction: South
Tarot: Wands
God: Byelobog
Angel: Michael
Issues, Intentions & Powers: determination, obstacles, strength, willpower

Dusk/Twilight

Zodiac: Cancer
Solar System: Venus
Celebration: Mabon
Runes: Feoh, Jera, Peorth
Element: Water
Direction: West
Tarot: Cups
Angel: Gabriel
Animals: Beaver, Coyote, Fox, Rabbit, Wolf
Birds: Blackbird, Dove, Owl
Issues, Intentions & Powers: banish, change/s, endings, the otherworld/underworld, sorrow

Midnight

Zodiac: Taurus
Solar System: Earth, Venus
Celebration: Yule
Runes: Is, Tyr, Ur
Element: Earth
Direction: North
Tarot: Pentacles
Angel: Auriel
Issues, Intentions & Powers: crossroads, endings, release

Tarot Cards

Tarot is an intricate divination system consisting of 78 cards divided into major and minor arcana cards. Heavily relying on classical mythology and symbolism, tarot is thought to allow one to receive answers to the events in question by interpreting messages based on how the cards are dealt. This can be done utilizing card spreads like the classic Celtic cross or a simple 3 card past, present, and future layout.

Oracle Cards

Less structured than tarot, oracle cards use a combination of artwork and written interpretations, sometimes including exercises. Oracle cards can be based on nearly any subject matter and are open to various styles and formats. Perfect for guiding without the intricacies associated with tarot.

Tarot/Oracle Library

Tarot/Oracle Library

Everyday Tarot Spread

1

2

Everyday Tarot Spread

Card 1 - Today's challenge
Card 2 - Solution to problems that may arise today

Impressions:

Beltane

1

2

3

4

5

Beltane

Card 1 - Seedling - What ideas/goals are you manifesting this spring?
Card 2 - Nurture - What steps will help your ideas and goals come to fruition?
Card 3 - Sun - How can you attract more abundance and positive energy?
Card 4 - Rain - How will your challenges and mistakes help you grow?
Card 5 - Bloom - What strengths within you will help you reach your goals?

Impressions:

New Energy

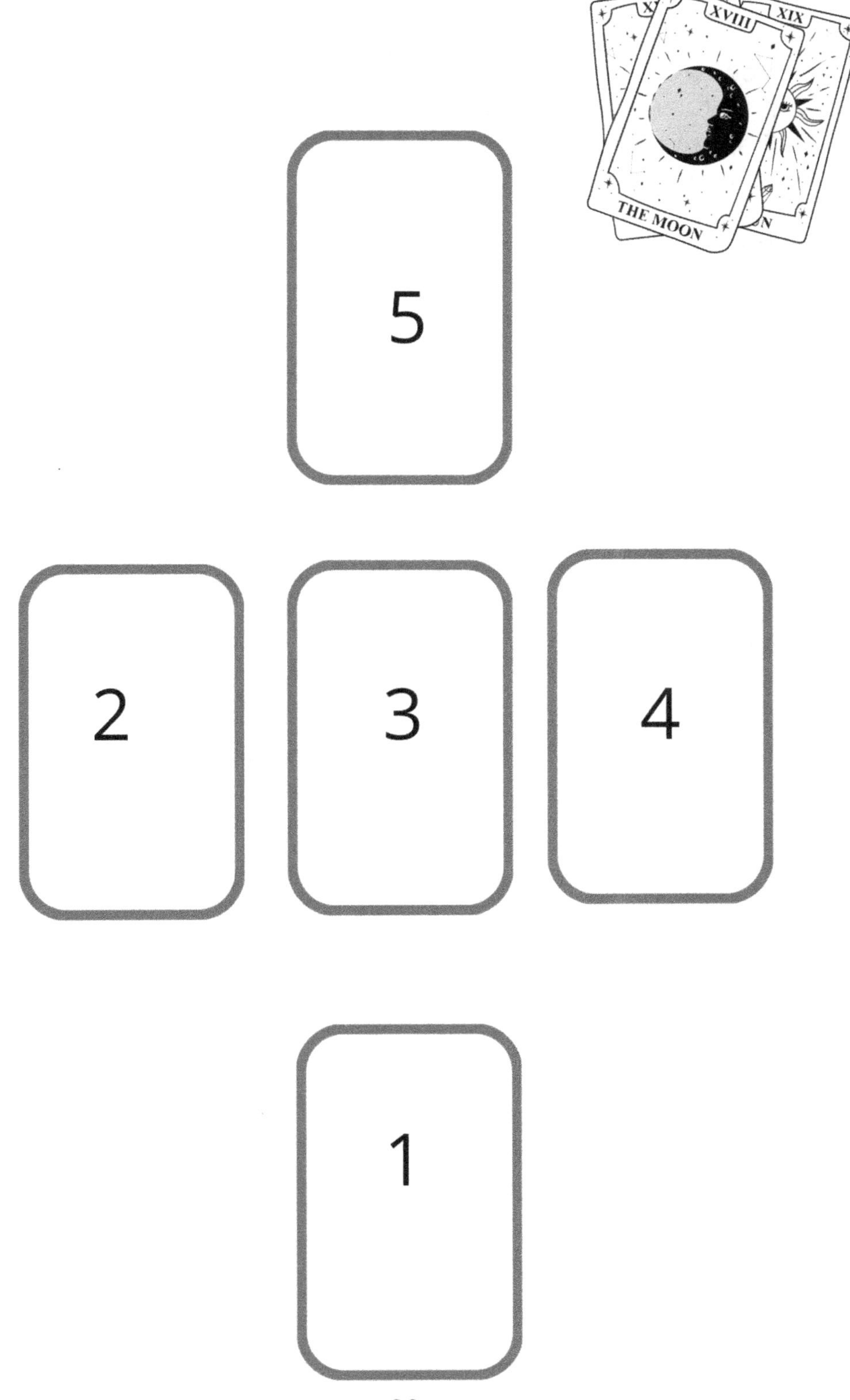

New Energy

Card 1 - What needs to be burned away?
Card 2 - How can you create space for this new energy and life?
Card 3 - Keys to an abundant year
Card 4 - Steps toward abundance
Card 5 - Messages from your ancestors

Impressions:

Morning Check-in Time

Morning Check-in Time

Card 1 - Something to let go and forgive from yesterday?
Card 2 - A piece of advice on navigating today?
Card 3 - Something to hold space for today?

Impressions:

Evening Check-In Time

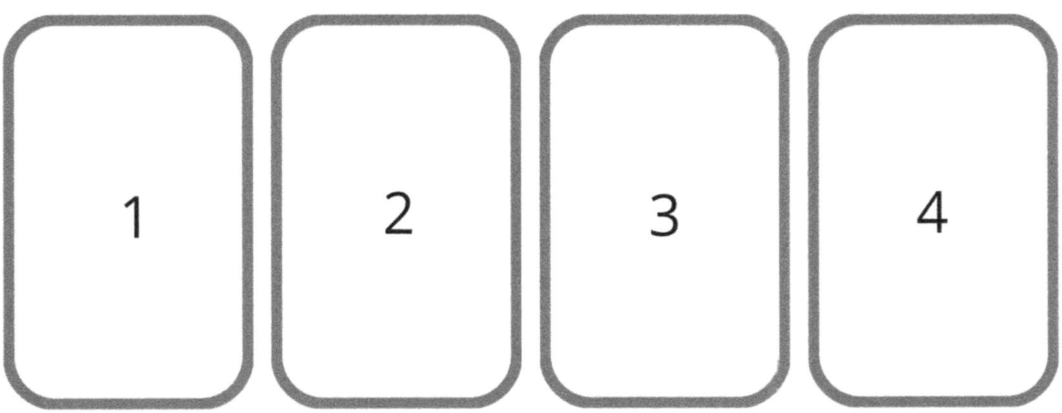

Evening Check-in Time

Card 1 - Energy to carry into tomorrow?
Card 2 - Something to reflect on from today?
Card 3 - Energy to release from the day?
Card 4 -Something for my dreams tonight?

Impressions:

Connecting With Nature

Connecting With Nature

Card 1 - What can I do for the Earth?
Card 2 - What is Mother Nature trying to tell me?
Card 3 - What is the best way for me to connect with Mother Nature?

Impressions:

Peaceful Trees

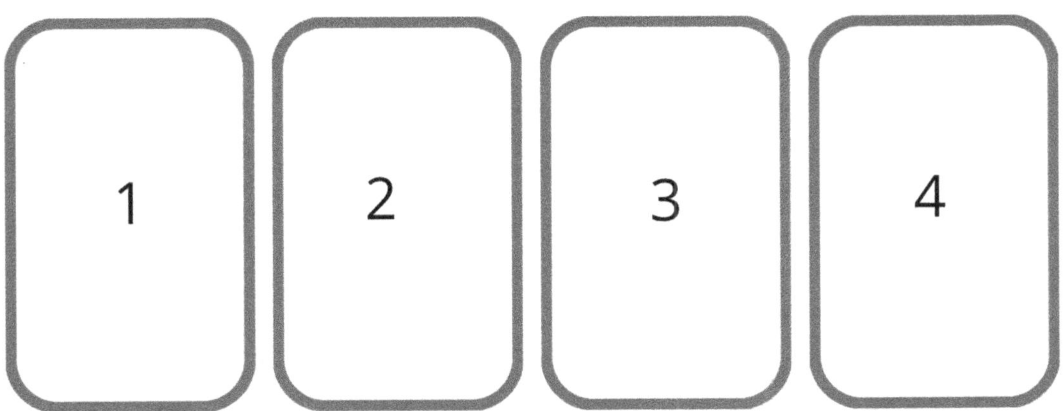

Peaceful Trees

Card 1 - Leaves: What feeds my soul?
Card 2 - Branches: What direction do I need to grow?
Card 3 - Trunk: What supports my well-being?
Card 4 - Roots: What anchors me in place?

Impressions:

Speak up

3

2

1

Speak Up

Cards 1 - Reminder from the past
Cards 2 - Message from the present
Cards 3 - Guidance for the future

Impressions:

Life Lesson Learned

1

2

Life Lesson Learned

Card 1 - The mistake you made
Card 2 - How can you learn from it?

Impressions:

Heads Up

1

2

3

Heads up

Card 1 - What is coming my way?
Card 2 - Best way to prepare?
Card 3 - Anything else I should know?

Impressions:

Empower

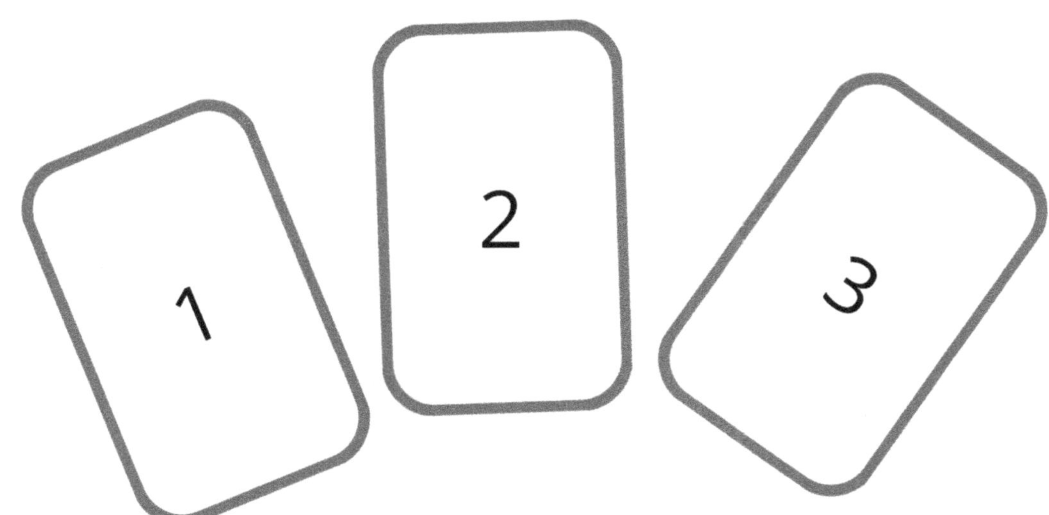

Empower

Card 1 - Know: What is my next step in understanding myself better?
Card 2 - Heal: How can I best improve my physical, mental, emotional, spiritual (or other area of) health?
Card 3 - Empower: How can I be more empowered?

Impressions:

Higher Self

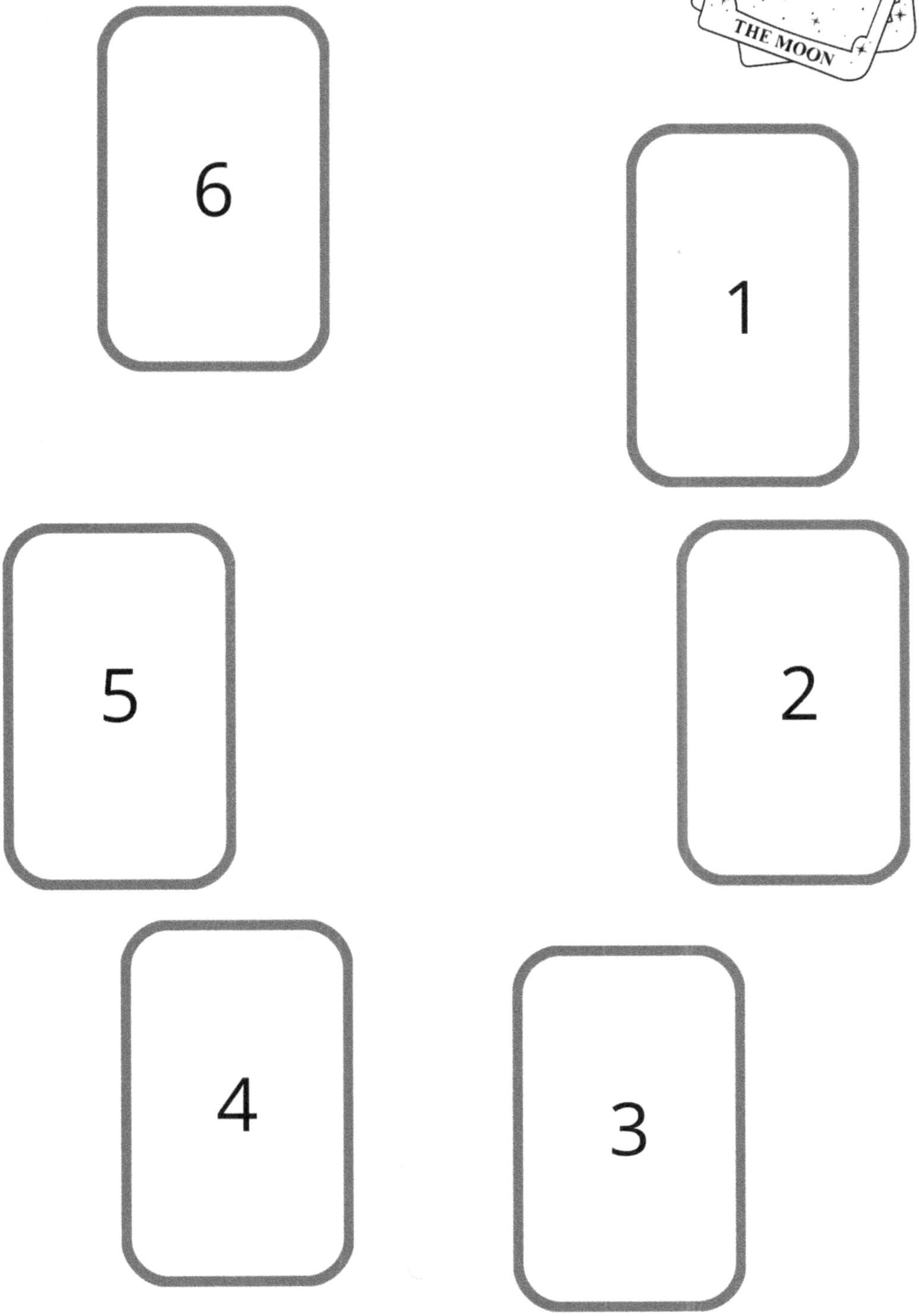

6

1

5

2

4

3

Higher Self

Card 1 - How can I reconnect with my higher self?
Card 2 - Something Beautiful about me
Card 3 - What do I need to heal?
Card 4 - Focus on this to begin the healing process
Card 5 - Outcome for healing yourself
Card 6 - Message from the Universe

Impressions:

Astrological Signs

Aries
March 21 - April 19
for those born under the sign of
The Ram

Taurus
April 20 - May 20
for those born under the sign of
The Bull

Gemini
May 21 -June 20
for those born under the sign of
The Twins

Cancer
June 21 - July 21
for those born under the sign of
The Crab

Leo
July 23-August 22
for those born under the sign of
The Lion

Virgo
August 23 - September 22
for those born under the sign of
The Virgin

Libra
September 23 - October 22
for those born under the sign of
The Scales

Scorpio
October 23 - November 21
for those born under the sign of
The Scorpion

Sagittarius
November 22 - December 21
for those born under the sign of
The Archer

Capricorn
December 22 - January 19
for those born under the sign of
The Goat

Aquarius
January 20 - February 18
for those born under the sign of
The Water Bearer

Pisces
February 19 - March 20
for those born under the sign of
The Fishes

Gemini

May 21 -June 20
Element - Air

Crystals - Tree Agate, Alexandrite, Aquamarine, Cat's Eye, Chrysocolla, Citrine, Emerald, Fluorite, Howlite, Jade, Green Jasper, Lodestone, Moonstone, Moss Agate, Clear Quartz, Sapphire, Serpentine, Tiger's Eye, Topaz, and Watermelon Tourmaline

June is a great month for those born under the sign of Gemini! This is the time when ideas come easily, and opportunities to engage with friends and family are abundant. Fun outdoor activities and adventures may be perfect for a Gemini's naturally curious outlook. It helps express their free-spirited energy. Additionally, June could show new, interesting horoscope readings for Geminis, all about embracing change and being on the lookout for new opportunities. They will have the courage to take advantage of these situations in order to grow as people. So make this June count Gemini, it could be a month full of adventure that you will want to take advantage of!

Cancer

June 21 - July 21
Element - Water

Crystals - Agate, Amber, Beryl, Calcite, Carnelian, Emerald, Moonstone, Opal, Clear Quartz, Rose Quartz, Ruby, Saffhire, Selenite, and Zircon

July is a month filled with magic. With the summer season in full swing, ideas and things to do are endless. This month, you'll be feeling extra empowered to take charge and follow ideas that align with your soul. You may also find that ideas come to life magically, like blessings from the stars. To make the most of this cosmic energy, try taking up something new and challenging yourself to explore ideas you've been harboring for a while.

African Zodiac

The African zodiac is a system based on the observation of people and everyday elements, and African cultures have used it for centuries. The symbols associated with each sign are based on things that are important in African cultures, such as family, daily life, and sacred nature.

Baobab
The Wealth of Amber
Family
Love Every Day
The Market
The Ancestor
The Judge
The Kola Nut
The Traveler
The Distance
Child of the World
The Harvest and the Granary

Alchemist Zodiac

The metals are numbered according to their position in the periodic table. In this sense, silver is 1, iron is 2, mercury is 3, zinc is 4, tin is 5, lead is 6, platinum is 7, nickel is 8, gold is 9, and copper is 0.

Silver
Iron
Mercury
Zinc
Tin
Lead
Platinum
Nickel
Gold
Copper

Arabic Zodiac

There are twelve, and they correspond with the signs of the Western horoscope. They have the name of medieval weapons: Lance, Slingshot, Axe, Dagger, Nail, Mace, Knife, Cutlass, Machete, Chain, Arab dagger, and Bow.

Lance
Slingshot
Axe
Dagger
Nail
Mace
Knife
Cutlass
Machete
Chain
Gumia
Bow

Aztec Zodiac

The Aztecs were a highly advanced civilization with a rich legacy in astronomy and astrology. They believed that God protected us and gave us a protection animal, which also determined our character. They created a whole explanation about how the day of our birth determines our character and our destiny. Aztec horoscope signs are represented by totems, which were usually chosen from the daily life of the members of this region. We can find totems of animals, plants, and even minerals and objects.

The Deer
The Cayman
The House
The Flower
The Jaguar
The Cane
The Rabbit
The Eagle
The Monkey
The Flint
The Dog

Celtic Zodiac

Celtic astrology is a system that uses the seasons and 21 different trees to divide the year. This system is based on the belief that our birth conditions our personality and character. This horoscope is related to the ancient Ogham wisdom, which uses the moon and trees to offer predictions about human life.

Poplar
Birch
Fir
Maple
Hazel
Chestnut
Elm
Apple Tree
Cherry
Beech

Hornbeam
Lime
Rowan
Cedar
Cypress
Walnut
Olive
Pine
Oak
Weeping Willow
Fig tree

Chinese Zodiac

Chinese zodiac, or shengxiao (/shnng-sshyao/ 'born resembling'), is represented by 12 zodiac animals. In order, they are the Rat, Ox, Tiger, Rabbit, Dragon, Snake, Horse, Goat, Monkey, Rooster, Dog, and Pig.

Chinese zodiac years begin/end at Chinese New Year (in January/February). Each year in the repeating zodiac cycle of 12 years is represented by a zodiac animal, each with its own reputed attributes.

Druid Zodiac

Druid astrology is an ancient tradition that dates back 7,000 years. The druids were highly skilled scientists and observers of nature during the Gallic period. They were responsible for keeping track of the changing seasons and celestial events. Their unique form of astrology is based on 13 trees, which they consider sacred symbols of wisdom and knowledge. This rich tradition has been passed down through the ages and is still practiced today. Thanks to the druids, we can still enjoy this ancient art.

Birch tree
Service tree
Ash tree
Alder tree
Willow tree
Hawthorn tree
Oak tree
Holly tree
Hazel tree
Grapevine tree
Ivy tree
Cane tree
Elder tree

Egyptian Zodiac

Characteristics of the personality and the mission of the signs according to your date of birth are divided into twelve signs with the names of gods.

Bastet
Selket
Apep
Ptah
Atum
Isis
Amon Ra
Horus
Maat
Osiris
Hathor
Anubis

Hindu Zodiac

The Hindu Horoscope, or Jyotish, is a form of astrology zodiac signs and the positions of planets to make predictions. Its signs (raashis) correspond with the 12 Western zodiac signs but focus on psychological aspects.

Mesha
Vrishaba
Mithuna
Karkata
Simha
Kanya
Tula
Vrishchika
Dhanus
Makara
Kumbha
Meena

Mayan Zodiac

The Mayan calendar is cyclical and organized into 13 lunar cycles of 28 days. Each lunar cycle is represented by a symbol with specific connotations.

Monkey
Falcon
Jaguar
Fox
Snake
Squirrel
Turtle
Bat
Scorpion
Deer
Owl
Peacock
Lizard

Native American Zodiac

The astrology of Native American Indians is based on the cycles of nature. Their totems or zodiac signs are animals that influence the daily life of Native American Indians. They're divided into four clans, each of which is influenced by an astrological element such as water, air, earth, or fire.

The Snow Goose
The Otter
The Wolf
The Falcon
The Beaver
The Deer
The Woodpecker
The Salmon or Sturgeon
The Grizzly Bear
The Crow
The Snake
The Owl

Orisha Zodiac

Orishas are semi-divine beings that represent different aspects of human existence. There are twelve signs in the Orisha Horoscope, each named after an Orisha and assigned according to a person's date of birth.

Oggún
Oko
Eleggua
Oshún
Changó
Yemanyá
Obatalá
Orula
Babalú Ayé
Agayú Sola
Ochosi
Inle

Tibetan Zodiac

The Tibetan horoscope is a system of astrology based on Buddhism's principles. It is believed that their past lives and experiences determine the destiny of humans. The Tibetan horoscope is made up of 12 signs, which are calculated according to the year of birth.

Snake or Cobra
Horse or Fire Guardian
Sheep or The Crystalline Water Spring
Monkey or The Jade Stele
Bird or Metal Gong
Dog or Lake Turtle
Pig or Copper Bracelet
Mouse or Black Buffalo
Tibetan Ox or New Moon
Tiger or The Exalted Sun
Rabbit or The Monk
Dragon or Comet

Wuykü Zodiac

The Tibetan Horoscope is an ancient form of astrology that originated in Tibet. Unlike other horoscopes, the Tibetan Horoscope only has four signs: the Spider, Scorpion, and Turtle. These animals were considered gods in Tibetan culture. The Acolytes, a group of people who studied predicting the future, are believed to have created the Tibetan Horoscope millennia before the birth of Christ.

Spider
Ant
Scorpion
Turtle

Types of Divination

Abacomancy, Aeromancer, Apantomancy, Arithmancy, Astrology, Augury, Automatic Writing, Belomancy (arrow divination), Bibliomancy, Bone reading (Osteomancy), Brontomancy, Capnomancy, Casting, Ceromancy, Chirognomy, Chiromancy, Cledonism, Conchomancy, Chirognomy, Crystal Ball Reading, Dactylomancy, Dice Divination, Dobutsu Uranai, Domino Divination, Dowsing, Etteilla Tarot, Graphology, Romani Fortune-Telling Cards, Haruspicy, Ifa Divination, Iching, Jiaobei/Poe Kau Cim, Kipper Cards, Lenormand, Libanomancy, Lithomancy, Mahjong, Mi Kayu Ura, Mirror, Scrying, Moleosophy, Necromancy, Nephomancy, Nggam, Numerology, O-Mikuji, Ogham, Oracle Cards, Ouija, Palmistry, Phrenology, Plastromancy, Playing Cards, Pyromancy, Rhabdomancy, Runes, Scapulimancy, Tarot, Tasseomancy, Teraphim, and Xylomancy.

Wow! I'm sure I missed some, but I'll leave it up to you to look up what they all mean.

Alternatives to "So Mote It Be"

"It is as I will It."
"As I speak it, so it is."
"This I command."
This is by my power."
"This I manifest."
"By me and the powers that be."
"Amen"

and my favorite
"Because I freaking said so."

Colors at First Glance

Bringing balance to our lives with color energy is easy. We can do it by wearing our favorite colors, painting rooms in calming colors, or adding different colors to our decor. If we pay attention to the colors around us and how they make us feel, we can use them to improve our lives. And increase our vibrations.

Black for banishing, protection, binding, releasing, and defense.

Green for money, prosperity, employment, fertility, growth, luck, abundance, and your Heart Chakra.

Red for strength, passion, courage, action, survival, love, and your Root Chakra

Yellow for intellect, confidence, travel, movement, joy, imagination, productivity, willpower, and your Solar Plexus Chakra.

Orange for attraction, energy, legal matters, ambition, vitality, opportunity, creativity, inspiration, and your Sacral Chakra.

White for protection, purification, peace, purity, tranquility, and balance.

Blue for healing, peace, forgiveness, communication, truth, calming, focus, memory, and your Throat Chakra.

Purple for spirituality, wisdom, peace, harmony, intuition, psychic abilities, divination, dreams, and your Third Eye Chakra.

But remember to do what feels right to you.
As always, You Do You, Boo!

Candle Color Usage

Using color in spells and rituals can be a powerful way to enhance their energy. Color energy is easy to use and can be woven into your candles, spells, and rituals.

Black - banishing, binding, cord cutting, and endings

Green - money, luck, prosperity, and growth

Red - passion, sexual love, health, and courage

Yellow - intelligence, mental health, memory, and confidence

Orange - happiness, justice, creativity, and flexibility

White - serenity, healing, renewal, and cleansing

Blue - wisdom, dreams, calm, and communication

Purple - divination, intuition, spirituality, and transformation

Pink - empathy, kindness, romance, and generosity

Brown - happiness, justice, creativity, and flexibility

Gold - fortune, enlightenment, talents, and strength

Silver - dreams, moon energy, enchantment, and inspiration

Aura Colors

YELLOW
Energetic, optimistic, confident, childlike, fun-loving, sensitive, happy, free-spirited, creative, generous, and connects with nature and animals.

ORANGE
Creative, independent, adventurous, risk-taker, resourceful, strategic, loves to test physical limits, mentally focused, and overcomes challenges.

BLUE
Loving, nurturing, compassionate, sensitive, forgiving, loyal, spiritual, emotional depth, teaching, caretaker of people and the planet.

RED
Intense, passionate, hard-working, grounded, literal, raw courage, sensual, honest, self-confident, experience the world through touch.

GREEN
Healing, teaching, organized, entrepreneurial, highly intelligent, driven, successful, perfectionist, empowers others, ability to accomplish goals.

MAGENTA
Non-conformist, creative, intelligent, free-spirited, eccentric, original, likes to be the center of attention, strong-willed, unique, and innovative.

TAN
Detail-oriented, practical, cautious, private, calm, clean, logical, intuitive, committed, values love, gentle, analytical, controlled.

VIOLET
Artistic/creative, visionary, loves to take chances, enjoys travel, charismatic leader, humanitarian, inspirational to others, big ideas.

LAVENDER
Enchanting, daydreamer, fragile, sensitive, imaginative, creative, intelligent, gentle, intuitive, love to change directions.

INDIGO
Wise, intuitive, belief in higher ideals + principles, peaceful, creative, non-judgemental, spiritually gifted, sensitive, enlightened consciousness.

WHITE
Gifted healer, highly spiritual, quiet, sensitive, one with nature, adaptable, highly intuitive, loves simplicity, meditative, calming.

Aura

Are in constant motion with every breath

They are not always the same color.

Are a physical representation of the energy surrounding your physical body

It may have one or more colors per layer.

Are not a perfectly rounded shape

They are multidimensional, above, below, and all around you.

They are composed of layers that may blend into each other.

Surround every living thing (human, plant, animal)

Need regular cleaning

Can rip and tear due to physical injury

Need maintenance to repair rips, holes, and tears

It can expand up to 30 feet outside your physical body.

Help you to feel external energies.

Are a natural part of your body

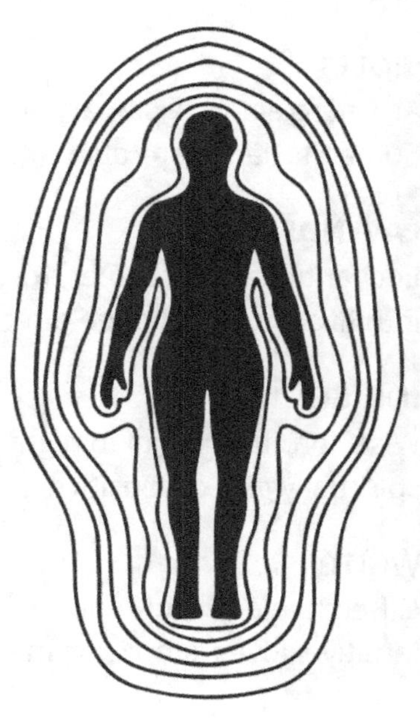

Starting on the outside and moving inward

1 Ketheric Template
2 Celestial/Divine
3 Etheric Template
4 Astral
5 Mental
6 Emotional
7 Etheric

Chakras

CROWN CHAKRA

SAHASRARA

Represents spiritual consciousness and transformation

THIRD EYE CHAKRA

AJNA

Responsible for spiritual communication, awareness, and perception.

THROAT CHAKRA

VISUDDHA

It governs self-expression, communication, and the ability to speak one's truth.

HEART CHAKRA

ANAHATA

Governs people's love for themselves and those around them, supporting empathy, compassion, and forgiveness.

SOLAR PLEXUS CHAKRA

MANIPURA

Represents confidence, self-esteem, and personal power.

SACRAL CHAKRA

SVADHISTHANA

It supports emotional and physical health aspects and governs many of the body's fluids, from the sex organs, the bladder, and the kidneys.

ROOT CHAKRA

MULADHARA

Good health in the body, a sense of connection to the Earth, and a feeling of support and stability in the physical world.

7 MAJOR BODY CHAKRAS

Crown Chakra
Third Eye Chakra
Throat Chakra
Heart Chakra
Solar Plexus
Sacral Chakra
Root Chakra

5 TRANSPERSONAL CHAKRAS

Stellar Gateway
Universal Chakra
Soul Star
Causal Chakra
Earth Star

Seven chakras govern our physical and spiritual bodies. First, the root, sacral, and solar plexus chakras are responsible for our physical reality. Next, the crown, third eye, and throat chakras connect us to the spiritual realm. And finally, the heart chakra is the bridge between the two dimensions. It is a reminder that we are both human and spiritual beings.

Crown Chakra: This chakra, located at the top of the head, is associated with spirituality and our connection to higher intelligence. It's represented by the color purple and helps us to achieve enlightenment. By opening this chakra, we can access greater knowledge and guidance.

Third Eye Chakra: The third eye chakra is a powerful tool for intuition and spiritual insight. It is located behind the middle of the forehead near the pineal gland. This chakra is associated with the color indigo and helps us to open up to greater awareness, psychic senses, and spiritual gifts.

Throat Chakra: The throat chakra is associated with the color blue. It governs our ability to communicate clearly and effectively. When this chakra is balanced, we can express ourselves truthfully and listen and understand others.

Heart Chakra: The heart chakra is located in the center of the chest and governs our ability to experience unconditional love. This chakra also influences our relationships and how we demonstrate compassion and hope. The color associated with the heart chakra is green.

Solar Plexus Chakra: This chakra is situated in the upper belly at the diaphragm. Its color is yellow, which guides our will and mental layers. It is also responsible for our energy, personal power, and issues related to the Ego.

Sacral Chakra: This chakra influences our emotions and creativity. It's located just a few inches below the belly button and is associated with orange. In addition, this chakra affects our views on intimacy, boundaries, and trust.

Root Chakra: This chakra is located at the base of the spine, in the pelvic region. It is responsible for our physical reality, safety, security, and survival instincts. It is often associated with the color red.

Balancing Act

Your chakras are responsible for your health and well-being. You'll feel physically and emotionally good when they're balanced and healthy. However, when one or more of your chakras needs to be balanced, it can lead to problems. To keep your chakras balanced, ensure they're all spinning in the same direction and size. Also, check that they're free of obstruction and appear bright and vibrant.

When one of your chakras is blocked, it means that it's not spinning as quickly or smoothly as the others. This can be due to a buildup of dense energies, making the chakra appear smaller than normal. In some cases, the chakra might spin in the opposite direction. If you have a blocked chakra, it's important to address the issue as soon as possible.

An overactive chakra is often spinning too quickly, appearing out of control. It may also appear larger than normal and begin to dominate the energy of neighboring chakras if left unbalanced. An overactive chakra can also change shape, becoming oval or oblong rather than a perfect circle.

Self-Healing Your Chakras

You can use several tools and techniques to open, heal and balance your chakras.

Yoga Poses: Yoga is an excellent way to get your chakras to open up and help your energy flow freely throughout your body. Yoga helps to move stuck and stagnant energy from your energy field, which can prevent the chakras from functioning properly. For example, if someone is having trouble opening their heart chakra, I recommend spending ten minutes a day doing back bending poses that help open their chest, heart, shoulders, and upper spine.

Essential Oils: Aromatherapy can be a helpful tool for recalibrating our thoughts, emotions, and energies. Scents containing earthy scents and tree properties can help the root chakra better align and focus a person's energy downward. This can be helpful for individuals who are struggling to keep their energy grounded.

Crystals: Healing crystals can balance, replenish and restore energy levels. People who love crystals also often like to bathe with them, infuse water with their energies, sleep with gemstones, or decorate their homes with rocks. When chakra healing, you can place a healing stone directly on or near the chakra you want to work with while meditating or resting.

Sounds: Singing bowls, tuning forks, and Solfeggio frequencies can be used to open and heal blocked chakras. Listening to certain sounds in nature can also be helpful. For example, listening to water sounds such as rain, waves, or waterfalls can help a person to connect more deeply to their sacral chakra and the watery properties of their womb.

Foods: Certain diets can help to open chakras or clear blocked energies. One example is eating more "yellow foods," such as peppers, lentils, squash, bananas, and corn, to assist with the healing of the solar plexus chakra.

Energy Work: You can do several daily things to help clear your energy and raise your vibration. This includes things like clearing your chakras and balancing your energy field. These activities can be beneficial in removing stuck energy and keeping yourself in balance.

Using A Pendulum To Check Your Chakras

One way to tell if your chakras are out of balance is to use a pendulum. This is a quick and easy way to check your chakras, and anyone can do it. To check your chakras with a pendulum, follow these steps:

Hold the pendulum in your dominant hand, and place it a few inches above the palm of your other hand.

Wait for the pendulum to stop moving, or command it to be still by saying, "stop" out loud. Then, make sure the pendulum has always stopped moving before asking it a new question.

Tell your pendulum, "Show me what a healthy chakra on my body looks like." Wait for the pendulum to respond and begin moving. Note the direction the chakra spins, how fast it spins, and how big of a circle it makes.

Once the pendulum has stopped moving, ask it to show you what each chakra looks like. For example, say, "Now, show me what my root chakra looks like." Then, take note of what the pendulum does. If it spins in the opposite direction, changes size, or barely moves, it could indicate a blockage in that chakra. If it starts spinning faster, makes oblong shapes, or spins in a large circle, it could indicate an overactive chakra.

Repeat this for each of your 7 main chakras.

CHAKRA	BLOCKED	BALANCED	OVERACTIVE
Crown	depression learning difficulties weak faith anger at divine brain fog	strong faith universal love intelligent aware wise understanding	dogmatic judgemental spiritual addiction ungrounded
Third Eye	poor judgement lacks focus poor imagination cant see beyond physical	imaginative intuitive clear thoughts and vision sees beyond the physical	nightmares delusions hallucinations obsessive see too many spirits
Throat	can't express self or speak out misunderstood secretive not a good listener	confident expression clear communicator creative diplomatic	opinionated load critical gossipy yell or talk over others harsh words
Heart	lack of empathy bitter hateful trust issues intolerant	peaceful loving compassionate tolerant warm open	jealous codependent self-sacrificing gives too much
Solar Plexus	low self esteem feeling powerless inferiority complex	confident feel in control personal power drive good self-image	power hungry domineering perfectionist critical
Sacral	low libido fear of intimacy no creativity isolated	passion creative healthy libido optimistic open	over emotional fixated on sex hedonistic manipulative
Root	fearful anxious financial instability ungrounded	safe secure centered grounded happy to be alive	greedy lust for power aggressive materialist cynical

Chakra Notes

Crown Chakra
To Know and Understand

Third Eye
To See

Throat Chakra
To Speak and Be Heard

Heart Chakra
To Love and Be Loved

Solar Plexus Chakra
To Act

Sacral Chakra
To Feel and Desire

Root Chakra
To Be Here and To Have

Psychic Abilities

Telepathy - is the ability to pass on information, ideas, impressions, feelings, moods, and thoughts between living beings without the involvement of known sensory organs.

Precognition - predicts future events that are already anticipated or experienced, whereby the prediction can relate to a few seconds or many years.

Mediumship - The term medium or channel refers to a person who can establish a connection to the spiritual world and is thus able to convey messages between people and supernatural beings such as angels, spirits, or the deceased.

Telekinesis - is the movement of objects through the power of human consciousness without the aid of the hands or other instruments that touch the object.

Apportion - This psychic ability is defined as the appearance or disappearance of an object without physical touch.

Clairvoyance - or clear seeing, is the ability to use paranormal senses to see images and visions. Clairvoyants use their gifts to obtain information, whether it is about an object, a person, future events, past events, or even a location.

Clairaudience - or clear hearing, is the ability to hear things psychically without using your physical ears. People with this ability receive information from spiritual beings through messages and sounds.

Clairsentience - means clear feeling or precise sensing. A person with this gift feels a person's soul, puts himself into their emotions, feelings, and perceptions, and interprets them.

Simplified Psychic Abilities

Clairvoyance - When you see stuff (clear vision)

Clairaudience - When you hear stuff (clear hearing)

Clairsentience - When you feel stuff (clear sensing and feeling)

Clairempathy - When you feel other people's stuff

Claircognizance - When you just know stuff (clear knowing)

Clairsgustance - When you taste stuff (clear taste)

Clairalience or Clairscent - When you smell stuff (clear smell)

Clairtangency - Pyschometry - When you get touched and stuff (clear touch)

Telepathy - When you can communicate through thoughts and stuff.

Telekenisis - When you can move things with your mind and stuff.

Psychic Notes

Types of Purification

The body gets purified by Water and Yoga.
Breath gets purified by Pranayama (Breath Regulation)
The mind gets purified by Meditation
Intellect gets purified by Knowledge
Memory gets purified by Thinking and Introspection
The ego gets purified by Selfless Service
Self gets purified by Silence
Food gets purified by Positive Thoughts
(While cooking & eating)
Wealth gets purified by Donation
Feelings get purified by Love and Surrender

What is Magic?

Magic is wearing a family heirloom for good luck and protection.

Magic is sleeping in your favorite shirt because it makes you feel safe.

Magic is growing your herbs and plants.

Magic is a deep breath, an "I am" affirmation, or a murmured assurance of "I can do this" before something big.

Magic is keeping a candle lit on your desk because you find it relaxing.

Magic is reading the energy behind the words.

Magic is opening your windows and playing your favorite music.

Magic is enchanting your child's blanket with extra love and protection so they'll always sleep soundly.

Magic is making a "monster under the bed" spray for your children.

Magic is talking to animals.

Magic is blowing out candles on your birthday while making a wish.

Magic is tossing a coin in a fountain and making a wish.

Magic is saying "God Bless You" to someone when they sneeze.

Magic is praying for a favorable outcome.

Magic is knocking on wood to call on the spirits for protection.

Magic is what you make it.

Ponder Points

In a grimoire, specific instructions may pertain to a particular tradition, or they may contain personal records intended only for the use of the individual author. Sometimes the grimoire (or sections of it) is passed down or copied from a master book. The term grimoire is generic and may be used in place of the title of the actual book, which is often kept secret.

Popularly known as the "book of shadows," it is a sort of Wiccan recipe book that includes spells and incantations. Some argue that a book of shadows resembles a diary or journal and that highly personal musings have no place in the more didactic grimoire. On the other hand, purists insist that the grimoire should be entirely instructional, full of information, annotation, and practical application. Fortunately, there is no correct or incorrect way of building, blessing, and using your grimoire for our purposes. Whatever works for you.

As a beginner witch, there are plenty of things to research! I've included some of these topics in this book or other books.

The history of witchcraft and of the Burning Times and the persecution of witches in general, types of witches, types of magick, types of spells, types of divination, talismans vs. sigils, seals, symbols, deities (For pagan witches), spirits, closed/open religions, and religions/faiths/spiritualities other than your own, lucid dreaming (Astral Projection), the elements, grounding, forging herbology, mycology & crystals, altars, astronomy, and moon phases, types of spells, and energy, The history, and environment of where you live, The history of countries that you have ancestral ties to.

Some extra credit topics:-)
Sacred geometry, what damages crystals, a crystal grid and how to make one, candle flame reading, bone correspondences, what is a poppet? How to use it, basic alchemical symbols, ways to break a hex, favorite cryptids, and their lore? What do you think about witchcraft? What is a liminal space? Scrying, ghost hunting, species of demons, forest bathing and earthing, wildcraft, traditional ways of living, candle making, animals and insects, cemeteries and the broader subject of death, DIY own personal care and beauty products, personal growth,l and living mindfully.

But more importantly, whatever tickles your fancy. You do you!!!

Spells vs. Ritual

Spells:
Powered by intention Done to bring about a specific outcome
Asking for something you want, sort of like a prayer
Almost always has a physical anchor
Less formal/structured
Done when there is a need

Rituals:
Also powered by intention
It may contain a spell but doesn't have to
Often done for a celebratory purpose
Tend to have a more structured plan to make them easier to repeat
Sometimes more formal
Often repeated yearly or monthly

Methods of Spells

To Banish - burn an effect to ash and sweep off the back doorstep, cast it out a window, or bury it in the ground and spit on it.

To Encourage - plant it by the front door/steps, bury it by a window, or place it on a windowsill.

To Hide - place in a black jar, cover with a cloth and bury, or wrap with a ribbon.

To Cleanse - bury it in a bowl of salt, burn herbs and pass through the smoke, or lay it in a moon water bath.

To Glamour - leave under the full moon, and hold its reflection over a mirror with herbs.

To Wish - place before a candle and blow it out, drown a coin in the water, or let seeds blow into the wind.

To Communicate - (with a spirit or deity), anoint a candle, leave out offerings, or open the front doors and windows.

Types of Spells

Banishing - Banish means to cast something or someone out of your life. If it's a person, the spell will stop them from seeing you or even thinking about you. Some practitioners use banishing spells to get rid of negative entities in general. Banishing spells are popular among folk magic circles such as Hoodoo.

Sweetening - Commonly known as honey jars, sweetening spells try to sweeten or mellow someone's attitude toward you. They can be cast on a specific person or situation (such as a legal case, a career problem, or a relationship). A representation of the target is placed in a jar (a name, personal belonging, sigil), and honey is added on top.

Binding - To bind means to control or limit the target's power. The idea behind this type of ritual is to symbolically tie up someone or something to restrict their actions and prevent them from harming themselves or others. While casting these spells on a person is not advisable, you could cast a binding spell on yourself, for example, to break a bad habit.

Protection - Feeling safe and protected is our most valuable gift. In ancient times, shamans and healers would help people to cure diseases, remove ailments and feel stronger. These rituals were complemented in many cases with the use of remedies such as food, beverages, cleanses, and more.

Freezing - Similar to binding spells, a freezer spell is typically used when we want to silence somebody. We call this to freeze someone's words or actions. The most common is to write down the target's name and put it in the freezer.

Good Luck - Inviting good luck is a way to empower ourselves. These spells can open doors by removing fear and increasing our willingness to take risks that lead to success. Attract good fortune by consecrating a lucky amulet such as a coin or a gemstone.

Types of Witches

Alexandrian
Ancestral/Hereditary
Art
Astronomy
Augury
Baby
Blood
Celtic
Ceremonial
Chaos
Christian
Correllian
Cosmic
Cottage/Hearth
Coven
Crystal
Death
Desert
Dianic
Divination
Druid
Eclectic
Elemental
Elf
Enchanter
Energy
Faerie
Fire
Folk
Forest
Garden
Gardnerian
Gothic
Green
Grey

Hedge
Hellenic
Hermit
Kitchen
Lunar
Music
Natural
Nature
Nocturnal
Norse
Pagan
Religious
Santeria
Satanic
Sea
Seasonal
Secular
Shadow
Shamanic
Sun/Solar
Storm
Swamp
Tech
Thelma
Thunder
Traditional
Urban
Voodoo
Wiccan
White

Gardnerian

The Gardnerian Witch follows the traditions of Gardnerian Wicca, which Gerald Garner created in the 1950s. This type of witchcraft has a hierarchical system with a high priest and priestess; these witches often practice in covens. To become a Gardnerian Witch, you must go through a variety of initiations. You must learn the traditions and culture of that branch of witchery and complete initiation into a coven to be considered a true witch.

Alexandrian

The Alexandrian Witch is similar to the Gardnerian Witch in that they both follow some of the same traditions, and both are based on Wicca belief systems. However, Alexandrian witchcraft has its own unique traditions and initiation processes. The Alexandrian Witch also practices more ceremonial magic than the Gardnerian, and many Alexandrians practice Oabalah as well.

American Folk Magic

Appalachian
Hoodoo
Ozarks
Pow-Wow

Ok, so, which witch are you? Sorry for the pun. Are you more confused now than you were before? I am, too, but what is a name? You know who and what you are, so that is all needed.

"A rose by any other name would smell as sweet" - Williams Shakespeare.

Types of Witches Notes

Witch Words

Affirmation: These are motivational phrases or words that inspire you.

Altar - A sacred space of devotional or ritual work. This space is usually a table, shelf, or corner where offerings are presented to spirits and where one may perform rituals or spell work.

Animism - The belief that objects, places, and creatures all possess a distinct spiritual essence or soul.

Arcane - From the Latin for "hidden" or "secret." The term is often applied to mystical secrets, and the word arcanum is used in alchemy and arcana in Tarot.

Ascended Masters: These enlightened Spirit Guides were ordinary humans who underwent a spiritual process and reincarnated as Ascended Masters.

Aspect - An archetype of a deity or entity. A form, facet, or persona of a deity. In astrology, an aspect is an angle planets make to each other in a chart.

Asperge - To cleanse and purify a space. This is usually done by spraying water around a room or using an herbal bundle to cleanse the area.

Astral Plane - The multi-dimensional plane within the astral realm where one can travel using their astral body.

Athame - A double-edged knife with a black handle, usually used in ceremonial magick and traditional Wiccan practices. It is associated with masculine energy and the elements of fire and air.

Auditory impressions: These are thoughts, ideas, words, phrases, or blocks of thought that pop into your head out of the blue. They are heard in your own voice in your own mind by those who are clairaudient and come from your Higher Self, Spirit Guides, spiritual team, and loved ones in heaven.

Aura: All living things have a glowing energy field of color around them. Auras reflect the state of the soul and change based on what you're feeling, if you're sick, or if you are stressed.

Besom - A broom made of twigs tied around a stick. Used in cleansing rituals and to invite beneficial energies to a space.

Binaural beats: They're scientifically proven to alter your brain waves and mental status and are used to help develop psychic ability. The beats are created with two tones that alternate in your left and right ears (you have to wear headphones with them). Sometimes it's just the tones, but most of the time, they include music or nature sounds as well.

Blot - A communal event where animal sacrifice is used as an offering to a deity or god. Members of the ritual feast on the sacrifice in celebration. In today's age, sacrificing a live animal is less common; there will be lots of good food and wine in its place.

Book of Shadows - Personal notebook kept by a practitioner of magick to record their work. This would include spellwork, rituals, personal wisdom, dreams, and observations.

Boline - A small sacred knife used to cut items during a ritual. In contrast to the "Athame," a "Boline" usually has a white handle.

Broom closet - One who practices Magick or follows a pagan lifestyle and keeps that aspect of their life to themselves. Being "In the broom closet" means you practice in secrecy from your friends and family.

Burning Times - A name given to the days of the Reformation, Inquisition, etc., when Witches were tried and executed by inquisitors, sometimes burned at the stake.

Casting the circle - To project a circle or cone of energy where the practitioner will contain the energy generated by their ritual or magick.

Cense - To perfume something ritually with the odor of burning incense, such as a room, person, or object.

Chakra: Picture 7 gorgeous spinning wheels of color running up and down your spine- from the tip of your head to the base of your tailbone. These energetic points are chakras, responsible for different parts of your existence. When your chakras are open, all is right in the world. But things like anxiety and sickness can block or close them.

Charge - Intentionally passing specific energy or intention to an object, person, or space. Items that have been charged are sacred or consecrated for a particular purpose.

Charm - From the Latin carmen meaning "song, incantation," but came to be a generic term referring to any type of magick. As a noun, it commonly refers to a small object that protects its wearer from evil. As a verb, it commonly refers to the act of using magick to exert control over a person.

Clairalience: It's the ability of "inner or psychic smelling."

Clairaudience: Translated to "inner Hear," those with clairaudient ability to receive psychic impressions through the auditory channel. They may hear intuitive messages from their Spirit Guides or their High Self.

Claircognizance: Translated into "inner knowing," those with claircognizant ability receive intuition with a strong sense of knowing. Their sense of knowing might not have any logical base to it, but they know it to be true.

Clairgustance: Translated psychic or inner tasting" Usually, this ability shows up when a medium is doing a reading.

Clairsentience: Translates into "inner feeling. Those with clairsentience receive psychic impressions in the form of sensing and feeling.

Clairvoyance: Translated, it means "inner seeing." Someone with clairvoyance receives intuitive impressions visually in the form of visions, images, and colors.

Conjure - Originally had to do with the taking of oaths. Its Magickal associations came when it was used to refer to binding demons to one's will. In time, "conjurer" became a generic term for a magick user.

Coven - A group of witches is called a Coven. A witch's magickal family may be considered their coven if they have formed a group to perform magick alongside each other.

Covenstead - A meeting space for witches to gather as a Coven.

The Craft - Refers to Witchcraft as a whole. One who follows the path of witchcraft follows the path of the craft.

Craft name - A name chosen by the practitioner for themselves within the magickal and spiritual community. This name can be a representation of their craft, abilities, interests or can sometimes be given to them by other members of their coven or elders.

Crown chakra: Located at the top of your head, it is associated with the color violet and is responsible for your connection to the universe.

Crystal: These gorgeous tools can be used in many ways. Crystals have strong, energetic properties, and people use their energetic vibrations to achieve certain effects.

Deosil - The clockwise motion of directing energy during a spell or ritual. This can be done with your hand, a wand, a knife, etc.

Dianic - A Wiccan type of group within the Goddess tradition, focused on female experience and empowerment, sometimes linked to feminism and led by women.

Diffuser: This device is how you get all the aromatic benefits of essential oils. You fill it p with distilled water, then add a few drops of essential oil. The diffuser breaks up the oil and releases a fine mist throughout the room.

Drawing down - Invoking a Goddess into one who possesses the ability and strength to handle the deity's energy. Drawing refers to divination using mistletoe, where a high-ranking political/religious class in some ancient Celtic cultures.

Eclectic - One who shapes their practices from many different cultures and belief systems. Someone who follows their own experimental journey rather than dedicating themselves to one predefined path.

Elder - One who has reached old age within the Pagan community. This person will typically guide and share their wisdom with others.

Elementals - Personified spirits of each Element. Traditionally: Gnomes, Undines, Sylphs, and Salamanders.

Empath: Empaths feel other people's energy intimately and deeply as if they are experiencing it themselves. It's a psychic ability connected with the gift of clairsentience (psychic feeling and sensing). Being an empath is different from just being empathetic.

Elder - One who has reached old age within the Pagan community. This person will typically guide and share their wisdom with others.

Elementals - Personified spirits of each Element. Traditionally: Gnomes, Undines, Sylphs, and Salamanders.

Esbat - Meeting of a coven outside of the Sabbats, where healing, feasts, psychic work, and rituals take place, sometimes in the Full Moon but not necessarily.

Esoteric - From Ancient Greek esoteriks, "belonging to an inner circle." It often refers to occult orders and belief systems like Gnosticism, Kabbalah, and Rosicrucianism, whose teachings are not shared outside of a group of initiates.

Essential oil: These oils are extracted from plants around the world, and because they are condensed, they offer a ton of benefits.

Equinox - This happens twice a year when the duration of the day is equal to the duration of the night (12 hours each). The equinoxes occur around March 2st and September 21st and correspond to spring and autumn.

Evil Eye - A particular look or stare that is believed to bring bad luck for the person at whom it is directed, for reasons of envy or dislike. It is a curse or legend believed to be cast by a malevolent glare and usually given to a person when they are unaware.

Familiar - An entity that has a spiritual bond with a Witch on a higher plane, sometimes said to shape-shift into a physical being such as a companion animal.

Familiars and a Pet...NOT the same thing. Nor should you want your beloved pet to be your Familiar. For a modern witch to lay claim to a Familiar spirit, the animal must have made a pact with the witch.

Great Rite - Wiccan ritual involving symbolic sexual intercourse (actual sex or symbolic) with the purpose of drawing energy from the powerful connection between a male and a female participant.

Green Witch - A practitioner who works with plants, flowers, and herbs, and studies herbalism, botany, and folk magick. Green Witches talk to nature for guidance and respect for every living being. Green Witchcraft is the discipline of tuning into the energies of Earth through herbs. It's an important piece in the puzzle of working with the Five Elements of Nature: Air, Water, Fire, Earth, and Spirit.

Grounding (spiritual grounding): In order to do your best energy, intuitive, and mediumship work, you need your energetic frequency to be high. Spirits and souks don't have psychical bodies weighing them down, so their energetic vibe is fast. Because of that, connecting with your intuitive abilities can leave you feeling like you are floating or drifting. Grounding reconnects you to the earth and your spiritual self to your physical self.

Guided meditation: This version of meditation uses voice prompts to lead you through a set meditation.

Heart chakra: This important chakra is located in the center of your chest and manages your feelings of love, openness, and empathy. Its green color is said to symbolize health, prosperity, and abundance.

Higher Self: Your higher self is the purest form of you. It is everything love and never concerns itself with trivial things. It has been around for a long time and knows your purpose in this lifetime. We can connect to our Higher Self through our intuition and meditation.

Kindred - Members of a community gather for mutual benefit and to share their beliefs.

Left-hand path - A type of practice that pursues the empowerment of the self over nature or any spiritual order. It focuses on the strength and will of the practitioner rather than on the communion or alignment with Divinity or nature.

Magic or Magick - Some prefer to use the term "Magick" to differentiate it from stage magic performed by illusionists. The word "magic" has its roots in Magh, which meant "to be able, to have power," later found in Latin magice, meaning sorcery. The correct term for stage magic is "illusionist," as it is not actual Magic but rather an illusion of Magic. Aleister Crowley chose to use Magick with a -k for his practices and rituals. The term has since been re-popularized by those who have adopted elements of his teachings, but not everyone.

Otherkin - Those who believe they have an aspect within them that is non-human. Examples: Vampires, werewolves, fairies, shape-shifters, etc.

Pendulum - A handheld device, usually a crystal or metal piece hung on a chain, used to receive yes or no answers.
Polytheism - The belief in many gods. A polytheist may worship multiple gods in their craft.

Quarters - The four corners and/or watchtowers associated with each cardinal direction in a magickal circle. They are symbolic structures called upon to guard over a circle during a ritual. The Four Quarters are spirits that rule over each direction: North, East,
South and East. Each is associated with one of the four classical elements: Earth, Air, Fire, and Water.

Reconstructionist - One who tries to recreate a single pre-Christian tradition, emphasizing historical accuracy over eclecticism, usually with a few exceptions.

Rede - From Middle English, meaning "advice" or "counsel," the Wiccan Rede provides the key moral system for Wiccans; "An it harm none, do what thou will."

Runes - The Scandinavian alphabet is mainly used today for divinatory purposes. Runes are usually inscribed on small stones.

Sabbat - Each of the eight Wiccan holidays is celebrated in a calendar year. The first sabbat is Yule, and then comes Imbolc, Ostara, Beltane, Litha, Lammas, Mabon, and Samhain. These festivals are considered sacred days, and it's tradition to celebrate them in good company.

Shadow Work - The shadow represents the repressed aspects of the personality that are rejected by the ego. Shadow work is an introspective practice where we face our pain instead of fighting it.

Sigil - A magickally charged seal, symbol, or glyph used in spells or charms.

Solstice - The time when the sun reaches its highest or lowest point at noon, resulting in the shortest and longest days of the year, typically around June 21-22 and December 21-22.

Summerland - A place beyond the material plane, similar to an afterlife, where souls go between incarnations.

Tradition - The beliefs, structures, history, rituals, and techniques followed and passed on for generations by a specific group of Pagans.

Warlock - From Old English for "traitor, liar, oath-breaker." It was sometimes used to refer to a person who was in league with the devil, and from there, it evolved (mainly in fictional work) into a male equivalent of "witch."

Wiccaning - Blessing a child or a newborn into the world by those who are part of the Wiccan community. A Neopagan ritual analogous to the christening or baptism of an infant.

Witch Word Notes

The Elements

The elements are another essential aspect of Witchcraft; we often call on them during spells and rituals. There are four primary elements, each of which has particular associations. Each element represents a different type of energy that you can harness.

Earth Elemental Magic The element of earth is the foundation of all life. The color green and the northern quarter align with the element of earth. It is potent in spells that require wisdom and spells for fertility, prosperity, strength, and wealth.

Air Elemental Magic The element of air is light, fuel for all living things. It is represented by the color yellow and the eastern quarter when casting a circle. Spells for renewal, change, intuition, and knowledge call upon the air.

Fire Elemental Magic The element of fire is a source of creation and destruction of life. It is represented by the color red and the southern quarter when casting a circle. Spells for passion, inspiration, intuition, creativity, and protection use fire.

Water Elemental Magic Water represents the flow of life. It is represented by the color blue and the western quarter when casting a circle. It is powerful in spells for healing, peace, and compassion.

Earth

Direction - North

Rules - Grounding, strength, healing, nature, animals, success, stability, sturdiness, foundations, empathy, fertility, death, rebirth, and wisdom

Time - Midnight

Season - Winter

Colors - Green, brown, black, white, and gold

Zodiac - Taurus, Virgo, and Capricorn

Tools - Pentacle, salt, crystals, dirt, herbs, wood, plants, and flowers

Virtues - Being centered, patient, truthful, dependable, and thorough

Vices - Dullness, laziness, and inconsiderable

Crystals - Emerald, jet, tourmaline, quartz, granite, bedrock, salt, peridot, onyx, jasper, azurite, and amethyst

Metals - Iron and lead

Plants - Cedar, cypress, honeysuckle, ivy magnolia, grains, patchouli, primrose, sage, nuts, and oak

Ruling planets - Venus and Saturn

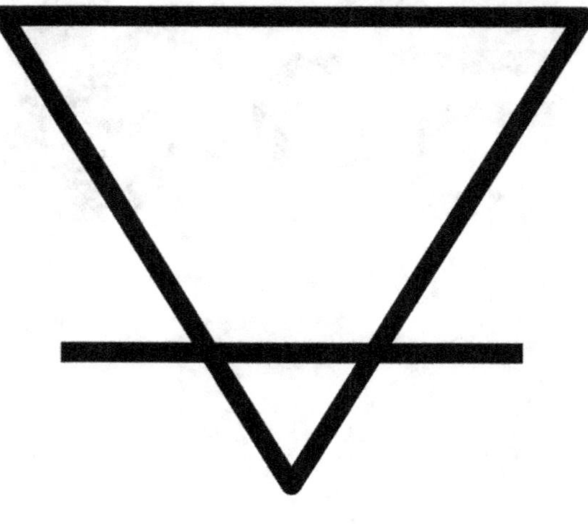

Earth

Symbol: P
Solar System: Earth, Saturn, Venus
Celebrations: Earth Day, Hunting of the Wren, Yule
Time of Day: Midnight
Runes: Is, Tyr, Ur
Colors: Black, Brown, Green, White Chakra: Root
Zodiac: Capricorn, Taurus, Virgo Season: Winter
Ogham: loho
Direction: North
Energy: Yin
Numbers: 4, 6, 8
Tarot: Pentacles
Trees: Ash, Blackthorn, Cedar, Cypress, Elder, Elm, Holly, Juniper, Locust, Magnolia, Maple, Oak, Olive, Pine, Pomegranate, Rowan, Spruce, Witch Hazel
Herb & Garden: Comfrey, Fern, Honeysuckle, Ivy, Jasmine, Mugwort, Primrose, Sage, Vervain Misc. Plants: Cinquefoil, Clove, Grains, Henbane, High John, Horehound, Mandrake, Patchouli, Reed
Gemstones & Minerals: Agate, Alexandrite, Amazonite, Amber, Andalusite, Apophyllite, Calcite (green), Cat's Eye, Cerussite, Chrysocolla, Chrysoprase, Diopside, Emerald, Fluorite, Hematite, Jade, Jasper, Jet, Kunzite, Malachite, Moss Agate, Peridot, Petrified Wood, Quartz (rutilated), Salt, Smoky Quartz, Staurolite, Sugilite, Tourmaline (black, brown, green, watermelon), Turquoise, Unakite
Metals: Lead, Mercury From the Sea: Coral (black)

Earth

Angels: Gabriel, Auriel
Goddesses: Anat, Ariadne, Artemis, Asherah, Bertha, Ceres, Demeter, Gaia, Kore, Nephthys, Persephone, Rhea, Rhiannon
Magical: Brownies, Dryads, Elves, Fairies, Gnomes, Pixies
Gods: Adonis, Arawn, Cernunnos, Dionysus, Geb, the Green Man, Khnum, Marduk, Mimir, Pan, Prometheus. Vishnu
Animals: Antelope, Armadillo, Badger, Bear, Boar, Buffalo / Bison, Cattle, Deer (stag), Dog, Elephant, Goat, Groundhog, Hippopotamus, Jaguar, Mole, Otter, Pig, Prairie Dog, Wolverine Birds: Blue Jay, Chicken, Crow, Goose, Sparrow, Swan, Turkey, Woodpecker
Reptile: Crocodile, Snake, Toad, Tortoise, Turtle Insect/Misc.: Dragonfly
Mythical: Dragon, Selkies
Ritual Tool: Pentacle
Sense: Touch
Principle: To Be Silent
Issues, Intentions & Powers: abundance, acceptance, agriculture, anxiety, balance, beginnings, business, comfort, communication, consecrate/bless, consciousness, creativity, cycles, death, endurance, energy (general, receptive), family, fertility, gentleness, grounding, growth, healing, hexes, the home, justice, life, magic (dragon), manifestation, money, nurture, the otherworld/ underworld, patience, peace, pregnancy/childbirth, prosperity, protection, purpose, rebirth/ renewal, relationships, the senses (smell, touch), sensuality, sex/uality, spirits (nature spirits), stability, strength, success, support, travel, warmth, wealth, weather, well-being, willpower, wisdom

Air

Direction - East

Rules - Mind, clarity, wisdom. knowledge, logic, abstract thought, wind, higher consciousness, divination, psychic work, intuition, and memory

Time - Dawn

Season - Spring

Colors - Yellow, gold, white, and light blue

Zodiac - Gemini, Libra, and Aquarius

Tools - Feather, wand, staff, incense, censer, pen, broom, and bell

Virtues - Intelligent, practical, and optimistic

Vices - Impulsive, frivolous, and easily fooled

Crystals - Topaz, amber, citrine, jasper, and agate

Metals - Tin and copper

Plants - Acacia, anise, aspen, clover, frankincense, lavender, lemongrass, myrrh, pine, vervain, and arrow

Ruling planets - Mercury, Jupiter, and Uranus

Air

Zodiac: Aquarius, Gemini, Libra
Symbol: A
Solar System: Jupiter, Mercury, Uranus
Season: Spring
Time of Day: Dawn
Celebration: Ostara
Ogham: Onn
Runes: Beorc, Hagal, Thorn
Direction: East
Energy: Yang
Colors: Blue (light), Gray, Lavender, Pink, Red, Silver, White, Yellow (bright, light)
Chakras: Crown, Heart, Throat
Number: 5
Tarot: Fool, Swords, Wands
Trees: Acacia, Alder, Apple, Ash, Aspen, Cedar, Chestnut, Elder, Elm Fir, Hawthorn, Hazel, Holly, Horse Chestnut, Laurel, Linden, Maple, Mesquite, Oak, Olive, Palm, Pine, Sycamore, Walnut, Yew
Herb & Garden: Agrimony, Anemone, Bergamot, Borage, Broom, Clover, Comfrey, Dandelion, Fern, Ivy, Lavender, Lily of the Valley, Marjoram, Marigold, Mugwort, Peppermint, Primrose, Sage, Spearmint, Thyme, Vervain, Violet, Yarrow
Misc. Plants: Anise, Bamboo, Bittersweet, Eyebright, Frankincense, Goldenrod, Horehound, Meadowsweet, Mistletoe, Myrrh, Nutmeg, Reed, Sandalwood, Star Anise, Wormwood
Gemstones & Minerals: Agate (tree), Ametrine, Angelite, Aragonite, Aventurine, Blue Lace Agate, Celestite, Chrysoberyl, Desert Rose, Moldavite, Opal, Quartz (clear), Sodalite, Sphene, Staurolite, Topaz (blue), Tourmaline (blue)
Metals: Aluminum, Mercury, Tin
From the Sea: Angel Wing, Jingle

Air

Goddesses: Amaterasu, Athena, Arianrhod, Hera, Nut, Phoebe Gods: Hermes, Khnum, Mimir, Mercury, Quetzalcoatl, Thoth, Zeus Magical: Elves, Fairies, Pixies, Sylphs
Angels: Michael, Raphael
Animal: Gazelle
Insect: Firefly
Birds: Albatross, Condor, Eagle, Falcon, Hawk, Seagull Mythical: Dragon, Sphinx, Thunderbird
Sense: Smell
Ritual Tools: Athame, Incense, Sword
Principle: To Know
Issues, Intentions & Powers: acceptance, action, Astral Realm, beginnings, business, clairvoyance, clarity, communication, concentration/ focus, consecrate/bless, creativity, divination, enchantment, energy, enlightenment, fairness, freedom, harmony, healing, imagination, inspiration, intelligence, intuition, justice, knowledge, learning, life, light, loss, magic (animal, dragon), memory/memories, the mind, money, motivation, order/ organize, power, protection, psychic ability, purification, relationships, release, the senses (hearing, smell, touch), shamanic work, spirits, spirituality, travel, visions, weather (general, lightning, storms), willpower, wisdom

Fire

Direction - South

Rules - Passion, drive, sexuality, motivation, creation, creativity, desire, enthusiasm, energy, protection, transformation, healing, destruction, heat, flame, and light

Time - High Noon

Season - Summer

Colors - Red, orange, gold, white, and hot pink

Zodiac - Aries, Leo, and Sagittarius

Tools - Censor, sword, dagger, wand, and candle

Virtues - Motivation, energy, drive, courage, willpower, and enthusiasm

Vices - Lust, excess, rage, aggression, hatred, and jealousy

Crystals - Amber, obsidian, rhodochrosite, ruby, lava, garnet, fire opal, bloodstone, and red agate
Metals - Gold, brass, and copper

Plants - Allspice, cinnamon, garlic, basil, juniper, hibiscus, nettle, onion, peppers, poppies, and thistles

Ruling Planets - Sun and Mars.

Fire

Symbol: 4
Zodiac: Aries, Leo, Sagittarius
solar System: Jupiter, Mars, Sun
Season: Summer
Time of Day: Midday
Celebrations: Beltane, Imbolc, Litha
Osham: Ur
Runes: Dag, Ken, Rad, Sigel
Direction: South
Energy: Yang
Colors: Crimson, Gold, Orange, Pink, Red, White, Yellow
Chakra: Solar Plexus
Numbers: 1, 3, 9
Tarot: Judgement, Swords, Wands
Trees: Alder, Ash, Beech, Blackthorn, Cedar, Cherry, Chestnut, Elder, Hawthorn, Holly, Horse Chestnut, Juniper, Laurel, Mesquite, Oak, Olive, Palm (dragon's blood), Pine, Pomegranate, Rowan, Walnut, Willow, Witch Hazel, Yew
Herb & Garden: Amaranth, Anemone, Angelica, Basil, Carnation, Chrysanthemum, Dill, Fennel, Garlic, Goldenseal, Gorse, Heliotrope, Hibiscus, Holy Basil, Lovage, Marigold, Pennyroyal, Peony, Peppermint, Poppy, Primrose, Rosemary, Rue, St. John's Wort, Snapdragon, Sunflower, Sweet Woodruff, Vervain
Misc. Plants: Allspice, Asafetida, Betony, Black Cohosh, Blessed Thistle, Bloodroot, Cinnamon, Cinquefoil, Clove, Coriander, Cumin, Deer's Tongue, Flax, Frankincense, Galangal, Ginger, Ginseng, High John, Mandrake, Mullein, Mustard, Nettle, Nutmeg, Pepper, Thistle, Wormwood From the Sea: Coral (red)
Gemstones & Minerals: Agate (banded, black, brown, fire, red, red-banded, snakeskin), Amber, Amet-rine, Apache Tears, Beryl (golden), Bloodstone, Calcite (orange, red), Carnelian, Citrine, Diamond, Garnet, Hematite, Herkimer Diamond, Jasper (red), Obsidian, Onyx, Opal (fire), Peridot, Pyrite, Quartz, Rhodochrosite, Rhodonite, Ruby, Sard, Sardonyx, Serpentine, Smoky Quartz, Spinel, Staurolite, Sunstone, Tiger's Eye, Topaz, Tourmaline (red), Tsavorite, Zircon (red)
Metals: Antimony, Brass, Gold, Iron, Steel Angel: Michael

Fire

Goddesses: Aine, Amaterasu, Bertha, Brigid, Danu, Durga, Freya, Hestia, Kupala, Pele, Phoebe, Sekhmet, Spider-Woman, Vesta Magical: Mermaids, Salamanders
Reptiles: Lizard, Salamander, Snake
Gods: Agni, Belenus, Brahma, Dionysus, Hephaestus, Horus, Inari, Indra, Khnum, Mimir, Nergal, Nord, Perun, Prometheus, Vulcan
Animals: Goat, Hedgehog, Horse, Lion, Porcupine, Sheep (ram), Tiger
Birds: Crane, Eagle, Falcon, Heron, Macaw, Peacock, Quail, Robin, Swallow, Woodpecker, Wren Insects is Misc.: Bee, Cicada, Firefly, Ladybug, Praying Mantis, Scorpion Mythical: Dragon, Phoenix
Ritual Tools: Censer, Wand
Sense: Sight
Principle: To Will

Issues, Intentions & Powers: action, activate/awaken, ambition, anger, authority, battle/ war, cheerfulness, communication, concentration/ focus, confidence, consecrate /bless, courage, creativity, defense, desire, destruction, divination, energy, faith, freedom, healing, honor, illumination, influence, inspiration, intelligence, intuition, justice, leadership, life, light, love, lust, magic (general, defensive, dragon, sex), the mind, motivation, passion, power, protection, psychic ability purification, purity, purpose, release, revenge, sex/uality, stimulation, transformation, truth, warmth, weather (general, lightning), willpower

Water

Direction - West

Rules - Emotion, intuition, psychic abilities, love, deep feelings, the unconscious mind, fertility, tides, lunar energy, self-healing, and reflection

Time - Twilight

Season - Fall

Colors - Blue, aqua, silver, and turquoise

Zodiac - Cancer, Scorpio, and Pisces

Tools - Sea shells, ocean water, seaweed, hag stones, chalice, cup, and cauldron

Virtues - Love, compassion, receptivity, flexibility, and forgiveness

Vices - Indifference, depression, instability, and moodiness

Crystals - Amethyst, aquamarine, beryl, blue fluorite, blue topaz, blue tourmaline, lapis lazuli, opal, pearl, and sodalite

Metals - Mercury and Silver

Plants - Aloe, apple, chamomile, ferns, gardenia, jasmine, lemon, lilac, lily, lotus, moss, passion flower rose, seaweed, thyme, and willow

Ruling planets - Moon, Neptune, Pluto, and Venus

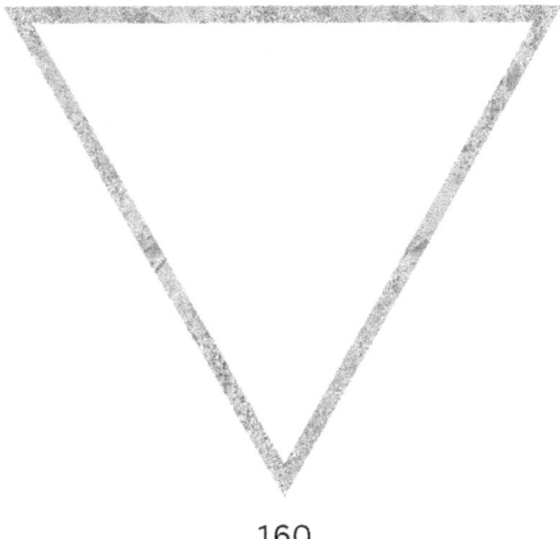

Water

Symbol: V
Zodiac: Cancer, Pisces, Scorpio
Solar System: Mercury, Moon, Neptune, Pluto, Saturn Season: Autumn
Time of Day: Dusk
Celebrations: Mabon, Neptunalia
Ogham: Eadha, Eamhancholl
Runes: Feoh, Jera, Lagu, Peorth
Direction: West
Energy: Yin
Chakra: Sacral
Colors: Aqua, Black, Blue, Gray, Green (blue, sea), Indigo, Lilac, Purple, Silver, Turquoise, Violet, White
Numbers: 2, 7
Tarot: Cups, Hanged Man, Moon
Trees: Alder, Apple, Ash, Aspen, Beech, Birch, Cedar, Cherry, Chestnut, Cypress, Elder, Elm, Hazel, Horse Chestnut, Locust, Magnolia, Mesquite, Mimosa, Myrtle, Olive, Poplar, Spindle-tree, Spruce, Sycamore, Willow, Witch Hazel, Yew
Herb & Garden: Aster, Blackberry / Bramble, Catnip, Chamomile, Columbine, Comfrey, Daffodil, Daisy, Feverfew, Foxglove, Gardenia, Geranium, Grape, Heather, Hibiscus, Hyacinth, Iris, Ivy, Jasmine, Lady's Mantle, Lemon Balm, Lilac, Lily, Monkshood, Morning Glory, Passionflower, Periwinkle, Poppy, Raspberry, Rose, Solomon's Seal, Spearmint, Strawberry, Thyme, Valerian, Violet, Yarrow
Misc. Plants: Aloe, Belladonna, Burdock, Cardamom, Coltsfoot, Cowslip, Dittany, Henbane, Lady's Slipper, Lotus, Meadowsweet, Moonwort, Myrrh, Orris Root, Reed, Sandalwood, Skullcap, Spikenard, Star Anise, Thornapple, Vanilla, Water Lily
Gemstones & Minerals: Alexandrite, Amethyst, Ametrine, Angelite, Aquamarine, Aragonite, Azurite, Beryl, Blue Lace Agate, Calcite, Charoite, Chrysocolla, Dioptase, Fluorite, Jade, Jasper (ocean), Jet, Kyanite, Labradorite, Lapis Lazuli, Larimar, Lepidolite, Lodestone, Moonstone, Morganite, Obsidian (gold sheen), Opal, Quartz, Rose Quartz, Sapphire, Selenite, Sodalite, Staurolite, Sugilite Topaz (blue), Tourmaline (black, blue, pink, watermelon), Tsavorite, Turquoise, Zircon (blue)
Metals: Copper, Mercury, Silver
From the Sea: Coral, Mother-of-Pearl, Pearl

Water

Goldesses: Amphitrite, Aphrodite, Bad, Boann, Brigantia, Chalchiuhtlicue, Coventina, Isis. Kupala, Ran, Sarasvati, Sedna, Tiamat
Gods: Aegir, Belenus, Ea, Khnum, Mabon, Manannan, Mimir, Neptune, Njord, Osiris, Poseidon, Prometheus
Magical: Mermaids, Norns, Undines
Angel: Raphael
Animals: Bat, Beaver, Cattle (cow), Dog, Hare, Hippopotamus, Horse, Moose, Otter, Polar Bear, Raccoon
Insect/Misc.: Dragonfly
Mythical: Dragon, Selkies
Birds: Albatross, Blackbird, Cormorant, Crane, Dove, Duck, Heron, Kingfisher, Seagull, Stork, Swan, Swift, Vulture
Reptiles: Crocodile, Frog, Salamander, Snake, Toad Marine Life: Dolphin, Manatee, Porpoise, Whale Ritual Tools: Cauldron, Chalice, Cup Sense: Taste
Principle: To Dare
Issues, Intentions & Powers: adaptability, agriculture, balance, beginnings, change/s, clairvoyance, compassion, consecrate/bless, consciousness (subconscious), creativity, desire, divination, dream work, emotions, empathy, energy (general, psychic, receptive), fertility, friend/ ship, grace, growth, healing, heartbreak, influence, introspection, intuition, life, magic (animal, dragon, moon), memory /memories, nurture, patience, power, pregnancy/childbirth, protection, psychic ability, purification, purity, rebirth/ renewal, reconciliation, reversal, secrets, sensitivity, sensuality, shamanic work, sleep, sorrow, spirituality, strength (inner), stress, transformation, weather (general, storms), well-being, wisdom

Symbols

Symbols have played a significant role throughout history, serving as a means of communication, expression, and identity. From ancient civilizations to modern times, symbols have been used to represent abstract concepts, convey religious beliefs, and create social cohesion. They have been etched into cave walls, inscribed on tablets, and emblazoned on flags. The power of symbols lies in their ability to capture the essence of an idea in a single image. They can evoke strong emotions, inspire action, and unite people across cultures and languages. The cross, for example, represents both religious devotion and colonial domination. Symbols are not static, they evolve with society, and the meanings they hold can change over time. Symbols remain a crucial aspect of communication and understanding their meaning and context is important for comprehending the complex ways in which humans communicate.

Hunab Ku

The Hunab Ku is an ancient Mayan symbol that is said to represent the Supreme God or the One Being, with 'Hunab' meaning 'one state of being' and 'Ku' meaning 'God.' It encompasses all opposites in the universe and unites them as one: male and female, dark and light, yin and yang, conscious and unconscious, internal and external—the list goes on. Some believe that the Hunab Ku acts as a bridge to connect these opposites.

The Hunab Ku symbol is a testament to the belief that it can unite opposing forces. It can be likened to the yin-yang symbol, with black spirals on one side and white spirals on the other. Much ado has been made out of it, especially because of the Mayan prophesy about the year 2012, when the sun will align with Hunab Ku (the galactic center of the universe or the black hole discovered by scientists).

Despite predictions about the future, the symbol is still considered powerful. It can be used to achieve balance and harmony in life because of its intrinsic powers of uniting or bridging opposites. It can also be used to connect one's inner being with one's external body or to achieve oneness with the universe.

Gordian Knot

This mystical knot traces its roots way back to ancient times. Legend has it that an oracle predicted that the next man driving an ox cart into the city of Phrygia would be its king. Gordia, then just a poor peasant, drove into the city, and priests declared him king. In gratitude and thanks to Zeus, he then tied his ox cart to a column using an intricate knot. Another oracle predicted that whoever could untie the "Gordian knot" would rule all of Asia. But while everyone else did not succeed in untying the complicated knot, Alexander the Great, using his wit and cunning, cut the knot in half using his sword in 333 BC.

The Gordian Knot also takes on a very mystical meaning in sacred geometry. This knot can actually be made from a Torus Tube (which resembles a donut shape), known in physics as the perfect shape. The Torus Tube was used as a symbol for the unity of consciousness with the universe. Although the Gordian Knot goes on for eternity, with no beginning and no end, there are three clear ovals shaped by this continuous line. These three shapes represent the Holy Trinity and its union and the three forces (positive, negative, and neutral) that comprise the universe. It is said that the Gordian Knot can help enlighten one's mind to see problems and difficult situations more clearly and with renewed hope and energy.

Medicine Wheel

Medicine Wheel, also called the Sacred Hoop, is an important part of Native American culture and spirituality. It is a stone structure that resembles a bicycle wheel. It has a circle of rocks in the center that is surrounded by an outer circle of stones. There are also 'spokes' made from lines of stones laid as coming out from the center and going on to the outer circle. Apart from physical construction on the land, the medicine wheel can also take the form of paintings or artifacts.

The term 'Medicine Wheel' was applied for the first time to the Big Horn, a medicine wheel found in Wyoming and believed to be the most southern and the biggest one in existence. A number of these structures have been sited all over southern Canada and the northern United States. These are supposed to have been used for ritualistic, healing, teaching, and astronomical purposes.

There is no certainty as to the meaning and function of the Medicine Wheel, and different Native American tribes are thought to have interpreted it differently. Generally used for healing and health, it symbolizes the cycles of life and embodies the cardinal directions- North, East, South, and West. The directions are represented by distinctive colors of white, yellow, red, and black. They also stand for the annual seasons (winter, spring, summer, and fall), the natural elements (wind, earth, fire, and water), and the aspects of life (spiritual, physical, mental, and emotional).

The Medicine Wheel is considered to symbolize peaceful interaction between the living beings inhabiting the Earth. Its circle shows everything as part of a cosmic whole and represents the balance between personal and natural powers. The wheel can be used for self-realization, finding your purpose in life, and bringing fulfillment and enlightenment into it.

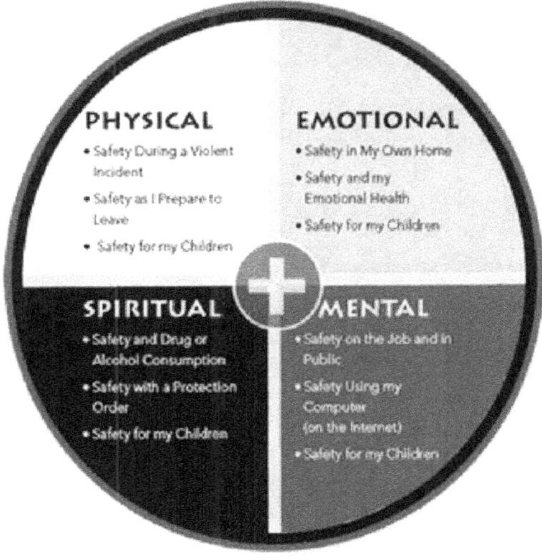

Bindi

One of the most well-recognized body adornments worn by Hindu women in the Indian sub-continent, the Bindi Symbol is a bright-colored dot applied near the eyebrows on the forehead. Typically, this dot is red in color, though it can be in other colors too. The word 'Bindi' has been derived from the Sanskrit 'Bindu'which means a dot or a drop.

The application of this mark is a tradition that goes centuries back when a married woman applied red turmeric powder (Kumkum) in a round shape on the forehead to reflect her marital status. The red color is believed to represent true love, honor, prosperity, and strength. The Bindi has strong spiritual significance. It symbolizes good fortune and feminine power that protects a married woman and her husband in ancient India; it was considered an essential element of feminine personal grooming. At times, even decorative leaves were cut into attractive shapes and pasted on the forehead.

The Bindi's positioning between the eyebrows has important implications. This region is believed to be the seat of wisdom and latent knowledge. The mystics call it 'Ajna Chakra,' the place that controls the levels of concentration one reaches through meditation. It is said that meditation awakens the dormant energy lying at the base of the spine and raises it to the brain. The place between the eyebrows is seen as a potential outlet for this strong energy. Applying the Bindi is believed to help retain this energy within the body and enhance one's intellect.

With time, the Bindi has lost much of its religious connotation and become more of a style statement and a decorative accessory. Non-Hindu and unmarried women also use it freely, and it is no longer restricted in shape, design, or color.

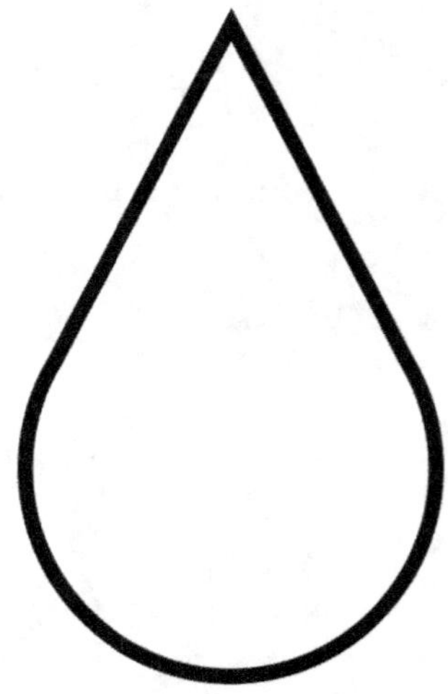

Chai

One of the most well-known symbols of Judaism, Chai is a Hebrew word that means 'life' or 'living.' The word is spelled with two Hebrew letters – 'Chet' and 'yud'. Traditionally, every Hebrew letter has been assigned a numerical value. 'Chet' has been given the number 8, and 'Yud' has got a value of 10. Together, they make 18, which has become the number of Chai.

The Jewish culture has always placed a special focus on life; loving and celebrating life has been an integral part of Judaism. As such, the word Chai holds much significance for the Jews, and it has come to symbolize the value of life and hope that sustains it. It also represents the personal will to live and is a reminder to the Jews to live and protect life.

"Le-Chaim," meaning 'to life' is a popular Jewish toast that is said at celebratory occasions to welcome all the good things that are anticipated in the coming times. The word Chai also features in another oft-repeated Jewish phrase, "am Yisrael chai," which means "the people of Israel live" and is a sort of prayer for the survival of the Jews for long into the future.

Due to its association with Chai, the number 18 is considered a spiritual and auspicious number by the Jews. They have a custom of giving out money in multiples of 18 for donations or at the bar mitzvah, weddings, and other festive events. This is seen as giving a gift of life and good luck.

The Chai symbol makes a popular jewelry piece. It is believed to have luck-bearing and protective properties and is worn by men as well as women. It is also widely seen in paintings, sculptures, tapestries, and plaques.

חי

Shield of Trinity

The shield of the Trinity symbol, also known as the Scutum Fidei, is a Christian symbol depicting the concept of the Holy Trinity. This diagrammatic representation has been found to have been in use as long back as the twelfth century for helping proclaim the fundamental Christian doctrine that the Almighty God is manifest in 3 distinct ways – as the Father, the Son (Jesus) & the Holy Spirit.

The classical Shield of the Trinity emblem is shaped as a downward-pointing triangle that is formed by three same-length bars and has a circle at each vertex. A fourth circle is in the center of this triangle, and it is joined by equal-length bars to the outer circles. The three circles on the outside have one Latin word written in each – Pater (Father), Filius (Son), and Spus Scus (Holy Spirit) and the circle in the middle carries Deus (God). The inner connecting lines have Est (is) written in them, while the outer ones have Non-Est (is not). The links in the diagram are non-directional, and the words may be read from any beginning point and in any direction. This beautiful staging of words and formation of sentences emphasizes the undivided, unending nature and eternity of the Holy Trinity.

There are many versions of the Shield of the Trinity. Some of these variations include having the triangle pointing upwards, putting curved bars in place of straight bars, putting triangles in place of circles, or having a star in the middle instead of a triangle or circle.

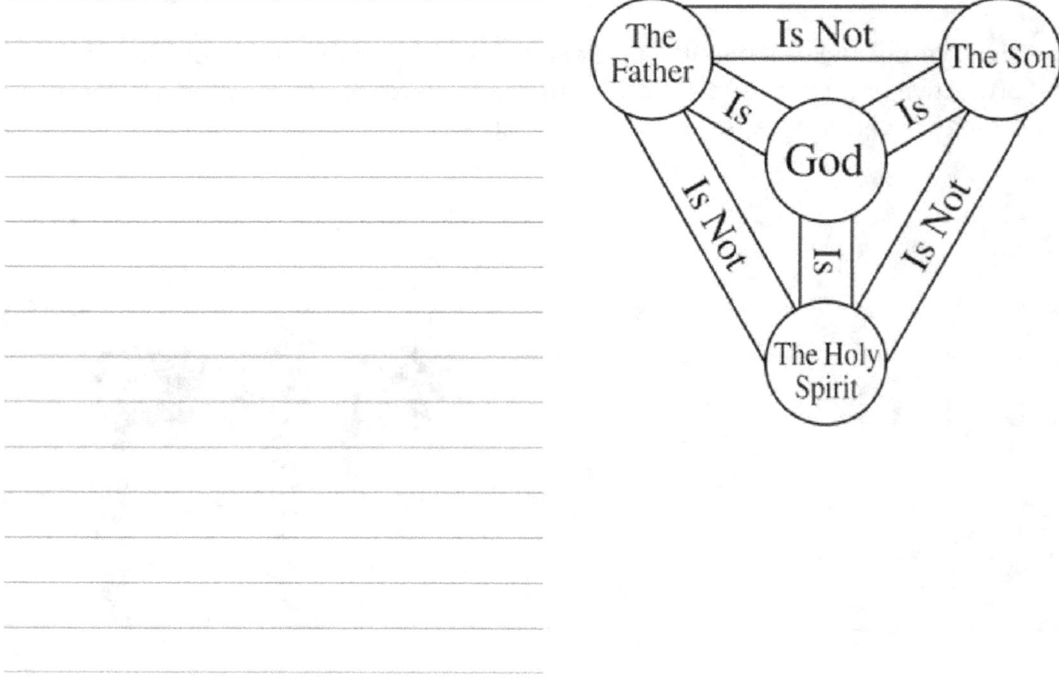

Eye of Providence

An ancient symbol of omniscience and divine providence, the Eye of Providence represents the eye of God, the singular divine power that has created the entire universe. The symbol shows a human eye enclosed in a triangle. In Christianity, the triangle represents the Holy Trinity, and as such, the Eye of Providence symbolizes the divine entity looking over humankind and providing it benevolent guidance.

At times, the Eye is also depicted as surrounded by clouds or bursts of light. Both of these images are representative of holiness and divine glory, and so, here, too, the symbol signifies that the Almighty is keeping a watchful eye on His creation.

Contrary to these beliefs, some people believe the symbol represents the eye of Lucifer or Satan, whose supernatural powers influence what happens in the world.

Besides being prevalent in Christianity, this concept of the 'All-seeing eye' can be found in several other religions and cultures. For instance, the Buddhists refer to it as the 'Eye of the World'; in Caodaism, it represents the image of God; and the Egyptian revere the Eye of Horus as a symbol of power and protection.

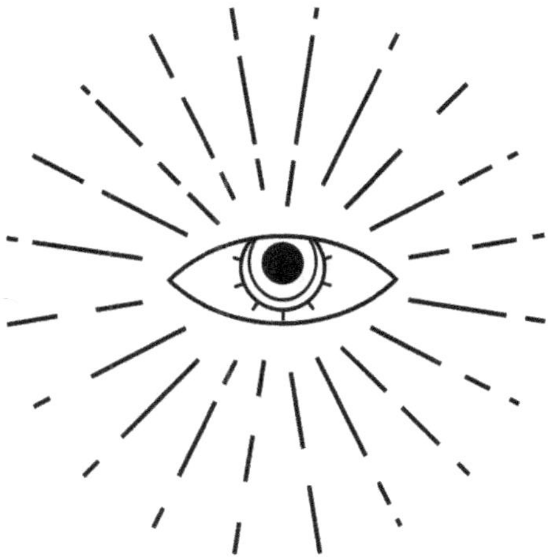

Star of David

Also known as the Shield of David (or Magen David in Hebrew), this Star of David symbol originated in ancient Jewish tradition. History books record that the earliest uses of this symbol were seen as a hexagram or the joining of two equilateral triangles. Records say that hexagrams were used as decorative motifs in synagogues as far back as the 3rd to 4th century. A Shield of David symbol was also noted on a Jewish tombstone, dating as far back as the third century CE.

It has been primarily used as a symbol of the Jewish religion—many Jews wear Star of David pendants or jewelry, and even the flag of Israel has a blue Star of David at the center. But this symbol does have a deeper mystical meaning. Some believe that the six points of the star represent God's rule over the universe in all directions: north, south, east, west, up, and down. Others believe that the two triangles, which point in opposite directions, are symbols of the duality of human nature or the relationship between God and man.

Maat

Maat (also known as Ma'at, Mayet, or Maae't) is the Egyptian Goddess symbolizing cosmic order, truth, justice, morality, harmony, stability, and balance. Depicted as a woman wearing an ostrich feather on the head and holding an ankh in one hand and a scepter in the other, the Goddess is said to be the daughter of the Sun God, Ra, and the consort of the Moon God, Thoth. Maat was revered even by the Gods.

The Goddess is symbolically represented by an Ostrich Feather. It is a strong Egyptian belief that after death, the dead are judged in the Hall of Maat, where their conscience (heart) is weighed against the feather. A heart heavier than the feather denoted a life of wicked deeds, and such a soul would be devoured by Goddess Ammit, while balanced scales indicated an honorable life, and such a soul would be welcomed by God Osiris.

Besides being venerated as a deity, Maat is also embraced as a concept or principle that keeps the universe in order and without which everything would perish. The ancient Egyptians thought that Maat bound the universe, nature, and man in unity. They believed that truthfulness, honesty, fair dealings, and correct ritual and public life were necessary to create cosmic harmony. Not adhering to the Maat principles would cause a disturbance in this harmony and plunge all creation into chaos.

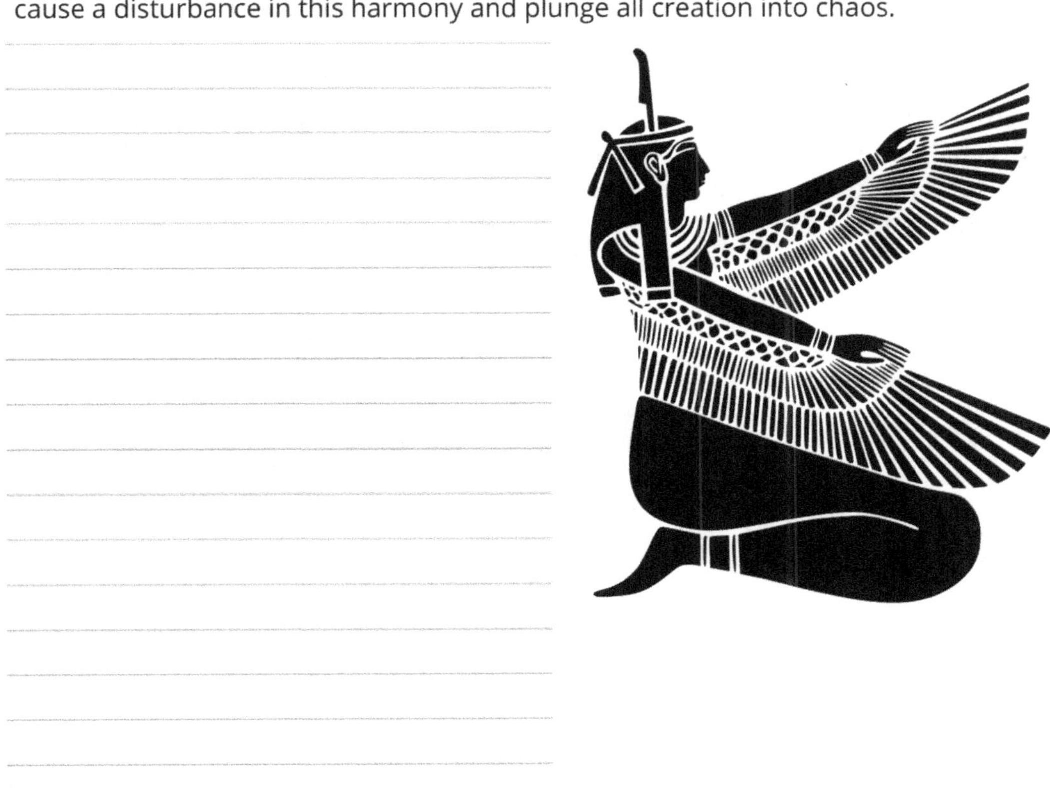

Faravahar

Faravahar or Farohar is a well-known emblem of the Persian identity as well as a symbol of the Zoroastrian faith. 'Faravahar' is a Middle Persian or Pahlavi word and is derived from the ancient Iranian/Avetsan word 'Fravarane,' meaning 'I choose'. The term is also associated with the 'Fravashi,' the guardian angel and guide, which is actually the divine, uncorrupt, and unpolluted part of the human soul. The Fravashi is the higher individuality that transcends to Heaven when human life on earth is over.

The winged disc symbol of Faravahar is influenced by the Egyptian winged sun that symbolizes divine kingship. All parts of it represent a basic Zoroastrian philosophy. The circle in the center symbolizes the immortality of a person's soul and the eternity of the universe. The human body coming out of it represents mankind. Its upward-pointing hand indicates that the way to Heaven is through righteousness, while the ring, on the other hand, represents faithfulness and honoring of promises.

The two wings, one on either side, have 3 layers of feathers each that stand for the pillars of Zoroastrianism – good words, good reflection/thought, and good deeds. The symbol's lower part also has three parts representing bad words, bad thoughts, and bad deeds that bring misfortune and misery to any individual. The two streamers/loops on the left and right signify the duality of good and evil, respectively.

Thus, Faravahar embodies the conflicting forces of good and bad and represents the Zoroastrian philosophy of promoting one's positive force and suppressing the negative. It is a reminder to the Zoroastrians of the purpose of their life, and that is to live in a good way that helps in the spiritual progression of the soul so that it unites with the Supreme Lord of Zoroastrianism, Ahura Mazda.

Raven

Raven is a scavenger bird that has primarily been associated with battlefields, where it appears to pick at the mangled remains of fallen soldiers. Despite this rather dark association, the raven has been a symbol of much finer attributes in various cultures across the world.

Raven is widely believed to be a harbinger of cosmic secrets and a bearer of magical forces. It is regarded as a divine messenger that reveals omens and foretells the future. It is a keeper as well as a communicator of deep mysteries. The Raven is symbolic of powerful wisdom, vast knowledge, great mental clarity, and high energy. The Native American holy men invoked the Raven to get clearer visions and called upon it for opinion and advice. It is a magical symbol in Native American mythology that says that a raven created the Earth by dropping stones in the sea and making islands. Southwestern tribes like the Navajo, Hopi, and Zuni considered the raven to be a bringer of light and a bird of creation that brought sunlight to the humans.

The ancient Greek and Roman cultures believed the raven to be a solar animal (despite its color). They affiliate it with Apollo as well as Athena, deities associated with the sun, light, and wisdom. The African cultures revere the raven as a guide. In Chinese and Japanese cultures, it is a messenger of the gods and also represents the sun.

In Norse mythology, the raven symbolizes the mind and intelligence. Legends of the Norse God Odin (also called the Raven God) depict two ravens, Hugin and Mugin, accompanying Him. Hugin is representative of the power of thinking and active pursuit of knowledge/information. Meanwhile, Mugin is symbolic of the intuitive ability of the mind.

Apps I Researched

My Moon Phase
Moonly
Co-Star
Stellarium Mobile - Star Map
Stars and Planets
Globe 3D - Planet Earth
Star Registration - Night Sky
Solar Walk Lite Planetarium 3D
Labyrinthos
Crystal Gemstones
PictureThis
Growit
WiccaCalendar
TheCornellLab
Cafe Astrology.com
Horoscope
Sigilscribe.me
Headspace
InsightTimer
Down Dog
Audible/Kindle/Kindle Unlimited

Apps To Research

Mystic Mind Community

Why Join The Mystic MindCommunity?

We bring together spiritual people seeking more connection, the ability to share their own experiences, and learn from online Challenges, Live Events, Courses, and each other!

The concept for building this Spiritual Social Network is so we can grow together in a supportive, inclusive, and fun Spiritual Metaverse covering a wide range of spiritual resources.

Some of what you will find inside our Spiritual Social Network:
Spiritually-minded community
Inclusive of all paths & modalities
A safe space to gather
Chat with members
Free Challenges to participate in with others
Groups to explore
Open Topics to interact with
Free learning tools & resources
Live videos
Live events
Online courses
Masterminds
Guest speakers/interviews from the spiritual world.
Support on your path
Staying connected via our mobile device app options
...oh, and we're pretty fun!

You can be a part of the community discussion with both your Desktop/Laptop or via your mobile device if you are on the go!
To join this wonderful community is only $1.00 a month.

The Mystic Mind Mentorship Circle

• Are you looking for more support in your Spiritual Journey?
• Are you interested in understanding and practicing solid foundations from which your intuitive and psychic abilities can soar?
• Are you interested in understanding your energy and how learning to master it can enhance your gifts?
• Are you interested in connecting with like-minded spiritual people to share this spiritual journey with?
• Are you looking for mentors who are professional, active practitioners?
Yes? Then I invite you to you join the Mystic Mind Mentorship Circle!
When you join, you get Group Mentoring + Community + Mini Masterclasses!

Basic Level Plan: $47/mo | Gold Level Plan: $111/mo
Part 1: You Get Mentoring

The mentoring environment is designed to give you access to other like-minded individuals in the group and the instructor to develop your psychic & intuitive abilities. Some members observe, some participate, and some volunteer to be a part of a growth activity. You participate at the level you feel comfortable. Suppose you can't make the live sessions, no worries. All live sessions are recorded, and the replay will be available to you.

Part 2: You Get Community
Community is an integral part of psychic & intuitive development. Students have told me many times that they wish they had a "community" to share their growth with.

WE CAN SUPPORT EACH OTHER.

The Mystic Mind Mentorship Circle is a supportive environment of like-minded sensitive individuals that lift each other up. We don't compete; we co-create!

Part 3: You Get Mini Masterclasses
When you join the Mystic Mind Mentorship Circle, you will receive immediate access to all the past live lessons as well as all pending mini-masterclass lessons and support sessions. This is an evergreen mentorship group, so you are not limited by time. These mini masterclasses are designed to give you the tools and techniques used by professional spiritual practitioners. They are taught in a way that is easy to understand, safe, and easy to implement.

The Mystic Mind Podcast

The Mystic Mind Podcast is a creative exploration to help support you in your intuitive and spiritual development journey and add a little fun!

I mean, we have to have fun on this journey, right?

As a professional Energy Healer and Spiritual Teacher, I share some of what I've learned along the way during my spiritual development journey for over a decade. In this podcast, you will find shows on Intuitive Development and/or reflections, Angels, Divination, Energy Work, special guests, interviews, and more.
Also, have you joined our Mystic Mind Community? :)

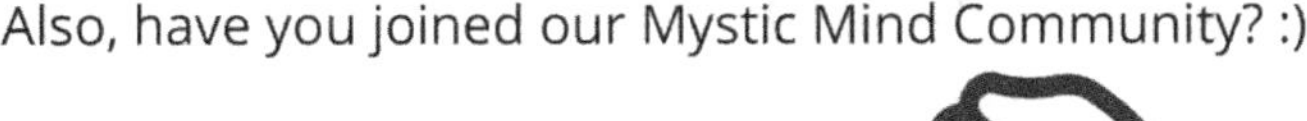

Colby Parrish

(727) 831-8077

Facebook: The Wondering Fool -Spiritual Advisor
Instagram: Thewonderingfool333
TikTok: TheWonderingFool333

Hours of Availability
Tuesday through Saturday, 11 am-8 pm
Available for Private Parties

Service Menu
General Psychic Readings
30 min/$60
45min/$90
60min/$120

Tarot - Oracle - Lithomancy
3 Card Single Message
Pull/ $20
Couples Readings
40min/$80
Personal Monthly
Forecast/$120

Numerological
Chart/$150

Available for private parties and events.

Service Payments
PayPal- Solice333@yahoo.com
cashapp-$boywitch333
venmo- @Colby-Parrish-3

He is my spiritual adviser, so I highly recommend him and his services.

Jamie Wareham

www.lightworkerpath.com
Email: lightworkerpathsite@gmail.com

Service Menu
Reiki + Sound Healing Sessions
Soul Coaching Sessions (spiritual life coaching)
Intuitive Development
Mentorship Programs
Reiki Level 1,2 & 3 Attunement
Certification Courses
Spiritual/Energy Development Classes

She is a fellow writer who co-authored The Voyage & The Return: The Path to Self Discovery (see my book section). Moreover, I've taken her classes, and they were interesting and helpful. She's super knowledgeable about energy work, angel spirit guides, meditation, and reiki healing.

Here is a profound quote from her book "Some of the best teachers are ones who have journeyed into the *heart of darkness* and come through it all like the powerful Phoenix they are! A rebirth into something else, something stronger, something that yearns to help others through their own forms of darkness."

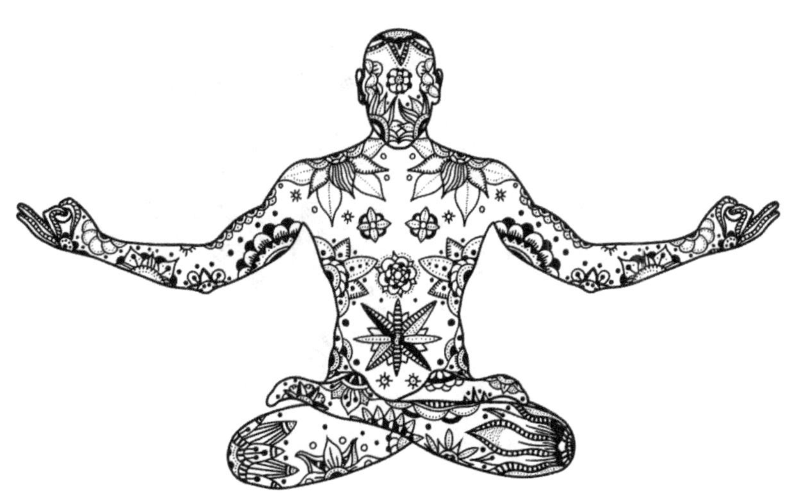

Readings with The Auric Diviner - Psychic Medium - Anthony

Service Menu

Reading Sessions
(psychic, tarot, mediumship)

30 minutes - $60
45 minutes - $90
60 minutes $120

Aura Rendering
Sessions

30 minutes - $70
45 minutes - $100
60 minutes - $130

Mini $30
Mini tarot reading

Email: Aurarenderings@gmail.com
Instagram: @the_auric_diviner
TikTok: @theauricdiviner

I have personally had a reading from him, and he was spot on:-)

Whimsical Cauldron and Crafts

www.whimsicalcauldronandcrafts.com
Email: Whimsicalcauldron2019@gmail.com
Facebook: Whimsical Cauldron and Crafts, LLC
they have an online store and go live on Facebook on Tuesdays, Wednesdays, Thursdays, and Fridays every week.
They sell crystals, minerals, specimens, jewelry, herbs, sage, etc.
They also feature other vendors and their merchandise.

I have purchased almost everything they have for sale and can confidently say they are a great small business for high-quality crystal needs. They are kind and patient, especially when I first learned about crystals. If they didn't have something I was looking for, they would get it for me.

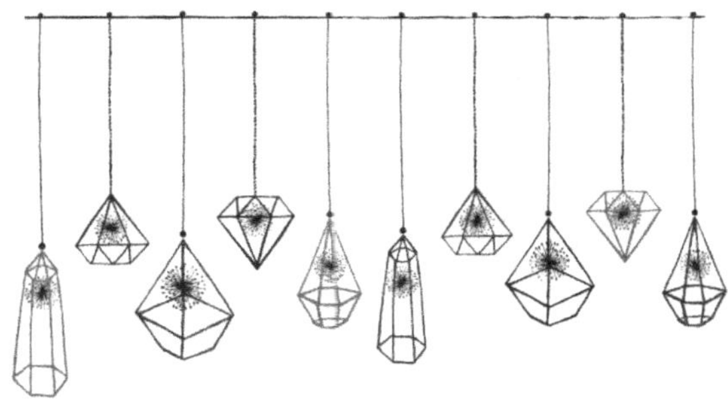

Botanicals Beauty

Botanicals Beauty provides herbal-infused beauty products for all-natural enthusiasts. We offer luxurious, artisan-crafted face masks, hair masks, whipped shea butter, talc-free body powder, and more. Our handmade products are infused with herbs and oils that you need without the toxins that you don't. Create a herbal hair tonic using Bamboo and Marshmallow Root, a hair mask using Ginger Root and Avocado, a face mask using Bee Pollen and Calendula, and moisturize your skin with shimmering body oils...Self-care has never been so refreshing.
Botanicals Beauty is a woman-owned, black-owned business.

Goat Milk with Cocoa and Shea Butter
Handmade Coconut Milk Soap
Scented Body Shimmer Oil Moisturizer
Scented Floral Body Oil Moisturizer
Whipped Shea Butter with Herb Infused Oil
Whipped Sugar Scrub
Zodiac Body Oil Moisturizer
and
Calendula, Chamomile, Hibiscus, Lavender, Neem, or Peppermint Infused Oil

I love her Gypsy-scented products.

Red Headed Scents

Your one-stop shop for small batches, 100% soy
candles & wax melts, all-natural sugar scrubs, and other handmade gifts.
etsy.com/shop/redheadedscents
Nashville, Tennessee

I started out as just a crafter making gifts for family and friends until enough of them urged me to start selling my products to share with everyone! All of my products are soy wax based, so they are clean burning in your home. Most of the fragrances I currently carry are custom blended in my kitchen, and everything is hand-poured in small batches. Plus, the entire product line has gone dye-free since melted soy wax can be used as a lotion or for massage.

Her unique Yule fragrance is called Winter Nights. You can enjoy it in candle or wax melt form at $7.50 and $4.00, respectively.

I had the great opportunity to meet her at an author's book promotion event. I bought a few scents, and after trying them, I immediately fell in love. They are the only candles and wax melts that don't make my allergies act up. So now I'm a customer for life. Oh, and they keep their scent longer than any other wax melt I have bought.

Below are some of her other scents:

Lemon Rosemary
Apple Cider Donuts
Lime in the Coconut
Julie's Kitchen
Vanilla Coconut
Citrus & Sage
Cedar & Leather
Evergreen
Apple Cider Donuts
Citrus & Sage
Cedar & Leather
Green Apple
Raspberry Sorbet
Peppermint
Vanilla Coconut
Lavender
Strawberry Mimosa

Leather & Sandalwood
Flannel & Blackberry
Evergreen
Caramel Pumpkin
Sandalwood & Bourbon
Autumn Nights
Peppermint
Green Apple
Lavender
Raspberry Sorbet
Lavender Teakwood
Strawberry Mimosa
Tropical Punch
Lavender Teakwood
Raspberry Sorbet
Peppermint
Vanilla Coconut
Lavender Teakwood

Witchy You-Tubers

Harmony Nice
(great for beginners)

White Witch Parlour
great for spellwork

The Witch of Wonderlust
basic information

Molly Roberts
great for positivity and basic magic workings

Stargirl the Practical Witch
excellent for tarot and divination

Behati Life
great for divination and astrological work

Owlvine Green
great for general witchcraft

Gather Thyme
great for general witchcraft and herbs

Asia Suler
great for herbalism

Witchy Subscription Boxes

Third Eye Creations
fromthirdeye.com

My Garden Box
mygardenbox.com

The Witches Moon
thewitchesmoon.com

Nine Of Earth
nineofearth.com

Awakening in a Box
awakeninginabox.com

The Magickal Earth
themagickalearth.com

Box of Shadows
myboxofshadows.com

Third Eye Creations

fromthirdeye.com

Third Eye Creations is a great place to buy unique and exciting gifts. They have a storefront in The Marketplace of Tarpon Springs, Florida, including a magickal apothecary, a DIY Candle bar, and their online shop. You can also find their products at local businesses around the area.

Hey, have you heard of Sabbat Boxes? These cool subscription boxes contain everything you need to celebrate each sabbat on the Wheel of the Year. I've been using them for a while now, and they're fantastic. Each box has multiple items related to the sabbat, making the celebration easy and fun. Plus, the quality of the items in these boxes is awe-inspiring. I'm always excited to see what's inside.

Some of the awesome stuff she sells includes spell candles that smell great and burn clean, plus her tup teas are perfect for many different spells. She also has sabbat boxes and witch kits available.

My Garden Box

mygardenbox.com
and they have an online store

My Garden Box
My Garden Box offers a fun, seasonal plant project and is very popular with families and crafters. Includes a themed collection of a plant(s), quality container(s), potting & care instructions, w/a letter about each collection, plant label(s), growing media, fertilizer, gardening tools, supplies, and/or functional decor. From bonsai to hanging plants and everything in between!

Monthly Subscription Cost starts at USD 50.00

The Plant Club
Celebrate new Plant Stories with us each month! We lovingly pack your monthly plant box to arrive safely at your door. Every plant has a story, and with so many plants in the world, there are so many plant stories to discover! We include our feature plant of the month along with your complete 'Plant Story.' In addition, your monthly membership box comes with an id tag, goodie kit, soil, and decorative planter.

Monthly Subscription Cost starts at USD 50.00

Succulents Monthly
From their quirky forms to their easy care, succulents spread joy, and it's our privilege to share them with you. Each month, you'll receive our featured succulent selection, easy-to-follow care and assembly instructions, and curious facts about and fun descriptions of your new succulent variety. In addition, we include plant care and detail about your succulent along with an id tag, goodie kit, soil, and decorative planter.

Monthly Subscription Cost starts at USD 50.00

Air Plant Box
Nature's best home decor! Three unique and beautiful air plants shipped directly to you every month! My Air Plant Box includes a blend of specialty air plants every month, ready to display in your container or decor. In addition, every box includes id cards and care instructions to ensure your air plants thrive in their new home.

Monthly Subscription Cost starts at USD 25.00

House Plant Box
You'll receive a beautiful and unique plant selection from our greenhouses each month. So enjoy the benefits of live plants. Each plant is selected based on a host of criteria, including coloration, character, foliage, form, seasonality, and diversity. In addition, we include plant care and information with each monthly plant.
Monthly Subscription Cost starts at USD 25.00

Tikes Garden Box
Everything a young grower needs to build rewarding and enriching seasonal plant projects. Plant(s) included with every box. With visually illustrated instructions, simple garden care tips, and properly portioned ingredients, assembly is fun & easy! Indoor and outdoor projects, based on the season. Recommended ages: 6 - 10 (under 6 with adult supervision).
Monthly Subscription Cost starts at USD 35.00
Remember, you can cancel anytime, and they make perfect gifts.

What exactly is a spirit guide?

Spirit guides are nonhuman or human entities that reside in the spiritual realm and make their wisdom available to the living. They take various forms, including guardian angels, animal or nature spirits, elves and fairies, saints or ascended masters, and ancestors or descendants who have crossed the spiritual realm. According to believers, spiritual guides assist humans in their daily lives even though they are unaware of the guides' presence. Those interested are[21] encouraged to seek out their guides to gain practical and mystical information, healing abilities, and protection from harm.

So here are my thoughts:
If you take comfort in believing in spirit guides, go right ahead and do it. Once again:

Live your life!
You Do You Boo!

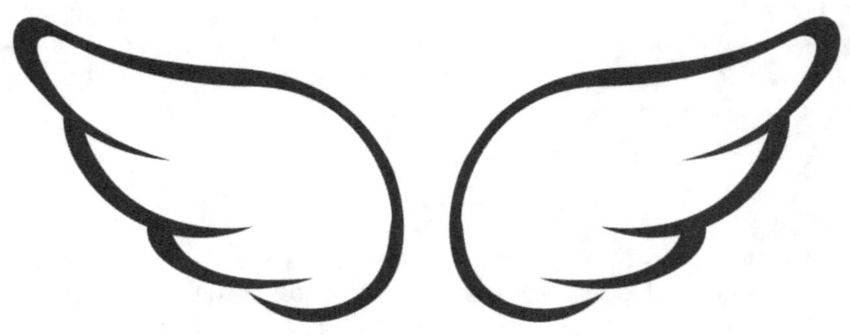

Types of Spirit Guides

Ascended Masters
Humans like us but who have transcended the spiritual plane (ex: Buddha)

Star Beings
Star beings are galactic entities whom you may have already known from the past

Animal Spirit Guides
Totems or Power Animals that provide healing & support during tough times

Nature Spirits
Ethereal personifications of nature who have come since the beginning of time

Ancestral Guides
They are spirit guides coming directly from our genetic lineage

Angelic Spirit Guides
More commonly known as your guardian angel

Elementals
Spirits who possess earthly elements, such as Earth, water, fire, and air72

Animal Guides at a Glance

Elements: A strong connection to Mother Earth, playful humor, easy to relate to and connect with.

Talents: Alignment with our inner nature, protection, and enhanced instincts.

Traits: You're protective of family and community, physically oriented, and strongly connected to the natural environment.

Bear

The bear is a powerful symbol of strength, gentleness, and intuition. This fierce yet gentle animal appears when we need to step back from the hustle and bustle of life to restore balance. By getting enough rest or reflecting on our beliefs, we can reconnect with our true selves at a deeper soul level. Bear also encourages us to look beyond physical appearances and find the truth within ourselves. In times of feeling lost or needing healing, Bear reminds us that it is essential to have inner balance and practice self-care to live according to our own path.

Deity Associations: Artemis, Artio, Brigid, and Diana

Bees

The bee symbolizes the importance of setting your mind to the task and achieving success, even if it seems impossible. It serves as a reminder not to rest too much or get busy if you procrastinate. The sweet end result can be highly rewarding. Bee also encourages you to keep a busy environment organized and running smoothly without escalating your temper. Moreover, it symbolizes hidden wisdom we should seek when facing challenging tasks.

The queen bee indicates looking for growth opportunities where you can find appreciation, respect, and creative freedom. Lastly, having the bee come into your life means that no matter how challenging or seemingly insurmountable the project is, there are always solutions ready to be discovered. Remembering this will give you a sense of contentment after completing the job or enjoying its results.

Bee provides assistance in difficult projects and seemingly intractable situations. It is important, however, to take a step back and take the time to appreciate any accomplishments achieved. If you are constantly running from project to project without feeling fulfilled, then this can be a sign of taking on too much work, leading to an exhaustion of effort that should be reserved for celebrating successes.

Deity Associations: Cybele, Demeter, Diana, Iris, Apollo, Krishna, Ra, and Vishnu

Cow

The Cow symbolizes leisure, relaxation, and taking things slow. If you see a cow, it's time to take a step back and enjoy the simple things. You may be trying to do too much at once and must remember to take care of yourself. Like a cow, you have a lot of stamina and can keep going even when you're tired. The Cow also has excellent vision and can see what's coming from all sides. This means you must be aware of your surroundings and think before acting. Finally, the cow reminds you to be strong in the face of adversity and trust your intuition to guide you to safety.

The Cow helps you to stay grounded and focused so that you can help others. In addition, it can teach you patience and persistence while still moving forward.

Deity Associations: Krishna and Manannan

Donkey

A donkey's appearance indicates spiritual advancement, encouraging growth in intuition, empathy, and divine connection. It may also warn those prone to overextend help and goodwill - don't let yourself be taken advantage of. Intelligently examine any risky situation before committing to it; you have both the analytical skill and inner insight required to make the right decision with self-preservation in focus. Being cantankerous or unreasonable is not recommended; use your reason and gut instinct together for optimal protection.

As someone who embodies the donkey's qualities, you have a strong and enduring character. You are both gentle and kind yet also fiercely protective when necessary. People tend to be surprised by your assertive behavior because of your propensity for helping others. Allow the donkey's boldness and protection to give you strength when it is needed to stand up for yourself and put your foot down when saying no is necessary.

Deity Associations: Epona, Apollo, Dionysus, Hephaestus, Pan, and Set

Dove

The white Dove is a potent signifier of peace, love, and devotion. It evokes images of peacefulness and calm, inviting us to embrace our loved ones. Dove is also a reminder to show appreciation for those we sometimes take for granted. Let them know how you feel about them in a great way - don't let it go unsaid! Furthermore, the Dove symbolizes mending broken relationships with people that we may have been arguing over misunderstandings - be the bigger person and strive to make peace with them.

Moreover, Dove implies eating nutritious foods while cleansing both your body and spirit. Believe in the power of hope to bring forth positive solutions - be clear-minded and speak only words of positivity during such times. You have the capacity within you to embody loving kindness towards all living things; let that energy guide you through life's challenges and keep hope alive in your heart.

All will be made right within your world if you embrace the Dove's messages. Dove is a sign of new beginnings and can help you with yours.

Deity Associations: Aphrodite, Astarte, Demeter, Freya, Holle, Inanna, Ishtar, Isis, Maia, Rhea, and Venus

Eagle

The appearance of an eagle symbolizes power, direction, and freedom - all of which you possess. You think beyond the moment and have a long-term view of things; coupled with your determination, you arrive at opportunities to take action and excel with skill. There may be the need for physical or emotional protection that requires you to step up with strength and confidence. Your leadership capabilities are undeniable, making you respected and followed by those who know your inspiring character. Finally, the eagle reminds you to use your wisdom and insight in approaching what lies ahead.

The eagle energizes, gives you an expanded view of situations so you can see what direction you should take, and encourages you to soar to great heights.

Deity Associations: Isis, Justitia, Agni, Ares, Belenus, Jupiter, Lugh, Odin, Pan, and Zeus

Frog

When a frog appears, it is a sign that you must focus on one thing and do it well. Unfortunately, frogs tend to jump from one project to another, and this warns you that there are better times to be focused. Instead, you need to concentrate on the most serious situation in your life and give it your full attention. It's time to be serious, hold your ground, speak your mind, and let your emotions out. This is a time of cleansing, transformation, and future growth. Relationships can be restored at this time. New opportunities can be locked down.

The frog totem is associated with many positive traits, such as being a great listener, reliable, and deeply connecting with others. If you have the frog as your totem animal, you probably find it easy to express your feelings, and you're comfortable with taking risks. The frog can also help you create new beginnings for yourself.

Deity Associations: Chalchiuhtlicue, and Coatlicue

Hare

Hare symbolizes independence, speed, and the will to survive. This animal is a sign of abundance, fertility, and good fortune. If you see a hare, it means that you are different than you appear on the surface. You have a stronger core essence than others give you credit for. While you usually prefer to handle disagreements with finesse, you will fight hard to get your point across and defend others or your territory if necessary. This is often a surprise to those around you because they didn't know you had it in you to react in such a take-charge manner.

Deity Associations: Aphrodite, Artemis, Freya, Hecate, Hera, Ostara, and Eros

Goat

When a goat appears, it's an important reminder to stay mindful and practical in your pursuits. Like the Goat, be determined and resilient—remain fearless and confident in your decisions. Sometimes you can take risks, but now is a time for making calculated choices on your journey toward success. Listen to the advice of others, but if it doesn't seem right for the situation, look within yourself for other solutions.
Let Goat remind you to stay focused and open-minded about what you can achieve—it's a sign that with strong will comes great rewards. Make sure not to overindulge or give up too easily; perseverance pays off, so always believe in yourself when it seems hard. Additionally, use this opportunity as a chance to take an introspective look at your current emotions and need

Deity Associations: Aphrodite, Artemis, Athena, Cailleach, Bheur, Freya, Holle, Agni, Bacchus, Dionysus, Faunus, Hermes, Mercury, Pan, Pushan, Silvanus, Thor, and Zeus

Goose

The presence of the Goose is a reminder to focus on family, love, affection, fertility, and self-enlightenment. It's important to recognize when it's appropriate to follow or lead while also being aware not to become distracted by external influences. The Goose has an incredibly loud honk which serves as a form of communication, always ensuring we consider our purpose in life and true direction. Goose is mindful of potential threats and will react accordingly for protection. With its wisdom, Goose allows us to make the best out of any situation we encounter.

Deity Associations: Aphrodite, Bertha, Hera, Isis, Juno, Amun, Brahma, Geb, Odin, Osiris, and Ra

Horse

The horse conveys messages of loyalty, friendship, trust, and collaboration. When you encounter a horse in your life, it's a sign that you need to take some time for yourself and escape from the confines of your routine. You should break free, follow your instinct for independence, and benefit from exercise to shake off any sense of restlessness. Horses also signal a journey ahead—it could be an actual voyage or an inner spiritual quest towards enlightenment—both require strong will and determination. When troubles arise, don't forget you have incredible persistence; you will never give up on the people who help nurture your growth or achieve your ambitious dreams. Keep that spirit alive!

Deity Associations: Aine, Artemis, Astarte, Athena, Demeter, Eos, Epona, Macha, Maeve, Modron, the Morrigan, Selene, Agni, Apollo, Arawn, Belenus, Buddha, Dionysus, Freyr, Gwydion, Hermes, Indra, Lugh, Mabon, Manannan, Mars, Neptune, Poseidon, Surya, and Vishnu

Leopard

The leopard is known to symbolize boldness and strength, as well as beauty. It emphasizes virtues such as patience and persistence; it hunts at the moment and lives fully in the present moment. Leopard encourages us to accept our uniqueness and reclaim our own power and self-confidence by trusting our knowledge of ourselves and others. We sharpen our instincts through insight and visions while dreaming and awake. Though you may find yourself gaining strange levels of insight into others, they never become aware that you can sense much more than what they have revealed with words. Trust the power of the leopard - it runs deep within us all.

Your clairvoyance is very strong, and if you've been ignoring it in the past, now you must embrace it and make it your own. It's not going to go away, so accept that it is part of you.

Deity Associations: Aphrodite, Bacchus, Dionysus, and Set

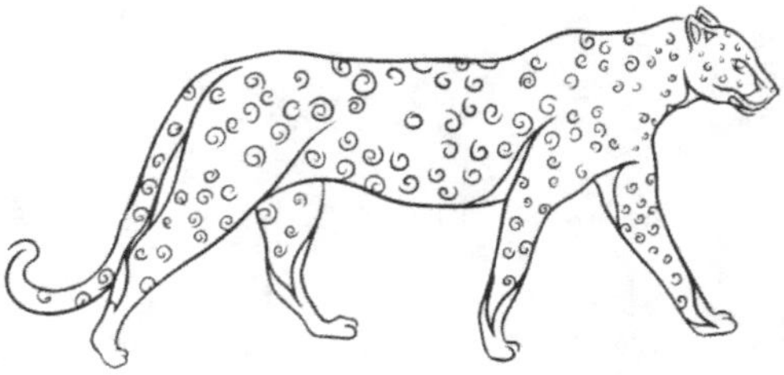

Lion

The lion is a powerful symbol when it comes to leadership and productivity. Those in a position of authority must learn to take the lead, delegate responsibilities, and look for guidance from wise role models — much like the lioness in her pride. Additionally, lacing around or procrastinating instead of doing the hard work can be a sign that you need to make changes to improve your personal power. Lion also helps with stress relief by releasing anger, aggression, and tension — making it easier to find a balance between work and home life.

It can give you the courage and assertiveness to face problems head-on instead of moving around them. But the lion also warns you when a situation is getting out of hand or is threatening your personal and emotional strength.

Deity Associations: Anat, Artemis, Astarte, Brigantia, Cybele, Devi, Durga, Hathor, Hera, Inanna, Ishtar, Isis, Parvati, Rhea, Sekhmet, Amun, Buddha, Dionysus, Helios, Khnum, Krishna, Lugh, Mithras, Nergal, and Vishnu

Lynx (Bobcat)

Lynx is an important symbol that shows you deeply understand the universe and its mysteries. This ancient knowledge implies that you must be discreet with other people's secrets, as they know you can see through their veil of lies or deceptions. In such moments, they will feel awkward in your presence because you can see them for who they really are.

Your inner strength allows you to remain silent even when presented with uncomfortable situations and demanding conflicts concerning others' secrets. People around you trust and admire your high inner vibration and often share their deepest thoughts with you, knowing they will remain around only between the two of them. To those who seek advice or wisdom, remember: You are wise and honorably serve as the keeper of secrets if asked to do so.

They unconsciously sense that you know their secrets and they're right. So you tend to speak your mind but are also cautious around people.

Deity Associations: Freya, Dionysus, and Lugh

Peacock

The peacock's presence indicates an exploration of spiritual domains such as intuition, transformation, and living with joy. Like the peacock, it is up to us to bring out our inner beauty and light through these pursuits. Additionally, this bird is also a teacher of resilience - its never gives up attitude tells us to continue with any mission we embark on persistently. Lastly, when attempting courtship, the peacock cleverly uses mimicry and deception to establish a relationship; mirroring this idea may benefit us in our love journeys.

The peacock's symbolism can be interpreted as an indication of vanity and pride. But on the other hand, it serves as a warning to turn down the level of ostentatiousness and increase one's level of humility. The peacock's loud call may sound like it is asking for help, but its meaning is actually the opposite: help is already here; all you need to do is seek assistance from the peacock itself.

Deity Associations: Devi, Hera, Hestia, Iris, Juno, Sarasvati, Amun, Brahma, Hermes, Horus, Pan, and Zeus

Raven

The raven is associated with speaking up, learning new skills, and deepening one's understanding of metaphysical topics. One can quickly accrue knowledge while the raven's intelligence aids in an enjoyable experience. Seeing a raven could indicate that a situation will arise soon where it is necessary to stand tall and let your voice be heard rather than staying silent. Ravens carry messages, dreams, and visions, so one should pay heed to their warnings and clues. Furthermore, the word 'raven' might suggest there is a secret you must keep for yourself or someone else, and it would be wise for you to remain vigilant about people's words or actions as they may betray or deceive you in some form. The "keeper of secrets" is embedded deep within the culture - when prompted by the raven's gentle whisperings, bear them close in your heart.

Keep it safe and secure inside you. Raven is metaphysical and symbolizes reaching through the darkness to find and resolve your inner conflicts, then letting your light shine bright. It's healing oneself from within.

Deity Associations: Amaterasu, Athena, Badb, Cailleach Bheur, Danu, Freya, Inanna, Macha, Maeve, the Morrigan, Rhiannon, Tiamat, Apollo, Asclepius, Lugh, Mars, Mithras, Odin, and Saturn

Swan

The swan is a powerful symbol of fidelity and lasting love. When one appears in your life, it's a sign that you're about to experience a significant new relationship. You may enter into a professional connection, find a close friend, or discover romance. Swan cautions against judging people on the basis of appearances - instead, look for their inner beauty and get to know them better. Your loyalty runs deep; therefore, if someone needs your assistance, you'll be there at any point in the future. Swan encourages expressing yourself with clarity and taking time each day for reflection in silence. End your day by whistling or humming a happy tune!

This will give you a sense of balance and keep you connected with your inner self. It assists when you need to have faith, see the mysteries in life, and reconnect with your bliss.

Deity Associations: Aphrodite, Bertha, Brigid, Nemesis, Sarasvati, Venus, Angus, Apollo, Brahma, Manannan, Njord, and Zeus

Wolf

The wolf embodies independence, boldness, a preference for being part of a pack or community, loyalty, curiosity, and strength. If you see a wolf in your life, then it's likely that new prospects are coming your way - make sure you trust in yourself while keeping clarity and integrity to take advantage of the opportunities when they arise. Also, don't shy away from making tough decisions to leave behind those things which no longer serve you. Be sure to reach out to family and friends with sincerity; display bravery if needed when standing up for what is right. Wolf encourages you to recognize the wildness within yourself and own it confidently!

You are very passionate and have a defined sense of social order, but you can be shy with others outside your immediate circle. If you're feeling like a lone wolf, isolated from the rest of the pack, now is the time to let go of past grievances and clear up any misunderstandings to regain the group's closeness.

Deity Associations: Artemis, Badb, Cailleach Bheur, Cerridwen, the Morrigan, Apollo, Gwydion, Hades, Mars, Odin, Osiris, and Zeus

Star Beings at a Glance

Elements: Cosmic consciousness, the ability to harness energies, and their attraction to technology.

Talents: Energy healing, a healthy detachment from human drama, and authenticity.

Traits: You have a persistent longing to go home, life on Earth is a mystery to you, and you're a cosmic ambassador.

Nature Spirits at a Glance

Elements: Playful creativity, manifestation skills, and the ability to heal the physical world (including our bodies and the environment).

Talents: Lightheartedness, a strong bond with animals, and a natural talent for magic.

Traits: You have a natural sense for power places and ley lines; you make an excellent peaceful warrior for the environment and are a natural healer.

Ascended Masters at a Glance

Elements: A wealth of knowledge about life on Earth, compassion for the human journey, the ability to connect people with their higher self

Talents: Discernment, wisdom, and gratitude.

Traits: You're a great teacher; you have lots of knowledge from past lives and a strong sense of responsibility.

Angels At A Glance

Elements: High-vibrational, loving, non-judgy.

Talents: Healing emotional issues, resolving fears, and compassion for all beings.

Traits: You're a compassionate soul who truly cares for others and can't be happy without everyone else is comfortable. You're a healer and bringer of peace.

Ascended Masters are believed to be spiritually enlightened beings who have evolutionarily transcended the need for physical incarnation and now exist in higher dimensions. Although there are many different Ascended Masters, they are all united in helping humanity awaken and evolve."

Akshobhya
Amaterasu
Amitabha
Amoghasiddhi
Apollo
Archangel Chamuel
Archangel Gabriel
Archangel Jophiel
Archangel Metatron
Archangel Michael
Archangel Raphael
Archangel Uriel
Avalokitesvara
Babaji
El Morya
Elijah
Jesus the Christ
Hermes Trismegistus
Horus
Krishna
Kuthumi
Lahiri Mahasaya
Lakshmi
Lanto
Mahakala
Manjushri
Melchizedek
Milarepa
Mother Mary
Ramana Maharshi
Ratnasambhava
Saint Francis of Assisi
Saint Germain
Shakyamuni Buddha
Shiva
Vairochana
Vajrakilaya
Tara
Paramahansa Yogananda

The thing is, everywhere I looked, there were different opinions and conflicting information. And some of it was just plain wrong.

I then searched for someone who might have the answer or some knowledge that could point me in the right direction.

I found Jamie Wareham, and she is a Reiki Master Teacher and Certified Angel Intuitive Practitioner (CAIP). Quantum Healer, Angelic Healer, Spiritual Life Coach, and Intuitive Reader.

www.AngelsTalk.com
www.LightworkerPath.com

I took her Angel course and was impressed by how much she knew. Also, I found her to be a kind and generous teacher who was willing to meet me at my basic level of learning.

And She has graciously given me some information on each archangel to share in this book.

The 15 Archangels

Angels have been of guidance to us as far back as man can recall. We may not always have used or known the word "Angel" that we know today, but the energy beings have been here. Archangels, specifically, were created to assist us on our life paths. If you ask them for help, they will guide you along your journey and illuminate ways to make following our true paths easier and filled with more joy.

Archangels will never punish, ridicule, chastise, or behave in any way that is negative or "mean." It is one of two things if you experience a feeling such as this. First, it could be our emotional aversion to change or growth. We may not want to hear the messages the Archangels are bringing us, but that does not constitute them being "mean." Secondly, if what you are "hearing" is negative, spiteful, condescending, etc., it is NOT from an Archangel. Let me repeat; it is NOT from an Archangel. I have heard some discussions and jokes around peoples' impression of a particular Archangel picking on or chastising them in some way.

Unfortunately, their encounters fell into either the first or second category above. That is just not how the Archangels work. Period. They have different personalities but do not carry egos and never get irritated with you or your actions. Instead, they are infinitely patient and will repeat signs for you if you ask them to clarify.

So, how do you work with the 15 main Archangels? This workbook can help you start to develop and track your connection to them. The more you work with them daily, the stronger your connection will be and the more Divine Guidance you will experience. As with all spiritual practices, developing a solid relationship with them is important. Don't worry about whether your request is "big" or "small"; that is not how they see things. Humans place values and labels on things that the Celestial Realms do not. It is more than ok to ask them to help you find a great parking spot, make it to an important meeting at just the right time or help you contact a past loved one. What matters to them is whether it is in alignment with your journey, not the perceived size or significance of your request. You will not "bother them" by communicating and talking to them. They were created to help us; let them.

Why Work With Angel Magic?

Archangels were created to assist humans. It's what they do. The #1 rule is that you must call on them for assistance. Additional rules are that they cannot interfere with life-or-death issues unless it is not your time, and it is important always to THANK THEM - even before the request is answered, as you are stating your trust in knowing you have been heard and your highest and best interest is in progress.

Archangels are extremely powerful celestial beings.
Angelic work will keep you ethical. Help from the Archangels always manifests for the highest and best good of all parties involved. (Ask for: "this or something better")
Archangel magic is SAFE. When working with the Celestial Realm, you cannot cause harm to yourself or others. It is arguably the best magic to start with while gathering your
ethical bearings. If you are meddling with others' affairs, etc. - the Angels will simply shut down your connection.

You cannot manipulate Archangels. They follow the rules of the Cosmos. You can ask them for help, seek guidance, and work with them, BUT you cannot tell them what to do or how to do it. Spirits can be manipulated, but Archangels cannot.

Archangels are non-denominational and neither male nor female. They are powerful Celestial Beings of Light, whom anyone can seek guidance from.

Work with Archangels during your Rituals and other magical work. Working with them will enhance your gifts.

While there are Angels beyond count, we commonly work with the most well know 15 Archangels are named throughout the world's many religions and spiritual practices - though they are non-denominational. They are neither male nor female but do hold more traditionally masculine or feminine energetic qualities and are sometimes referred to as "he" or "she." However, this distinction does not matter to the Archangels; therefore, call them whatever feels right to you.

Remember, it's about energy, not a physical body or attribute. The Archangels desire to create peace and love. They were created specifically to assist humans with their journey on earth. Call on the Archangels when you feel afraid or unsure. They will bless you with what you need. Take the time to thank the Archangels for all the love and light they create in your life.

1. Ariel
2. Azrael
3.Chamuel
4 Gabriel
5 Haniel
6. Jeremiel
7. Jophiel
8. Metatron
9. Michael
10. Raguel
11. Raphael
12. Raziel
13. Sandalphon
14. Uriel
15. Zadkiel

Archetypes

The term "archetype" means original pattern in ancient Greek. Jung used the concept of archetype in his theory of the human psyche. He identified 12 universal, mythic character archetypes that reside within our collective unconscious.

Jung defined twelve primary types that represent the range of basic human motivations. Each of us tends to have one dominant archetype that dominates our personality.

The 12 Jungian Archetypes
Ruler
Creator/Artist
Sage
Innocent
Explorer
Rebel
Hero
Wizard
Jester
Everyman
Lover
Caregiver

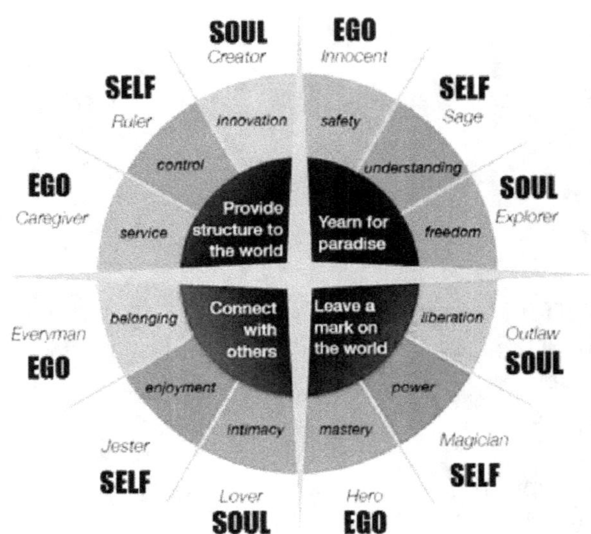

The 4 Cardinal Orientations

The 4 cardinal orientations that the archetypes are seeking to realize are:
Ego – Leave a Mark on the World
Order – Provide Structure to the World
Social – Connect to others
Freedom – Yearn for Paradise

The Ego Types

The Innocent
The Everyman/Regular Guy
The Hero
The Caregiver

The Innocent

Motto: Free to be you and me
Core desire: to get to paradise
Goal: to be happy
Greatest fear: to be punished for doing something bad or wrong
Strategy: to do things right
Weakness: boring for all their naive innocence
Talent: faith and optimism
The Innocent is also known as Utopian, traditionalist, naive, mystic, saint, romantic, and dreamer.

The Everyman

Motto: All men and women are created equal
Core Desire: connecting with others
Goal: to belong
Greatest fear: to be left out or to stand out from the crowd
Strategy: develop ordinary solid virtues, be down to earth, the common touch
Weakness: losing one's own self in an effort to blend in or for the sake of superficial relationships
Talent: realism, empathy, lack of pretense
The Everyman is also known as The good old boy, the regular guy/girl, the person next door, the realist, the working stiff, the solid citizen, the good neighbor, and the silent majority.

The Hero

Motto: Where there's a will, there's a way
Core desire: to prove one's worth through courageous acts
Goal: expert mastery in a way that improves the world
Greatest fear: weakness, vulnerability, being a "chicken"
Strategy: to be as strong and competent as possible
Weakness: arrogance, always needing another battle to fight
Talent: competence and courage
The Hero is also known as The warrior, crusader, rescuer, superhero, soldier, dragon slayer, winner, and team player.

The Caregiver

Motto: Love your neighbor as yourself
Core desire: to protect and care for others
Goal: to help others
Greatest fear: selfishness and ingratitude
Strategy: doing things for others
Weakness: martyrdom and being exploited
Talent: compassion, generosity
The Caregiver is also known as The saint, altruist, parent, helper, and supporter.

The Soul Types

The Explorer
The Rebel
The Lover
The Creator/Artist

The Explorer

Motto: Don't fence me in
Core desire: the freedom to find out whom you are through exploring the world
Goal: to experience a better, more authentic, more fulfilling life
Biggest fear: getting trapped, conformity, and inner emptiness
Strategy: journey, seeking out and experiencing new things, escape from boredom
Weakness: aimless wandering, becoming a misfit
Talent: autonomy, ambition, being true to one's soul
The explorer is also known as The seeker, iconoclast, wanderer, individualist, and pilgrim.

The Rebel

Motto: Rules are made to be broken
Core desire: revenge or revolution
Goal: to overturn what isn't working
Greatest fear: to be powerless or ineffectual
Strategy: disrupt, destroy, or shock
Weakness: crossing over to the dark side, crime
Talent: outrageousness, radical freedom
The Outlaw is also known as The rebel, revolutionary, wild man, misfit, or iconoclast.

The Lover

Motto: You're the only one
Core desire: intimacy and experience
Goal: being in a relationship with the people, work, and surroundings they love
Greatest fear: being alone, a wallflower, unwanted, unloved
Strategy: to become more and more physically and emotionally attractive
Weakness: an outward-directed desire to please others at risk of losing own identity
Talent: passion, gratitude, appreciation, and commitment
The Lover is also known as The partner, friend, intimate, enthusiast, sensualist, spouse, and team-builder.

The Creator

Motto: If you can imagine it, it can be done
Core desire: to create things of enduring value
Goal: to realize a vision
Greatest fear: mediocre vision or execution
Strategy: develop artistic control and skill
Task: to create culture, express own vision
Weakness: perfectionism, bad solutions
Talent: creativity and imagination
The Creator is also known as The artist, inventor, innovator, musician, writer, or dreamer.

The Self Types

The Jester
The Sage
The Magician
The Ruler

The Jester

Motto: You only live once
Core desire: to live in the moment with full enjoyment
Goal: to have a great time and lighten up the world
Greatest fear: being bored or boring others
Strategy: play, make jokes, be funny
Weakness: frivolity, wasting time
Talent: joy
The Jester is also known as The fool, trickster, joker, practical joker, or comedian.

The Sage

Motto: The truth will set you free
Core desire: to find the truth.
Goal: to use intelligence and analysis to understand the world.
Biggest fear: being duped, misled—or ignorant.
Strategy: seeking out information and knowledge; self-reflection and understanding thought processes.
Weakness: can study details forever and never act.
Talent: wisdom, intelligence.
The Sage is also known as: The expert, scholar, detective, advisor, thinker, philosopher, academic, researcher, thinker, planner, professional, mentor, teacher, contemplative.

The Magician

Motto: I make things happen.
Core desire: understanding the fundamental laws of the universe
Goal: to make dreams come true
Greatest fear: unintended negative consequences
Strategy: develop a vision and live by it
Weakness: becoming manipulative
Talent: finding win-win solutions
The Magician is also known as The visionary, catalyst, inventor, charismatic leader, shaman, healer, and medicine man.

The Ruler

Motto: Power isn't everything; it's the only thing.
Core desire: control
Goal: create a prosperous, successful family or community
Strategy: exercise power
Greatest fear: chaos, being overthrown
Weakness: being authoritarian, unable to delegate
Talent: responsibility, leadership
The Ruler is also known as The boss, leader, aristocrat, king, queen, politician, role model, manager, or administrator.

Other Personality Tools

Other Personality Profile tools to understand yourself and those around you:

The Myers-Briggs type indicator https://www.16personalities.com/personality-types

The DISC Profile https://discpersonalitytesting.com/free-disc-test

The Enneagram https://www.integrative9.com/enneagram

Tools of the Trade

No matter your traditions or practices, you can always find a use for magical tools. If you use any tool consistently in your work, it's automatically a magical tool. Simple as that.

Witches' tools are more than just practical; they're also magical. Each tool has its own energy that enhances spells and rituals. For example, candles represent the element of fire.

Altar
Athame
Bells
Bolline
Besom or Brooms
Candles
Cards (playing, tarot, oracle)
Cauldron
Chalice
Cord or Twine
Crystals and Crystal Balls
Dolls or Poppets
Flying Ointments
Horns
Labrys
Masks
Mirrors
Mortar and Pestle
Pentacle or Pentagram
Sieve
Staff
Sword
Tripod
Wand

Tool List

Animism, Power Animals, and Totem

Animism is the belief that all things in the universe, including animals, plants, rocks, and even words, possess a spiritual essence. This belief is prevalent among many Indigenous peoples and is in contrast to the development of organized religions. Animism focuses on the soul and the metaphysical universe.

Animism is a common religious perspective among indigenous cultures. It is the belief that everything, including inanimate objects, has a spirit. This perspective is so inherent to most indigenous peoples that they often do not have a word in their languages that corresponds to "animism" (or even "religion"). The term is an anthropological construct.

Power animals are spirit guides in animal form that can help you navigate through life's challenges and transitions. You can turn to these perceptive and trustworthy oracles for advice and counsel on any questions or concerns. They're exceptional teachers who will help you learn about both the spirit and the natural world. Working with them on a regular basis will enhance your personal life and expand your spiritual capacities immensely.

Power animals can appear in meditations, visions, dreams, shamanic journeys, or on the earth in their physical form. They can be mammals, birds, or reptiles, and even so-called mythical creatures such as unicorns or dragons can be power animals. However, they have no physical representations in the material world. However, since spirit animals' power is drawn from their instinctual and wild nature, it's uncommon for purely domesticated animals, such as pets, to be part of this group.

A totem (from Ojibwe: ᑑᑌᒼ or ᑑᑌᒻ doodem) A totem is a spirit being, sacred object, or symbol that serves as an emblem of a group of people, such as a family, clan, lineage, or tribe. The term totem comes from the Ojibwe language and culture, but belief in tutelary spirits and deities is not limited to the Ojibwe people. Similar concepts can be found in a number of cultures worldwide. The term has also been adopted, and at times redefined, by anthropologists and philosophers of different cultures.

Contemporary neo-shamanic, New Age, and mythopoetic men's movements not otherwise involved in the practice of traditional religion have used "totem" terminology for personal identification with a tutelary spirit or spirit guide. Again, however, this can be seen as cultural misappropriation.

What is Smudging

Smudging is the practice of burning sacred herbs or resins to cleanse, purify, and clarify a sacred space. This is done periodically before performing spells, rituals, divination, or any other spiritual practice. The smoke from the burning herbs or resins clears out any dense or negative energies, purifying the space so that it can be used for positive intentions.

The ceremony of using an abalone shell and feather represents all four of the earth's elements: water, air, earth, and fire. The shell represents water, the smoke represents air, the herbs or resins represent earth, and once they're lit, they represent fire. Feathers are used to lift the stagnant energy during a smudging ceremony. Feathers transform the art of space clearing by guiding the smoke and energy into the wind to be cleansed. In the traditions of Native Americans, feathers are considered sacred gifts from the sky, sea, and trees. The shell is used to hold the burning sage stick, and the feather is used to fan the smoke around the space/object/person. You can use the shell to catch any ash and also put the burning stick out when you're finished.

The past few years have certainly left many folks with the desire to rid their homes of negative energy. Smudging, also known as saging, has become a trendy wellness practice that folks use to cleanse their spaces, be it a bedroom, an entire home, or even a car. But if you tend to poke around smoke-cleansing social media circles, you've probably heard people ask (and might be wondering yourself): Is burning sage and smudging cultural appropriation?

The plant sage, or Salvia, grows all around the world in different colors and variants. Culinary sage (the kind you use in butternut squash and roasted chicken dishes), also known as garden sage, originally comes from the shores of the northern Mediterranean region. However, what most people are referring to when they talk about the popularized practice of smudging is white sage (Salvia apiana).

White sage grows naturally in the southwestern United States and northwestern Mexico and is particularly found along the coast of Southern California and in the Mojave and Sonoran deserts. Though not the only sage native to North America, white sage is by far the one most frequently used and sold by the wellness industry. It's also a sacred herb to several Indigenous communities, including the Lakota, Cheyenne, and Navajo. The Chumash people, for instance, who are native to central and southern coastal regions of California, use white sage in healing sessions to purify the central nervous system.

Wondering whether burning sage is cultural appropriation is a fair question — long story short, burning sage is problematic for a few reasons, the biggest being cultural insensitivity and environmental unsustainability. If you're not Indigenous and therefore hesitating to strike a match to cleanse the bad vibes out of your apartment, here's what you need to know about burning white sage.

Is Burning White Sage Bad?

Thanks to the recent trendiness of smudging, white sage is in high demand. The demand has become so great that many Chumash people (of what is now Southern California) are concerned that the plant is being overharvested. The United States Department of Agriculture (USDA) says that white sage has important medical benefits. It is used to cure colds and aid postpartum healing — and it's a crucial part of the surrounding ecosystem.

Overharvesting white sage and the threat of increased wildfires and urban development endangers Indigenous peoples' ability to access and use the wild plant in the ways they and their ancestors have done for thousands of years.

Leaving the root is important because that's how the plant grows back. If someone is harvesting white sage and doesn't know how to do so properly, they're preventing more plants from growing and thus endangering the plant species.

Smoke Cleansing vs. Smudging

White sage has become particularly popular with those who practice witchcraft or witchcraft-inspired wellness rituals. Sage, however, is not historically part of European witchcraft, from which many modern-day witch practices stem.

If you have used herbs to cleanse your space in the past and enjoy the ritual, you don't have to give it up in order to do so in a culturally conscious way. Smudging refers to a specific cultural and spiritual practice, but smoke cleansing offers an alternative to smudging for folks who aren't Indigenous. This form of cleansing can look a bit like smudging, but it's just the simple act of burning herbs, wood, incense, or other safe-to-burn materials that possess cleansing properties. The smoke is then waved over the area you want to cleanse.

Many cultures have historical and spiritual practices connected to smoke cleansing — everything from herbs and woods to incense and roots. For example, frankincense and myrrh were burned in ancient Egypt for prayer, and rosemary was historically burned in hospitals in France in order to clear the air of infection. It may even be personally fulfilling to find out if and what your ancestors burned for cleansing. But unless you are a descendant of Indigenous North American people, it likely wasn't white sage that they were burning, according to Keene.

However, the general act of smoke cleansing is not inherently spiritual or specific to a certain culture in the way that smudging is. If burning incense, herbs, or wood is part of your self-love practice and inner wellness work, there are safe-burning alternatives to burning sage for smoke cleansing, including lavender, pine, thyme, and cloves, each of which has its own unique properties and is not environmentally endangered.

As a note, if you're browsing your fave place to buy herbs and look at the options for smoke cleansing next to white sage, you might find Palo Santo ("holy wood" in Spanish). But you may want to hold off on buying that, too. Palo Santo sticks have been getting more popular as an alternative to sage, but buying this Central and South American tree bark used by Amazonian tribes can also be harmful in similar ways to white sage. Palo Santo has been added to the International Union for Conservation of Nature's (IUCN) list because though the tree is not yet nearing extinction, its recent overharvesting can put it on that path.

It's important that in the process of any cleansing, you're respecting Indigenous cultures and the ecosystem. That may include educating yourself and others about white sage, appropriation, and smoke cleansing; harvesting your own sage or other herbs sustainably; contacting brands to ask them to stop selling white sage without giving due to Native cultures; or using other plants entirely. Being intentional about how you implement this practice in your life — and being mindful of its origins and significance — is helpful for everyone.

Experts:

Ruth Hopkins, Dakota/Lakota Sioux writer

Dr. Adrienne Keene, assistant professor of American Studies and Ethnic Studies at Brown University, author of the blog Native Appropriations, and citizen of the Cherokee Nation

The Ethics Of Burning Sage, Explained
by Nylah Burton and Jay Polish
Updated: Feb. 24, 2022
Originally Published: July 19, 2019

Cultural Appropriation

So that leads me to talk about cultural appropriation for a second. It's when somebody from a dominant group takes something from a minority culture without understanding or respecting that culture. It's become a big issue in recent years.

Cultural appropriation is when dominant group members adopt elements of a minority culture in a way that is exploitative, disrespectful, or stereotypical. To really understand this concept, we need to have a clear definition of culture.

A culture is a group of people's shared beliefs, values, customs, and practices. It's not something you're born with—it's something you learn by being part of a particular society.

Cultural appropriation is when someone from a majority group benefits financially or socially from the culture of a minority group. It can also happen when someone from a majority group oversimplifies or belittles the culture of a minority group.

Cultural appropriation is when someone from a dominant group takes something from a minority group and uses it without understanding the cultural context.

Cultural appropriation is when people from dominant groups adopt elements of minority cultures without facing the same consequences as members of those minority groups.

When someone appropriates another group's culture without understanding or respecting it, it's a serious issue with far-reaching consequences. Even if it's not done on purpose, it can be really harmful.

An example:
I lived in New Mexico for a while and saw the Zia symbol everywhere. I thought it would be a cool tattoo to remind me of my time there. Unfortunately, I was wrong.
I found the following article while researching the symbol for one of my books. To say I was horrified was putting it lightly. I culturally appropriated the symbol by having it tattooed on my arm without understanding its culture and meaning.

The Zia Symbol

In 1925, New Mexico, which gained statehood in the United States in 1912, adopted a design for its flag featuring a sun symbol belonging to the Zia people. According to the tribe, the symbol was secret and stolen from the Zia, who lost both ownership and control over it, and was left to contemplate that the sun symbol is widely used and sometimes desecrated.

On the side of the World Intellectual Property Organization committee on the protection of traditional knowledge this week, the governor of the Pueblo of Zia explained the case of the sun symbol. An indigenous panel on the committee also provided their thoughts on gaps in the intellectual property system when it comes to protecting their traditional knowledge and folklore.

The side event was held yesterday on the margins of the 38th session of the Intergovernmental Committee on Intellectual Property and Genetic Resources, Traditional Knowledge and Folklore (IGC), taking place from 10-14 December.

The Governor of the Pueblo of Zia, Anthony Delgarito, explained how the distinctive sun symbol was stolen and later used on the state of New Mexico's flag and many other items nationally and internationally.

The Zia Pueblo is located among the mountains and red-earth canyons of northern New Mexico, about 40 miles northwest of Albuquerque. Pueblos were names given to the tribes by colonizers, Delgarito said, first by the Spanish and later by the Mexicans. The state of New Mexico hosts 19 pueblos, he said.

The state of New Mexico uses the Zia logo on both the flag and license plates. However, the sun symbol is an "exceptionally significant religious symbol," he explained, and it existed since time immemorial, well before the US was founded. "It represents the tribe itself," he said.

He added that archaeological evidence shows that the symbol has existed for several hundred years.

According to Delgarito, in 1923, the state of New Mexico, which at that time did not have a flag, launched a contest for a flag design.

As it happened, an anthropologist named James Stevenson in the late 1890s built a trusted relationship with the Zia and was allowed to attend their sacred ceremonies, Delgarito said. Stevenson stole pottery with the sun symbol, later displayed in New Mexico's capital, Santa Fe.

Another anthropologist living in Santa Fe, Harry Mera, was inspired by the sun symbol on display at the museum, entered the contest with his wife using the sun symbol, and won the flag contest.

In 1925, the design was officially adopted as the New Mexico state flag. The Zia sun symbol was appropriated without the consent of the Zia, Delgarito stated. It later became part of the public domain, still without consent from the Zia. He said the symbol was stolen from the Zia secret society, all the more significant since the symbol was used in religious healing and wellness processes.

The Zia sun symbol represents the four cardinal directions, the four seasons of the year, the four periods of each day (morning, noon, evening, and night), and the four seasons of life (childhood, youth, middle age, and old age). The center of the sun symbol stands for life itself, Delgarito explained.

The general public is using the Zia sun symbol without knowing its history or the religious significance behind it, he said. Zia at least wants respect for the symbol and that it is not desecrated. He said that the symbol was the taking of Zia's identity, which continues to be threatened by the ongoing exploitation of the symbol.

The Zia want the general public to ask permission to use the symbol and to contribute to a scholarship program fund so that children have the opportunity for a sound education, he said. However, the Zia has no control over how the symbol is used, he said, giving examples of desecration of the symbol: tattoos, gravestones, the embedding in the floor of the New Mexico State Capitol, and marketing, he said.

The Zia have learned from their misfortune with the sun symbol and now close their village during secret ceremonies, he remarked.

The Zia is trying to raise awareness among the New Mexican government and the general public about the significance of the sun symbol and the importance of not defaming it. He said that the Zia now has a protocol to follow if someone wants to use the sun symbol. An example of use Zia has agreed to is on the Southwest Airlines planes.

There is little the Zia can do about protecting their sun symbol, as it has been considered in the public domain for several years, said a speaker in a video shown during the side event.

Indigenous Panelists on Zia Case Discuss Public Domain

A panel of indigenous peoples at the IGC yesterday gave perspectives on gaps in the IP protection of traditional knowledge and traditional cultural expressions of indigenous peoples.

The three panelists mentioned the importance of the United Nations Declarations on the Rights of Indigenous Peoples [pdf], and in particular Article 31, which asserts the right of indigenous peoples to maintain, control, protect and develop their cultural heritage, TK and TCEs, and the right to maintain, control, protect and develop their intellectual property over their cultural heritage, TK, and TCEs.

Commenting on the Zia case, June Lorenzo, a lawyer advocating in tribal and domestic courts and legislative and international human rights bodies, said that in the late 1890s, Zia was at a very vulnerable point, as many other tribes were. A number of archaeologists came and took "what they could because they thought we were going to disappear as a civilization," she said, noting that the stolen pot was repatriated in 2000 or 2002.

In 1925, when the state of New Mexico adopted the Zia symbol, the Zia was not even considered citizens of the United States, she said, and could not vote. "So the idea that they should have objected to this [the use of the symbol] in 1925 ... is just absurd."

In the 1990s, the Zia began to organize and demand compensation, and then they challenged trademark applications, she explained. In one case, they only prevailed because of public outcry, and the company withdrew its application, she added.

According to Lorenzo, the idea of the public domain oftentimes is contrary to what indigenous peoples think.

"We don't have a belief that our epistemologies are supposed to be shared with the rest of the world," she said. "This idea of the public domain really threatens what we hold most sacred."

Prior Informed Consent key, Gaps in Tiered Approach

Elifuraha Laltaika, an expert member of the UN Permanent Forum on the Rights of Indigenous Peoples and executive director for Law and Advocacy for Pastoralists in Tanzania, remarked that TK cannot be separated from indigenous peoples' lives.

He stressed the importance of free prior informed consent of indigenous peoples and said it should be the central theme of any agreement to be reached. He also underlined the importance of benefit sharing, and the full and effective participation of indigenous peoples in the decision-making process, particularly when decisions will impact their lives with far-reaching consequences.

Q"apaj Conde Choque, an Aymar lawyer from Bolivia, said indigenous peoples want to have control over their TK, but gaps in the law make it difficult to exercise that control. He said that TK, for example, cannot answer the patentability criteria of novelty and industrial application.

Indigenous peoples are also creators and innovators, and those inventions could meet the patent or copyright requirement, he said, but the collective authorities holding that knowledge do not access the IP system because they do not feel that the protection by the current system fully satisfies Article 31 of the UN Declaration on the Rights of Indigenous Peoples.

In the audience, Preston Hardison, legal advisor for the Tulalip Tribe, commented on the "tiered approach" being considered in the draft articles discussed this week at the IGC. The tiered approach would differentiate the level of protection according to whether the knowledge is secret, sacred, narrowly diffused, or widely diffused.

He said that the tiered approach would not answer cases like the Zia sun symbol, which illustrates a violation of fundamental indigenous laws. According to Hardison, some indigenous peoples seek the recovery of some of their TK and TCEs because the "violations are so bad," so fundamental to who they are as people, that they need to recover control over their TK and TCEs. "That's not really what we are doing in the tiered approach," he said.

It should be noted that during the indigenous panel, a number of delegates left the plenary room, leaving the indigenous peoples to speak to a depleted audience.

Indigenous Knowledge Misappropriation: The Case Of The Zia Sun Symbol Explained At WIPO
11/12/2018 BY CATHERINE SAEZ, INTELLECTUAL PROPERTY WATCH

Smudging Herbs and Resins

ROSEMARY
Peace
Soothing
Clears Negative Energy
Clarity & Memory
Boosting

CEDAR
Clears Negative Energy
Renewal
Grounding & Protection
Uplifting
Spiritual Connection

LAVENDER
Clears Negative Energy
Peace of Mind
Relaxation
Happiness
Cleansing

SWEETGRASS
Clears Negative Energy
Cleansing
Purification
Attracts Positivity
Call in Spirits & Divination

YERBA SANTA
Clears Negative Energy
Purification
Renewal
Raises Vibration
Clarity & Empowerment

JUNIPER
Clears Negative Energy
Grounding
Healing
Attracts Positive Energy

CINNAMON
Energy & Motivation
Clears Negative Energy
Healing
Grounding

Resins

DRAGONS BLOOD
Clears Negative Energy
Cleansing
Healing
Protection
Enhance Productivity

FRANKINCENSE
Protection & Purification
Spiritual Awareness
Relieves Anxiety &
Depression
Clears Negative Energy
Healing

MYRRH
Antibacterial
Clears Negative Energy
Healing
Grounding
Spiritual Connection

Please make sure the following is ethically sourced

PALO SANTO
Antibacterial & Antiviral
Clears Negative Energy
Transmutes & Raises
Vibration
Deep Healing
Cleansing

SAGE
Antibacterial & Antiviral
Cleansing
Healing
Clears Negative Energy

Correspondence Flowers and Herbs

I have included worksheets to familiarize you with some correspondence associated with this season. Feel free to add others to personalize your unique way of celebrating this sabbat. In addition, I have included how to dry herbs and how to make an infusion oil.

Foraging Calendar

JANUARY, FEBRUARY, AND MARCH

Chickweed, Common Mallow Leaves, Common Sorrel, Cowberry. Crow Garlic. Dandelion Root. Garlic Mustard, Ground Elder, Hairy Bittercress, Nettles, Pignut, Sheep's Sorrel, Silver Birch Sap, Wild Garlic, Winter Cress, Wood Sorrel

APRIL, MAY, AND JUNE

Beech Leaves, Borage, Broom, Chickweed, Cleavers, Common Poppy, Dandelion Leaves and Roots, Dog Rose Flowers, Elderflower, Garlic Mustard, Ground Elder. Hawthorn Blossom, Hops, Nettles, Pignuts, Sheep's Sorrel, Spearmint, Sweet Cicely, Watercress, Wild Garlic. Wild Thyme, Wood Sorrel, Yarrow

JULY, AUGUST, AND SEPTEMBER

Acorns, Apples, Beech Nuts, Bilberries, Blackberries, Burdock, Chamomile, Chickweed, Chicory, Cleavers, Common Mallow, Dandelion Leaves and Flowers, Elderberry, Fat Hen, Garlic Mustard, Gooseberries, Hawthorn Berries, Hazelnuts, Horseradish, Juniper Berries, Nettle, Plums, Rowan Berries, Sheep's Sorrel, Spearmint, Sweet Chestnuts, Sweet Cicely, Walnuts, Wild Cherries, Wild Strawberries, Wild Thyme, Wood Sorrel, Yarrow

OCTOBER, NOVEMBER, AND DECEMBER

Chestnuts, Chickweed, Crab Apples, Hawthorn Berries, Horseradish, Nettles, Rosehips, Sheep's Sorrel, Sloes, Spearmint, Sweet Chestnuts, Walnuts

I live in the North Eastern United States; you may find different species depending on where you live.

Drying Herbs & Flowers

You can dry your fresh herbs and flowers using a couple of different methods:
Lay them on a towel or dry surface and use a stick to weigh them down. Use an old mesh produce bag! Place the herbs in the bag and set it in direct sunlight. Using a produce bag also allows you to flip the herbs so that they dry evenly and prevent them from blowing away.

Use two old window screens and sandwich them or tie the end of a bunch of herbs or flowers with a piece of string and hang it in a dry place in direct sunlight. When it's hot, your herbs will dry out completely within a day or two. At dusk, bring your herbs inside to prevent them from getting damp and dewy. They're ready to store when they are dry and crumble when crushed.

Bring the herbs indoors to dry if it's not hot and sunny. You can use a dehydrator on its lowest setting or an oven on its lowest temperature (170 or less). You can tie a bunch of herbs or flowers with a piece of string and hang it on a sunny window in your home. Use the old mesh produce bag again and hang the bag in a sunny window.

The trick is, DON'T dry your herbs and flowers in a cool or damp place. Unless the herbs are in direct sunlight or you're using a dehydrator or oven, I don't recommend drying them indoors, as it's easy for the herbs to mold. If your herbs or flowers mold during the drying process, do not use them! They now belong to the compost.

Storing: When your herbs are completely dried, transfer them to a jar with an airtight lid and store them in a cool place, out of direct sunlight. They will last for several months.

Use your dried herbs for tinctures, cooking, salves, balms, herbal teas, and potpourri!

Infusions

Infusion is a general term used to describe the method of soaking plant material in a liquid to impart flavor to the medium. Infusions can be made from various ingredients: leaves, stems, seeds, barks, and berries are common. Fruits and vegetables work well, too. The liquid in your infusion, also called the "menstruum," will vary with your intended use.
Water can be used to make an infusion. So can alcohol, oil, and sweet solutions be made from sugar, honey, and glycerin? Different methods for making infusions can be used to create beverages, medicines, and flavorings.

Cold infusions are made by steeping the material in liquid for a long while and letting time slowly and gently do its work. The process releases fewer tannins than hot infusions, so they lack the bitter flavors that hot infusions can sometimes have. Cold infusions retain more of the taste of the material being infused so that you won't lose the bright, fresh flavor of delicate herbs and fruits. Cold-brewed coffee and tea, known for their smooth flavor, are examples of cold infusions.

Hot infusions - are made by heating your infusing medium before introducing your flavoring agents. Hot infusions release more of the plant's volatile oils, sometimes with a pleasingly bitter note from the tannins that have been unlocked as well. This is an excellent method to use when you want faster results. Hot infusions work in minutes rather than the hours or days that cold infusions can take. They are also good at releasing flavors that cold water is too gentle to unleash. Tea and coffee are common hot infusions.

Flavored oils are often made by hot infusion. Mild flavored or neutral oil, such as organic canola or safflower oil, is gently heated until it is warm. Garlic or herbs are then added to the oil and allowed to steep to impart their flavors. The plant material is then strained out, and the oil is decanted for future use. Scented oils from fragrant plants such as lavender, rosemary, thyme, and citrus peel can be made from the hot infusion.

The oil should be refrigerated and used within several weeks. Although the oil has been strained, tiny particles of food material can remain suspended in the liquid and act as a vector for contamination.

Infused vodka - *Never heat alcohol. The flame can quickly leap into the pot and catch on fire.* Instead, clean out a glass jar or bottle, add some flavoring agents, such as a handful of berries or the husk of a vanilla bean, and cover them with vodka. Put the container in a cool, dark place for a few days, up to a few weeks, to allow the flavor to develop, shaking or turning the container every so often to distribute the liquid. Then, strain out the solids and decant the flavored concoction back into the container. Infused vodkas made with berries of any sort, a vanilla bean, grated ginger root, or chili peppers are always a hit. You can also sub out the vodka for any liquor that is at least 80 proof, which ensures that you are infusing, not fermenting or rotting, your flavoring ingredients. And don't throw out those solids! You can blend those vodka-drenched fruits into adult beverages and desserts or use them to flavor cooked foods, where the heat of the process will burn off the alcohol.

Infused vinegar - Uses the same method as infused vodka. However, you can use this infused vinegar to significantly affect vinaigrettes. Think strawberry vinegar in a spinach salad. Infused types of vinegar are terrifically diluted with water or seltzer (at a 1:8 ratio) to create a traditional beverage called a "shrub." Refreshing and delicious, shrubs were popular in Colonial times and are now seeing a comeback. So-called "drinking vinegar" popping up in gourmet shops is a shrub, sometimes with added sugar or fruit purees. But when you make them at home, you can see just how economical they are. You will get sixty-four ounces of vinegar from a few berries infused with eight ounces of the delicious shrub.

Infused water - Slice up anything you think would be flavorful to sip on and add it to your water jug, glass, or bottle. For example, cucumbers, citrus segments (or just their peels), and chunks of melon or pineapple are all delicious.

Extracts, Tinctures, Decoctions & Tisanes

Extracts are just highly concentrated cold infusions. Alcohol is the typical menstruum used to make extracts. Use the same method described above for making flavored vodka, using a high concentration of flavoring material to alcohol. For herbs, you'll want about a 1:1 ratio. For non-vegetal items such as nuts and spices, you can use less but still more than the straight infusion described earlier. For instance, instead of one vanilla bean in a 750 ml bottle of vodka for flavored liquor, you will need to use two or three beans in a cup of vodka. Citrus is another great extract option. Pack a pint jar half full of zest strips, cover it with a cup of vodka, and let it go. Allow your extracts to diffuse for much longer than flavored vodka or vinegar. Two to three months should do it. Strained and bottled, preferably in a dark bottle or kept in a dark place, they keep for a year or more.

Tinctures - are the strongest infusions and are often used for medicinal purposes. Dried or fresh herbs and flowers such as mint, calendula, or rosemary are infused to extract their oils and leave the plant material behind. Alcohol is also the most popular menstruum to make tinctures. The ratio of plant material to alcohol is the highest of all infusions: about 3:1 for most recipes but higher for some. Tinctures keep for up to five years.

Glycerine - Those sensitive to alcohol often use vegetable glycerin as their menstruum when making tinctures. Be sure to use culinary-grade glycerin and dilute it 75/25 with water. Then use 1:2 dried plant matter added to the glycerin mixture. Crush the herbs first to encourage infusion. Remove to a cool dark place for four to six weeks, then strain. You can store the infused glycerin in a cool dark place for six to twelve months.

Decoctions - are like hot infusions, except that you don't just pour hot water over the plant material; you simmer it for an extended time. This method is helpful for barks, such as cinnamon, dried hard herbs, and berries, such as elderberry, and roots and rhizomes.

Fruit peel "tea" can be made by simmering apple or pear peels in hot water until fragrant; sweeten and sip on a cold winter's night. Homemade cold remedies and other home cures, such as elderberry syrup, which often calls for woody herbs, barks, and dried items, are often created by decoction.

Tisanes - Hot herbal infusions and decoctions are sometimes called "tisanes." The term is used, in part, to differentiate such beverages from teas, which technically can only be made with leaves from the Camellia sinensis plant. Herbal "teas," therefore, are tisanes, not teas, unless they contain the leaves of the tea plant.

Infusion Solar Method

Fill a mason jar with desired dried herbs or flowers. Cover the herbs with a carrier oil of choice, e.g., olive, grape seed, almond,
or jojoba. Leave to infuse on a sunny window sill for 2-6 weeks.

Shake occasionally to agitate.

Using a very fine sieve or nylon stocking, strain the infusion, making sure to squeeze every last drop of precious oil out of the herbs and petals!

Store the oil in a cool dark place.

Infusion Slow Cooker Method

Fill a mason jar with desired dried herbs or flowers.

Cover the herbs with a carrier oil of your choice. e.g., olive, grape seed, almond, or jojoba. Place the jars in the slow cooker with a tea towel lined on the bottom (this will prevent them from moving around.)

Fill the slow cooker half full with water so the mason jars are about 3/4 covered. Turn the slow cooker on low heat and leave to infuse for 10-12 hours.

Using a very fine sieve or nylon stocking, strain the infusion and squeeze every last drop of precious oil out of the herbs and petals!

Store the oil in a cool dark place.
Use your infused oils for homemade balms, salves, cooking, and lotions!

Freezing Herbs

Freezing is an excellent method to preserve herbs; you'll have fresh herbs for the whole year. You can have whatever you want whenever you want:-)

Cut up your chosen herb and add 2-3 tablespoons of olive oil.

Put in blender and blend for 3- 4 minutes.

Put in freezer storage bags to use throughout the year.

Or, if you are going to use them soon, you can put them in an ice cube tray for later.

My daughter does this with her DIY baby food, which works great.

DIY Terrarium

Supplies:
A clear container of your choice
Pebbles, small river stones, or expanded clay balls that are used in hydroponics.
Charcoal (activated charcoal, horticultural charcoal, or lump charcoal will all work as long as the product does not contain any additives)
Potting soil (choose a well-draining soil to prevent it from getting compacted and waterlogged)
Decor (wood, rocks, or other decorations)
Plants

Planting tools: a spoon, long-handle tweezers, or even chopsticks can come in handy when planting in thin-mouthed containers

Directions:
Start by covering the bottom of the container with a 1-inch layer of pebbles or crushed stone. This drainage layer is used to keep the soil from becoming waterlogged and swampy.

Add chunks of charcoal to the stone or cover it with a 1/8-inch-deep layer of crushed charcoal to cover the pebbles. This helps with filtration and any odors.

Next, add 2 to 4 inches of sterilized potting soil on top of the charcoal, depending on the size of your container and the size of the plants.

Now you get to be creative and design your miniature landscape. If your container is large enough, the soil can be molded into hills and valleys to add interest; add rocks and small logs for a natural-looking setting. You could even add lakes, paths, statues, and driftwood.

Finally, it's time to plant. Look for dwarf or low-growing plants with the same light, humidity, water, and temperature requirements. Combine different sizes, shapes, colors, and leaf textures to make things interesting.

Select plants that don't mind wet foliage, such as moss, ferns, or prayer plants. Plant a woodland scene, use flowering alpines, get carnivorous, or go totally tropical.

Once the terrarium is planted, cover its top with a pane of glass. If the sides fog up from excess humidity, leave the top open a crack so that some of the moisture evaporates from the container. A sealed terrarium will go for months, even years, without needing water. Place your terrarium out of direct sunlight to avoid overheating; fluorescent lighting is ideal.

You will want to display your terrarium where it is sure to be noticed because it may just give the room-as well as your plants-a little atmosphere!

Some of the most popular houseplants are tropical, making them ideal candidates for a terrarium. Plants such as miniature ferns, peperomias, African violets, and some types of orchids are all good choices. In addition, many woodland plants and mosses can thrive in a terrarium environment.

When choosing plants for terrariums, it's important to consider their mature size and ability to tolerate moisture. Smaller plants with a high soil moisture and humidity tolerance will do best in sealed terrariums.
Some plants that grow especially well in terrariums are:
Ajuga
Aluminum plant
Artillery plant (Pilea)
Baby's tears
Bird's nest sansevieria (for open terrariums only)
Bloodleaf (Iresine herbstii)
Bromeliads (young plants only)
Button fern
Carnivorous plants: Venus fly traps, sundews, butterworts, cobra lilies, and tropical pitcher plants are all carnivorous plants that like humidity. (However, most non-tropical species need to experience a period of colder weather to thrive.)
Chinese evergreen (young plants only)
Creeping fig
Earth star (Cryptanthus)
Flame violet (Episcia dianthiflora)
Mosses
Oxalis
Pellionia
Peperomia
Polka-dot plant (Hypostes)
Rabbit's foot fern
Small-leaf ivies
Snike moss (Selaninella)
Strawberry begonia
Swedish ivy
Variegated aloe (for open terrariums only)

Taking Care of Your Terrarium

Once established, your terrarium will be very low maintenance.

Don't plant too closely; allow some room for growth. Your terrarium won't look instantly lush; plants need time to adjust and settle in.

Water after planting; soil should be damp but not soaked.

Place your terrarium where it will get bright light but not in direct sun, which will cook your plants. Artificial light is excellent.

Leave the terrarium open for a few days while the plant leaves dry off, then put on the cover and keep a close eye on the plants.

Excessive condensation, moldy plants, and limp yellow leaves are signs of overwatering. Open the cover and let your terrarium dry out a bit if that occurs.

No condensation and plants with wilted leaves are signs of underwatering. Check the soil and water lightly if it seems dry.

Leggy growth is a sign that your terrarium is not getting enough light.

It's normal to see small insects crawling around in your terrarium after a while. Usually, these are springtails, beneficial insects that help break down dead plant material. They're your terrarium's clean-up crew!

Florida Water Recipe

Ingredients:
16 oz of vodka
3-5 tablespoons of floral water (orange, rose, lavender, etc.)
8 drops of Lavender EO
10 drops of Lemon EO
10 drops of Orange EO
5 drops of Bergamot EO
5 drops of Cinnamon EO
5 drops of Clove EO
3 drops of Benzoin EO
Fresh rose petals & fresh rosemary (optional)

Add your vodka and floral water to a bowl and smell each EO before adding it to your bowl. Let your nose and spirit tell you if you should add more or less than what's in the recipe.

Combine all ingredients in a spray bottle

Shake well before each use

Remove rose petals and rosemary if you wish

Keep your customized Florida Water on hand to energetically cleanse your aura, car, home, workspace, altar, etc.

I like using it on my floors, windows, and doors. But you can use it in your bath or laundry to clean your tools and crystals or make it into a spray.

Cascarilla Powder

Cascarilla powder is an easy-to-make essential ingredient for protective magic Cascarilla.
(as-ka-ree-ah) is made of powdered eggshell and used primarily for protection and spiritual cleansing. It originates from hoodoo and Santeria but has become popular throughout America due to its accessibility. Cascarilla powder can also help create spiritual barriers (similar to salt), add blessings, aid in protection, and is a great nutritional addition for plants in the garden!

Florida water also has protective qualities and complements the Cascarilla very well.

Tip: When you crack an egg, run the shell under the kitchen faucet to separate the membrane from the body. Removing the membrane makes a higher-quality powder.

Ingredients:
2 dozen eggshells, dried
Food processor or mortar and pestle
½ teaspoon of Florida water (see recipe)
Small glass jar / sealable container

Directions:
Bake the eggshells at 200* for approximately 30 minutes to further dry them out. This step allows excess moisture to cook off, making a more delicate powder. This step is significant if you plan to grind the shells by hand using a mortar and pesto! You might notice the color change slightly if you're using white eggshells. Don't' worry-your powder will still come out white.

When the egg shells are dry, grind them into a fine powder using a mortar, pestle, or food processor. Add about 1/2 teaspoon of Florida water and process until you have a fine, sand-like consistency. Store the cascarilla powder in a jar or pack it into chalk.

For Cascarilla chalk, mix 1 tablespoon of flour with 1 tablespoon of loose cascarilla powder and mix thoroughly. Add a tablespoon of warm water and mix until the ingredients have combined just enough to form a ball in your hands. Roll the mixture into sticks about 1/2 to 1 inch in diameter and let them dry for 3 to 5 days. Alternately, you can roll the mixture into balls and place them in a small-pack paper condiment cup (this is the easiest method). Store the chalk in a glass, plastic, or metal container to protect it from breaking, and keep it in a cool dark place.

Note: You can enhance the magical properties of your cascarilla powder by adding additional or specific herbs. Use caution when adding; too much of these and the mixture will not stick together and form chalk.

You can use it in spells and in making sigils and magical symbols.

Apple

Pyrus spp

Folk Name: Fruit of the gods, Silver branch, Tree of love

Magical Properties

Love
Divination
Making wands (wood)
Tarot reading
Scrying
Garden magic
Immortality

Physical Properties

It May:

Prevent cancer
Diabetes
Dysentery
Fever
Heart problems
Warts
Vitamin C-deficiency condition called scurvy

Use Caution:

Planet - Venus

I am a powerful being, full of magic and potential.

Apple

Pyrus spp

Folk Name: Fruit of the gods, Silver branch, Tree of love

Some Suggested Uses:

Apple Incense

Ingredients:

- Dried apple blossoms, seeds, and/or bark
- Resin tears like copal or frankincense (optional)
- Essential oils (optional)

Equipment:

- Mortar and pestle
- Charcoal tablet for incense
- Heat-proof vessel (such as a cast iron or copper cauldron)

Instructions:

1. Collect dried apple blossoms, seeds, and/or bark.
2. Grind the dried apple blossoms, seeds, and/or bark in a mortar and pestle until they are a fine powder.
3. If desired, add a ground-up resin tear like copal or frankincense to the mixture for a more pleasant aroma.
4. Optionally, add a drop of essential oil to the mixture.
5. Light a charcoal tablet for incense and place it in a heat-proof vessel.
6. Sprinkle the apple blossom powder mixture onto the charcoal tablet.
7. Enjoy the aroma as the incense smolders and use it to enhance your divination practices, magical rituals, or spellwork.

Note: Always use caution when working with fire and burning incense, and make sure to keep the charcoal tablet and heat-proof vessel on a stable surface.

Mugwort

Artemisia Vulgaris

Folk Name: Artemis herb, Felon herb, Sailor's tobacco, Old man

Magical Properties

moon cycles
women's health
childbirth
Prophetic dreams
Protection
Astral projection
Healing

Physical Properties

It May:

Alleviating muscle aches and pains

Planet - Venus

Use Caution: Some of Mugwort's active components, such as thujone, can be toxic in excessive doses, causing liver damage, nausea, and convulsions.

I honor the cycles of the moon and use its energy to manifest my desires.

Mugwort

Artemisia Vulgaris

Folk name: Artemis herb, Felon herb, Sailor's tobacco, Old man-

Some Suggested Uses:

In Asia, mugwort flavors tea and rice dishes promoting digestion.

Mugwort Infused Olive Oil Recipe:

Ingredients:

- Fresh mugwort
- Olive oil
- Glass jar
- Cheesecloth or dishcloth
- Rubber band
- Chopstick

Instructions:

1. Allow the fresh mugwort to wilt for half a day.
2. Chop the mugwort into tiny pieces.
3. Place the chopped mugwort in a glass jar and fill it to the top with olive oil.
4. Remove any air bubbles by moving the mixture around with a chopstick.
5. Add more olive oil to completely cover the plant material.
6. Cover the jar with cheesecloth or dishcloth and secure it with a rubber band. Do not use an airtight lid to allow the humidity to evaporate.
7. Place the jar in a sunny window for five to six weeks and stir occasionally. Ensure that all of the plant material is covered with oil to prevent mold from forming.
8. After five or six weeks, filter the oil and discard the plant material into the compost bin.
9. The infused oil will have a deep green color, the darker the green, the more potent the medicine.
10. Store the infused oil in a cool, dark place. It will keep for three to six months.
11. Use the oil to massage sore muscles or restless legs and enjoy the soothing benefits of mugwort.

Lemon

Citrus Limon
Folk Name: Ulamula, Lymon

Magical Properties
Cleanse magical objects
Longevity
Love
Purification
Break negative ties with your past

Physical Properties
It May:
Vitamin C
May lower cholesterol
It may help to lower blood pressure
Reduce appetite
Reduce sugar cravings
Treats sore throat, colds

Use Caution:

Planet - Moon

I am surrounded by love and light, and negativity cannot touch me.

Lemon

Citrus Limon
Folk Name: Ulamula, Lymon

Some Suggested Uses:

Cleansing: Create a cleansing floor wash by boiling 1 tsp. lemon peel in a cup of boiling water before adding the water to your favorite cleaning solution. You can use this to cleanse your ritual space.

Cleanse your aura by soaking lemon slices or lemon leaves in a bath tea before adding it to your ritual bath.

Surprisingly lemon is an ingredient in Florida water.

Strawberry-Lemonade Smoothie
Ingredients:
½ teaspoon lemon zest
1 lemon wedge, peeled
4 large strawberries
2 cups fresh baby spinach (or other leafy green)
1 banana
1/2 cup water
Directions:
Add all the ingredients to a blender, and blend to desired consistency, blend with ice if desired

Yarrow

Achillea millefolium
Folk Name: Arrowroot, Death Flower, Thousand seal, Wound wort

Magical Properties
Handfasting & Weddings
Divination
Love
Visions
Divining the identity of future lovers
Protection Spells
Dreamwork
Love Magic

Physical Properties
It May:
Wound healing
Digestive aid
Menstrual aid

Planet - Venus

Use Caution: Don't use during pregnancy

I embrace my intuition and trust my inner voice to guide me towards my truth.

Yarrow

Achillea millefolium

Folk Name: Arrowroot, Death Flower, Thousand seal, Wound wort

Some Suggested Uses:
Yarrow Blessing:
"I will pluck the yarrow fair
That more benign will be my face,
That more warm shall be my lips,
That more chaste shall be my speech,
Be my speech the beams of the sun,
Be my lips the sap of the strawberry.
May I be an isle in the sea,
May I be a hill on the shore,
May I be a star in the waning of the moon,
May I be a staff to the weak.
Wound can I every man,
Wound can no man me."
— CARMICHAEL

Yarrow Protection Spell
Ingredients:
1 tablespoon dried yarrow leaves and flowers
1 cup boiling water
1 teaspoon honey (optional)
A pinch of salt
A small saucepan
A strainer
Instructions:
Cleanse yourself and focus on your intention.
Boil 1 cup of water and add the yarrow. Steep for 10 minutes.
Strain the mixture into a cup, add salt and honey.
Hold the cup, take three deep breaths and visualize a protective shield.
Repeat the incantation: "Yarrow, protect and guide me, bring what I seek."
Drink the potion, focusing on your intention.
Dispose of the remaining yarrow in a natural place.

Note: *Always practice magic safely and responsibly using only fresh, organic ingredients. Consult a healthcare professional before consuming herbal remedies.*

YlangYlang

Cananga odorata

Folk Name: perfume tree, cadmia, canaga

Magical Properties
Reconciliation spells
Fertility
Turn negative energy more positive
Aphrodisiac

Physical Properties
It May:
Hair and skincare
Help anxiety
Help acne
Antibacterial
Antidepressant
Antifungal
Anti-inflammatory
Antiseptic
Antispasmodic

Use Caution:

Planet - Jupiter

I am grateful for the abundance in my life, and I attract more abundance with ease.

Ylang-ylang

Cananga odorata

Folk Name: perfume tree, cadmia, canaga

Some Suggested Uses:

Blessing: May the sweet scent of ylang-ylang be a blessing to us all. May it bring forth peace and calm, balancing our emotions and lifting our spirits.

Serenity Spell

Ingredients:

Ylang Ylang Oil

Relaxing music

A white candle

Directions:

Meditate on a quiet night after a relaxing bath infused with ylang-ylang in a peaceful place where you won't be disturbed. Diffuse some ylang-ylang oil, play relaxing music, and use a white candle to aid concentration. Imagine you are surrounded by white light above you. Thank the angels for their presence and ask for help to overcome discomfort and negativity. Request the angel to cleanse your soul and grant you serenity. As you meditate, imagine negativity leaving and new energy filling your body. Allow the serene energy to flood your energy centers. Intensify your prayer as you sense the energy. Feel a new strength fill you from head to toe, bringing light and love. Forgive yourself and show gratitude to your angel for their help.

Chickweed

Stelaria media
Folk name: Adder's mouth, Passerina, Starwort, Winterweed

Magical Properties
Courage
Balance
Wisdom
Inner peace
Fidelity
Healing
Love
Protection
Lunar energy
Endurance
Amplification
Safe travel
Abundance
Luck

Use Caution:

Physical Properties & EO
It May:
Help dry skin and irritating eczema
Anti-inflammatory
Antipyretic
Laxative

Planet - Moon

I am in tune with the natural world and its rhythms, and I use this knowledge to heal and transform.

Chickweed

Stelaria media
Folk name: Adder's mouth, Passerina, Starwort, Winterweed

Some Suggested Uses:

Chickweed can be eaten as part of a mixed edible weed salad. It tastes much like alfalfa and has a cool, juicy crunchiness to match.

Love, Peace, and Harmony: A Magical Chickweed Potion Recipe

Ingredients:
- 1 cup fresh chickweed
- 1 cup distilled water
- 1 teaspoon honey
- 1 teaspoon dried lavender
- 1 teaspoon dried rose petals

Instructions:
- Begin by cleaning and drying the chickweed.
- In a small saucepan, bring the water to a boil.
- Once boiling, remove the pan from heat and add the chickweed, lavender, and rose petals.
- Allow the mixture to steep for 10-15 minutes.
- Strain the mixture through a fine mesh strainer or cheesecloth.
- Stir in the honey until it dissolves.
- Allow the potion to cool before drinking.

This potion is said to have magical properties, such as bringing love, peace, and harmony to the person who drinks it. You can also add different dried herbs or essential oils to enhance the effects of the potion and make it your own.

Chamomile

Matricaria Recutita
Folk Name: Maythen, Manzanilla, Whig Plant, Ground Apple

Magical Properties
Calming
Love
Healing
Reduce stress
Money
Prosperity

Physical Properties
It May:
Healing
Immune boosting
Anti-inflammatory
Protect skin
Soothe menstrual cramps
Ease diarrhea
Reduce headache
Aid indigestion
Help colic in babies

Use Caution:

Planet - Sun

I release any negative energy or limiting beliefs that no longer serve me, and I welcome positivity and growth.

Chamomile

Matricaria Recutita
Folk Name: Maythen, Manzanilla, Whig Plant, Ground Apple

Some Suggested Uses:
Chamomile is used to attract money, and gamblers sometimes use a hand wash of the infusion to ensure winnings. It is used in sleep and meditation incense, and the infusion is also added to the bath.

Blessing: With the gentle touch of chamomile, we call forth its healing energy. May it bless us with peace, soothe our worries, and bring calm to our minds and spirits. So mote it be.

Chamomile Calmness Spell
Ingredients:
- Dried chamomile flowers
- A white candle
- A mortar and pestle
- A small dish
- Matches or a lighter

Instructions:
- Grind the dried chamomile flowers into a fine powder using the mortar and pestle.
- Place the powder into the small dish.
- Light the white candle.
- Hold the dish of chamomile powder in your hands and close your eyes.
- Visualize a sense of peace and calm spreading through your body.
- Repeat the following incantation three times: 'Chamomile, herb of peace, Bring calmness and release, Let my worries fade away, And bring serenity to stay.'
- Sprinkle the chamomile powder around the candle, creating a circle of peace.
- Sit quietly and breathe deeply, allowing the scent of chamomile and the flame of the candle to soothe and calm your mind.
- When you feel at peace, snuff out the candle and keep the chamomile in a safe place.
- Use this spell whenever you need to bring peace and calm into your life.

Dandelion

Taraxacum officinale
Folk Name: Blowball, Cankerwort, Lion's tooth,White endive

Magical Properties
Divination
Call Spirits
Wishes
Clear stuck energy
Psychic powers
Send messages to loved ones telepathically

Physical Properties
It May:
anti-inflammatory and anti-cancer properties
Provides several B vitamins along with vitamins C and vitamin E

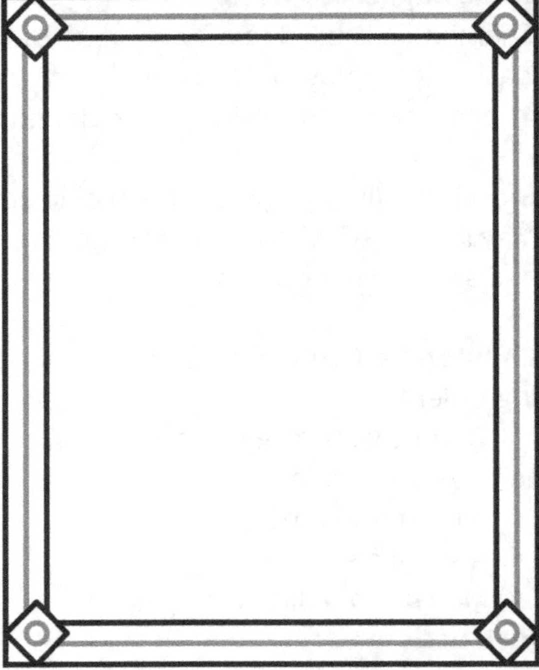

Planet - Jupiter

Use Caution: Do not use dandelion if you are taking a blood thinner, such as warfarin.

I honor the spirits and ancestors who have come before me, and I draw on their wisdom and guidance.

Dandelion

Taraxacum officinale

Folk Name: Blowball, Cankerwort, Lion's tooth, White endive

Some Suggested Uses:

Every part of the dandelion plant, from the flower to the leaves and even the root, is both edible and medicinal.

Dandelions are a mild laxative that encourages proper, healthy digestion while stimulating your appetite and balancing bacteria in your intestinal tract.

Dandelion Blossom Elixir Recipe

Ingredients:

- 35 dandelion blossoms
- 10 lemons
- 3 liters of boiled water
- Honey or brown sugar to taste

Instructions:

1. Gather the dandelion blossoms in a pure and serene location, avoiding any areas contaminated by dogs or traffic fumes.
2. Wash the dandelion blossoms thoroughly and remove the stems.
3. Put the dandelion blossoms in a large jug and pour over 1/3 of the boiled water, covering it with a saucer or plate to keep the steam in.
4. You can stir the mixture, focus on your intention, and let it steep for a few minutes until the water cools slightly.
5. Stir the mixture again, and top up the jug with the remaining boiled water. Cover the jug with the saucer and let it stand for 1 hour.
6. Strain the mixture and discard the dandelion heads.
7. Pour the elixir into glasses and sweeten with honey or brown sugar, as desired.
8. Enjoy the magic of the dandelion blossom elixir, filled with health and happiness.

Note: If making this elixir as a group, have everyone in the room stir the mixture to imbue it with collective energy and intention.

Mint

Mentha spp.
Folk Name: cornmint, corn mint, water mint,

Magical Properties
Promote lust
Call good spirits
Safe travels
Money
Protection
ExorcismDreams
Communication
Psychic work
Strength

Physical Properties
It May:
Relieve headaches
Help stomach problems
High in Vitamin A
May improve brain function

Use Caution:

Planet - Mercury

I am a healer, and I use my magic to bring love, light, and positivity into the world.

Mint

Mentha spp.
Folk Name: cornmint, corn mint, water mint,

Some suggestions:

Money Spell Using Mint
This spell leverages the magical properties of mint to attract prosperity and abundance. You can perform this spell whenever you'd like. However, please be careful when you use candle magic.

Ingredients:
- A green candle
- Mint oil or dried mint (for added power, it's recommended to use both)
- Cinnamon (optional, but it enhances the spell's potency - use either cinnamon oil or dried cinnamon)
- Fire-resistant surface or bowl

Instructions:
1. Apply the mint oil to your green candle
2. Mix the dried mint with cinnamon powder or anoint the candle with cinnamon oil
3. Roll the anointed candle in the dried herb mixture
4. Place the candle in a fire-resistant bowl, securing it by melting wax on the bottom if desired.
5. Light the candle and close your eyes. Visualize abundance and prosperity flowing toward you like a golden river. Believe that you have already received the wealth you desire. The more specific and focused your intention is, the more likely it will manifest.
6. Repeat the following chant three times:
7. Then, allow the candle to burn down completely, and repeat the spell as needed.

Marigold

Tagetes

Folk Name: Maribel, Arely, Mariel, Mirabelle, Emerald

Magical Properties

Prosperity
Blessings
Purification
Peace
Meditation
Youth
Calming
Sleep
Energy
Clearing
Joy
Healing
Inspiration
Money

Physical Properties

It May:

Anti-inflammatory
Soothes Anxiety
Reduces Stress
Boosts Immune system
Relieves Menstrual Cramps
Can Reduce Swelling
Treats Nausea
Indigestion
Soothes Stiff Muscles
Promotes Good Sleep
Helps Skin Irritation
Soothes Sore Throat

Use Caution:

Planet - Jupiter

I trust in my own power and the power of the universe to manifest my dreams into reality.

Marigold

Tagetes
Folk Name: Maribel, Arely, Mariel, Mirabelle, Emerald

Some suggestions:

Fresh marigolds will cleanse and disperse negative energy in the room they are placed in.

A yellow dye has also been extracted from the flower of the plant by boiling.

To prepare an infusion using dried flowers, add 1-2 teaspoons of the flowers to one cup of boiling water. Allow the mixture to infuse for 10-15 minutes before drinking. You may consume the infusion up to three times daily.

To create a compress, mix 2 tablespoons of dried flowers or 3 fresh flowers with 1 pint of boiling water, and let it cool. Soak a compress in the solution and apply it to the affected area. You can use the compress at least twice daily.
It is crucial to ensure that you use the correct type of marigold and prepare it appropriately.

Rose

Rosa spp.
Folk Name:

Magical Properties
Prosperity
Blessings
Purification
Peace
Meditation
Youth
Calming
Sleep
Energy Clearing
Joy
Healing
Money

Physical Properties
It May:
Anti-inflammatory
Soothes Anxiety
Reduces Stress
Boosts Immune system
Relieves Menstrual Cramps
Can Reduce Swelling
Treats Nausea, Indigestion
Soothes Stiff Muscles
Promotes Good Sleep
Helps Skin Irritation
Helps Blood Sugar
Soothes Sore Throat

Use Caution:

Planet - Venus

I am worthy of love, abundance, and happiness, and I attract these things into my life effortlessly.

Rose

Rosa spp.
Folk Name:

Some suggestions:
The primary usage of rose water is as a skin toner, which can help to heal various skin conditions such as burns, mouth ulcers, chapped hands, and puffy eyes.

Rose Hip Tea
Ingredients:
- 2 1/2 teaspoons of cut rose hips
- 1 cup of water

Instructions:
1. Put 2 1/2 teaspoons of cut rose hips into one cup of water.
2. Bring the water to a boil and simmer gently for 10 minutes.
3. Strain the mixture and drink the tea as needed.

Rose Hip Syrup
Ingredients:
- 1 cup of cut rose hips
- 2 cups of water
- 1/2 cup of honey

Instructions:
1. Add 1 cup of cut rose hips and 2 cups of water to a pot and bring to a boil.
2. Reduce the heat and let it simmer for 30 minutes.
3. Strain the mixture and add 1/2 cup of honey to the liquid.
4. Bring the mixture to a simmer until the honey dissolves and the mixture thickens into a syrup-like consistency.
5. Remove the syrup from the heat and let it cool before storing it in a glass jar.
6. Take the rose hip syrup as needed.

Pine

Pinus spp,
Folk names: Eastern White Pine: "Weymouth Pine," "Soft Pine," "Pumpkin Pine

Magical Properties
Healing
Fertility
Protection
Exorcism
Money

Physical Properties
It May:

Use Caution:

Planet - Mars

I embrace my uniqueness and trust in my own abilities and talents to bring me success and fulfillment.

Pine

Pinus spp.
Folk name: Ponderosa Pine: "Bull Pine," "Western Yellow Pine," "Blackjack Pine"

Some Suggested Uses:

Pine needles are burned during the winter months to purify and cleanse the house.

Scattered on the floor, they drive away evil and, when burned, exorcise the area of negativity.

They are also used in cleaning baths.

Pine needles are burned to reverse and send back spells.

Pine Needle Tea
Ingredients:

- 2 cups of water
- 1/4 cup of fresh pine needles (or 2 tablespoons of dried pine needles)
- Honey, lemon, or other sweeteners (optional)

Instructions:

1. Gather fresh pine needles from a tree that is known to be safe for consumption. If you use dried needles, ensure they are properly stored and fresh.
2. Rinse the needles to remove any dirt or debris.
3. Use a sharp knife or scissors to chop the needles into small pieces.
4. Add the chopped pine needles to a pot with 2 cups of water.
5. Bring the water to a boil, then reduce the heat to low and let it simmer for 15-20 minutes.
6. Strain the tea to remove the needles.
7. Add honey, lemon, or other sweeteners to taste, if desired.
8. Serve hot, and enjoy your pine needle tea.

Note: It is important to be cautious when consuming pine needle tea, as certain pine species can be toxic or cause allergic reactions. Make sure to properly identify the pine species you are using, and consult a healthcare professional before consuming pine needle tea if you have any concerns or medical conditions.

Blackberry

Rubus villosus

Folk Name: Bly, Bramble, Cloudberry, Thimbleberry

Magical Properties

Healing

Money

Protection

Physical Properties

It May:

Cancer

Diarrhea

Whopping cough Colitis

Toothache

Anemia

Psoriasis, Sore throat

Mouth ulcer

Mouthwash

Hemorrhoids

Minor bleeding

Use Caution:

Planet - Venus

I am a channel for positive energy, and I use this energy to create positive change in the world.

Blackberry

Rubus villosus
Folk Name: Bly, Bramble, Cloudberry, Thimbleberry

Some Suggested Uses:

Blackberry leaves can be incorporated into various practices for their metaphysical benefits.

You can use them in spells aimed at attracting wealth.
Include them in incense blends or infusions to enhance protection.

Additionally, blackberry leaves are known to have healing properties, so they can be added to charm pouches for this purpose, or an infusion can be made to add to bath water for a soothing and restorative soak.

Blackberry vines can be woven into protective wreaths, especially in combination with Rowan and Ivy.

The thorns and leaves can also be added to mojo bags and other preparations for general household protection and prosperity.

Cinnamon

First, a little history: Cinnamon has been used in various ways for thousands of years. The Romans burned it in funeral ceremonies, believing the aroma was sacred and pleasing to the gods. Because it was hard to come by, during the Middle Ages, wealthy Europeans served cinnamon at feasts so their guests would know that no expense had been spared. Later, it became a focus of the spice trade, eventually leading to white explorers' discovery of North America.

Cinnamon has been around for a long time - the embalmers of ancient Egypt used it to prepare bodies for their journey to the afterlife some two thousand years ago. It's even mentioned in the Old Testament as an ingredient in anointing oil in the book of Exodus:

The History Channel's Maryel Synan says, "The Arabs transported cinnamon via cumbersome land routes, resulting in a limited, expensive supply that made the use of cinnamon a status symbol in Europe in the Middle Ages. As the middle class began to seek upward mobility, they, too, wanted to purchase the luxury goods that were once only available to the noble classes. Cinnamon was particularly desirable as it could be used as a preservative for meats during the winter. Despite its widespread use, the origins of cinnamon were the Arab merchants' best-kept secret until the early 16th century. To maintain their monopoly on the cinnamon trade and justify its exorbitant price, Arab traders wove colorful tales for their buyers about where and how they obtained the luxury spice."

Magical Uses for Cinnamon
Cinnamon is good for protection, magic, and workings related to passion, prosperity, and power.

Cinnamon is an ingredient in the famous "fiery wall of protection" blend and other cleansing and protective incense. Still, it is most commonly used to bring good fortune and prosperity to a business.

If you own a business, tuck a few cinnamon sticks under the cash register or in your money box. Another great option is to sprinkle bits of ground cinnamon into your wallet or purse - in addition to being excellent for prosperity magic, it will smell fantastic all day long! Finally, try using a paintbrush and a bit of water to add a light dusting of cinnamon to your paper money - this is believed to help multiply your fortune.

Rosemary Water

Protection Spray

Rosemary is known for its cleansing and purifying properties. It can help to eliminate negativity and create a more positive environment.

Ingredients:
Rosemary sprigs
Salt

Directions:
Add boiling water to rosemary in a bowl
Add some salt
Allow to cool down
Strain and fill the spray bottle

I have an EO for that!

To remove grease stains, use lemon EO
Put a few drops of lemon EO on the grease stain, gently rub the EO in to break up the grease, and toss it into the wash. Be sure to check the clothes when they come out of the wash to ensure that the grease stain is gone; if not, repeat.

To get rid of spiders, use peppermint EO.
Have you noticed spiders starting to build artistic creations around your home that rival Charlotte's web? Spiders hate the peppermint smell, so use a little peppermint EO to encourage them to find a new home—Mix 15 drops of peppermint EO and a cup of water in a spray bottle. Shake well and then spray all around your home (inside and out) where spiders hang out or might enter your home. Spray your baseboards around doors, windows, porches, corners of rooms, etc. Be careful not to use too much. You don't want to saturate your drywall and carpets. The goal is not for them to be wet; that could cause mold to grow. You want to get the smell of peppermint into the area so that the spiders will relocate elsewhere.

DIY Toner
Add a few drops of melaleuca (tea tree) EO to witch hazel for an excellent toner. Shake it up every time before you use it to mix the witch hazel and EO.

Feeling tired and low energy? Put a drop of lemon and peppermint EO in the palm of your hands, rub them together, and inhale deeply for about 30 seconds.

Put a few drops of EO on clothespins and clip them to the underside of all your **floor vents.** When your heating or air conditioning runs, air will flow over the clothespins, and your whole house will smell great!

For plump lips
Add 1-2 drops of peppermint EO to a lip gloss tube. Mix well using the lip gloss wand to ensure the EO is distributed evenly throughout the entire lip gloss tube. Apply as normal. Thanks to the peppermint, you're lips will feel slightly tingly and look more full!

Add scent (and therapeutic benefits) to store-bought lotion
Do you love the smell of scented lotions, but you're trying to avoid artificial fragrances and toxins? Add a few drops of EO to an unscented store-bought lotion.
Here are some EO combinations to try:
eucalyptus and spearmint (great stress buster)
bergamot and grapefruit (energizing and uplifting)
orange, cedarwood, and ylang-ylang (calming and balancing)
lavender and lemon (fresh and clean)

Get rid of that funky **smell in your shoes** by using just a cotton ball and EO. Add a few drops of EO, put the cotton ball in your shoes, and leave overnight.

Make your cuticle oil.
Fill a 15ml bottle with olive oil and add 10 drops of frankincense EO. Top with your choice of original 15ml top, glass dropper, or roller ball. Shake to mix. Apply to cuticles and massage in.

Freshen as you vacuum
Put a few drops of your favorite EO (or EO combination) on a small piece of a napkin, tissue, or cotton ball, and then vacuum it up. As you vacuum, your whole house will smell AMAZING! Add a few drops in each new bag you put in your vacuum; no bag? No problem. If your vacuum has a washable filter, put some EO on the filter.

If you are happy and you know it
Smell orange EO straight from the bottle, or use it in your diffuser for an uplifting aroma.

Keep pantry bugs away.
Wipe down shelves with a mix of white vinegar and a few drops of essential oil. Citronella, eucalyptus, melaleuca (tea tree), and peppermint all work.

Superpower your mopping
Add a few drops of pine, lemon, or melaleuca (tea tree) EO to your mop water. They have powerful disinfectant properties and also leave your room smelling great.

Kickstart your moisturizer
Add 1 drop of geranium EO to your face moisturizer to promote youthful-looking skin.

Sleepy time
When washing your sheets, add a few drops of lavender EO to the rinse cycle. Lavender is calming and promotes a sound and peaceful night's sleep.

Freshen your clothes
Do you have clothes that need to be freshened up,
Put a few drops of EO on a clean cotton washcloth and toss that washcloth into the dryer along with the clothing to be freshened. Run through the dryer on the fluff cycle, and your clothing will be as fresh as if you just picked it up from the dry cleaner.

Kickstart your toothpaste
Add EO to toothpaste. Add 1 drop of rosemary and 1 drop of peppermint to a couple of ounces of natural toothpaste to help support healthy gums, give you an immunity boost and fight bad breath.

Clean your microwave
Microwave a bowl with about a cup of water and 5 drops of lemon EO for about 3 minutes. Use a potholder to remove the boiling water bowl and clean your microwave.

Lemon EO can be used to **get rid of adhesive** sticky messes- like removing labels from bottles, unsticking stickers that your kids used to decorate your refrigerator, and removing gum.

Correspondence Crystals

I have included worksheets to familiarize you with some correspondence associated with this season. Feel free to add others to personalize your unique way of celebrating this sabbat.

Cleansing vs. Charging

Cleansing:
Removes past energies
Item is restored to its natural state
Crystal-like quartz & selenite can cleanse other crystals/tools

Charging:
Adds purpose or intention
Programs a tool for a specific energy
Charged crystals can be used to add energy to other items.

Like you need to be clean so do your crystals.

Due to their energetic nature, crystals hold onto energy patterns with which they come in contact. Therefore, when your crystals have made their way to you, they have been in many hands and places. This is why it is essential to cleanse your crystals. Crystals are effective at healing because they can pick up or absorb subtle negative energies, imbalances, and psychic debris; and remove them on your behalf. There are many ways to cleanse crystals and stones.

A few crystals never need cleansing. For example, citrine, kyanite, and selenite are self-cleaning. Clear Quartz and Carnelian cleanse other crystals.

Here are some of the most effective and safe methods.

Cleansing with Water
While water is a beautiful cleanser for humans, we must be cautious when using it to cleanse our stones or crystals because it can be harmful to delicate or soft crystals. Water works best with polished stones or hard crystals. Never use water to cleanse rough stones, soft crystals, or natural geodes. The more delicate the crystal, the more fragile the cleansing process should be.
The water method for cleansing crystals or stones is quite simple. Hold the crystal or stone under fresh water for a few seconds. Never use saltwater to cleanse crystals or stones because the salt can penetrate microscopic fissures in the surface of the crystal and cause extensive damage to the structure, as well as take the shine off of the stone.

Water Bath: Place the crystal in a bowl of water. Allow the stone to sit for several hours, letting the water gently pull away and absorb the accumulated energy. After this clarifying bath, let the crystal air dry and dispose of the water. Keep in mind, though, that some stones can be damaged by water.

Cleansing

Cleansing With Moonlight
Moonlight is a favored and safe way to cleanse any crystal type (rough or polished) since they do not come into contact with anything other than soft moonlight. Place your crystals or stones outside on a table or inside near a window that is bathed in the moonlight for a few hours. Make sure dew does not get them wet. In the morning, your crystals will be ready to go to work.

Cleansing With Sound
With reverberating sound, it can be used to cleanse crystals or stones. You can use any of a variety of instruments. I suggest a tuning fork, singing bowl, bell, chime, tingsha, or your voice chanting a prayer or mantra. Allow the sound to wash over the crystals or stones and actively visualize them, releasing all of the old energies onto the sound waves.

Cleansing With Sunlight
Sunlight is a powerful crystal and stone cleaner, but only for certain types. A few crystals and stones will fade (just like some fabrics) with continued exposure to sunlight. These sunlight-fragile crystals and stones include Ametrine, Aventurine; Apatite, Amethyst; Chrysoprase; Kunzite, Sapphire, Fluorite, Rose Quartz, and Smokey Quartz. Do not place these crystals or stones in sunlight for more than a few minutes to be safe.

Like you need a boost of energy, so do your crystals.

Think of it like charging your phone; neglect it long enough, and it will die. So here are some basic techniques for charging your crystals.

Quartz Points: Place the crystal that needs charging on a flat surface and surround it with three or more quartz crystals, with the points facing inward. Quartz directs and amplifies energy, so aiming it at your stone channels positive energy into it.

Sunlight: Set your stones in direct sunlight for several hours. Some crystals can fade in prolonged sunlight, affecting their magical power. To avoid fading, shorten the time they're left in the sun to just a few minutes.

Moonlight: The full moon is also an essential source for charging. Place your crystals outdoors or on a windowsill; even if it's a cloudy night, the moon's energy will find them and fill them with power.

Candles: Light white candles in a small circle on your magic work area, altar, or sacred space. Place your crystal in the center and light the candles.

Plants: Place the crystal at the foot of a healthy tree where it can touch the roots or bark.

Herbs: Mugwort is an herb used in witchcraft to increase psychic powers. It's often used to charge tools used in magic. You can boil a bit of dried mugwort into a tea, let it cool, and place the crystal in it for several hours. You can also keep some dried mugwort in a container and place the crystal in it, covering it completely and letting it sit for several hours. Other herbs for charging crystals include rose petals, rosemary, and sage.

Crystals Everywhere

In your purse, pocket, or bra
In a crystal grid
In a dreamcatcher
Hang by a window or on the sill
In your garden
In a zen garden
On a necklace or bracelet
In a pot with your inside plants
In spells: sachet, bottles, candles, balls, then hang anywhere
Under your pillow
In an infused water bottle (only certain ones)
On your altar
Hang from your pet's collar
Use in your bath water (only certain ones)
Use to help with anxiety or pain

"I think I'll just buy one crystal," said no one EVER.

Crystal Shapes

Clusters
radiates unity throughout the space and charges other crystals

Pyramids
anchoring crystal and powerful for manifesting desires

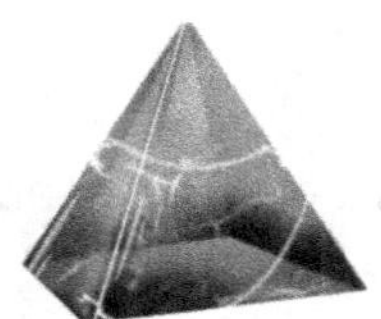

Cubes
consolidates energy, grounding & meditation, and connect to the energy of the Earth

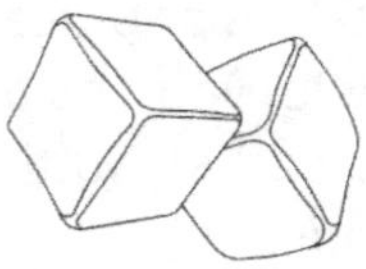

Double Terminated
absorb negative energy, grounding, break down old patterns, and promotes psychic ability

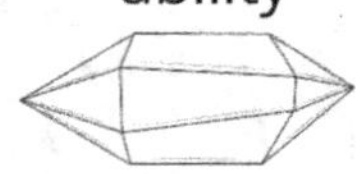

Twin
grounding & harmonizing energies, and balances yin & yang energies

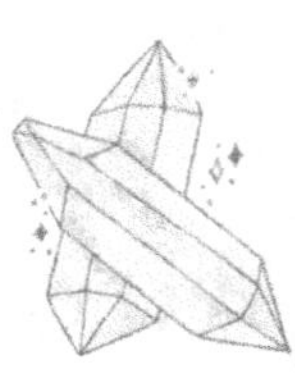

Points
concentrates & directs energy

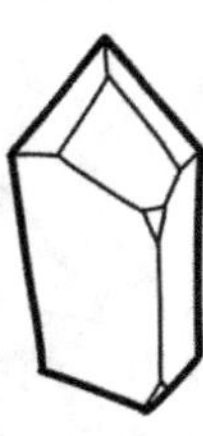

Crystal Shapes

Wand
healing rituals,
moving &
directing energy

Egg
healing, fertility,
and
balance

Spheres
emits energy
equally
from all direction,
and
ideal for scrying

Druzy
charging, relaxation &
harmony, purify &
amplify body's
natural healing
properties

Geode
amplifies,
conserves &
releases energy,
and
Internal healing

Isis
feminine energy,
healing
emotional
hurt and distress

Choosing the Shape of your Crystal

1 - Look up the energetic properties of your crystal.

2 - Consider the shape and if it offers benefits such as enhancing any of the
properties you are interested in.

3 - Consider if the crystal shape suits your chosen way to work with the stone.

Rose Quartz

Magical Properties
Peace
Harmony
Acceptance
Trust
Love
Healing
Empathy
Receptivity
Intimacy
Romance
Who doesn't need self-love

Classification
Origin
Rarity

Draw or Paste your crystal

Crystal Pairs With
Don't Mix With Sun
Cost
Got it from

Notes: Heart Chakra
Taurus and Leo Sign
Archangel Ariel

Identification
Color(s)
Transparency
Lustre
Crystal System
Chemical

I release any fear or doubt that holds me back, and I trust in my own strength and resilience.

Bloodstone

Magical Properties
Abundance
Alignment
Organization
Smooth energy flow
Generosity
Idealism
Good fortune
Purification

Classification
Origin
Rarity

Draw or Paste your crystal

Crystal Pairs With Many
Don't Mix With
Cost

Got it from:
Notes:
Planets - Mars
Chakra **-** Base
Signs - Aries, Libra, Pisces

Identification
Color(s) -
Transparency -
Lustre -
Crystal System -
Chemical

I am deeply connected to the earth and all living beings, and I honor and respect them.

Emerald

Magical Properties
See visions
Truth
Protect against unwanted spells
Ward off unwanted enchantment
Creativity enhanced

Classification
Origin
Rarity

Draw or Paste your crystal

Crystal Pairs With
Don't Mix With
Cost

Got it from:
Notes:
Planets -
Chakra - Crown
Signs - Aries

Identification
Color(s) -
Transparency
Lustre -
Crystal System -
Chemical -

I am open to receiving divine guidance and wisdom, and I trust in the universe to provide for me.

Yellow Jasper

Magical Properties
Deflecting jealousy
Positive energy

Classification
Origin
Rarity

Draw or Paste your crystal

Crystal Pairs With
Don't Mix With
Cost

Got it from:
Notes:
Planets - Saturn
Chakra - Base Chakra, Solar Plexus
Signs -Leo, Taurus

Identification
Color(s) -
Transparency -
Lustre -
Crystal System -
Chemical -

I am a magical, powerful, and magnificent being.

Red Jasper

Magical Properties
Fertility
Deter bad luck.
Healing
Balance
Courage
Strength

Classification
Origin
Rarity

Draw or Paste your crystal

Crystal Pairs With
Don't Mix With
Cost

Got it from:
Notes:
Planets - Mars
Chakra - Root and Sacral chakra
Signs -Aries

Identification
Color(s) -
Transparency -
Lustre -
Crystal System -
Chemical -

I release all fear and doubt and embrace the unknown with excitement and curiosity.

Orbicular Jasper

Magical Properties
Nurturing Protective
Encourage patience
Release emotional blockages
Soothing past sorrows

Classification
Origin
Rarity

Draw or Paste your crystal

Crystal Pairs With
Don't Mix With
Cost

Got it from:
Notes:
Planets - Earth
Chakra - Heart Chakra
Signs -Capricorn

Identification
Color(s) -
Transparency -
Lustre -
Crystal System -
Chemical -

I can manifest my desires and creating my own reality.

Mookaite Jasper

Magical Properties
Strength
Stability
Quiets the mind
promote goal reaching
Self Confidence
Inner strength
Removes challenges
Encourage versatility

Classification
Origin
Rarity

Draw or Paste your crystal

Crystal Pairs With
Don't Mix With
Cost

Got it from:
Notes:
Planets - Saturn
Chakra - Root, solar plexus, navel
Signs - Capricorn

Identification
Color(s) Red, yellow, mauve
Transparency
Lustre
Crystal System -
Chemical

I am a channel for divine energy and share my light with the world

Leopard Skin Jasper

Magical Properties
Courage
Mentally brave
Confidence
Increase agility
Sparks creative problem-solving

Classification
Origin
Rarity

Draw or Paste your crystal

Crystal Pairs With
Don't Mix With
Cost

Got it from:
Notes:
Planets - Venus
Chakra - Root, Sacral, and Heart Chakra
Signs -Capricorn and Leo

Identification
Color(s) -
Transparency -
Lustre -
Crystal System -
Chemical -

I am aligned with the cycles of the earth and the seasons of the year.

Kambaba Jasper

Magical Properties
Inner peace
Tolerance
Focus during meditation
Intention setting
Release negative thoughts
Increase prosperity
Increase money flow

Classification
Origin
Rarity

Draw or Paste your crystal

Crystal Pairs With Many
Don't Mix With
Cost

Got it from:
Notes:
Planets - Saturn
Chakra - Heart
Signs - Capricorn

Identification
Color(s) Blue and Green
Transparency
Lustre
Crystal System -
Chemical

I trust in the power of transformation, and allow myself to evolve and grow.

Dalmation Jasper

Magical Properties
Amplify herbal remedies
Good focus
Prosperity
Protective charm against financial scams
Encourage teamwork
Determine which friends

Classification
Origin
Rarity

Draw or Paste your crystal

Crystal Pairs With
Don't Mix With
Cost

Got it from:
Notes:
Planets -Earth
Chakra - Root chakra
Signs - Virgo

Identification
Color(s) -
Transparency -
Lustre -
Crystal System -
Chemical -

I am filled with love and compassion for myself and others.

Cobra Jasper

Magical Properties
Relaxation
Contentment
Compassion
Nurturing
Consolation
Tranquility
Healing
Completion

Classification
Origin
Rarity

Draw or Paste your crystal

Crystal Pairs With
Don't Mix With
Cost

Got it from:
Notes:
Planets -
Chakra - Base Chakra, Heart Chakra, Crown Chakra
Signs -Leo, Virgo, Scorpio

Identification
Color(s) -
Transparency -
Lustre -
Crystal System -
Chemical -

I release all past hurt and forgive myself and those who have wronged me.

Some of My Fav Crystals

Amethyst - Great Healing Stone
Sunstone - Great Pick Me Up
Selenite - Cleansing
Rose Quartz - Self Love
Clear Quartz - Programmable
Lava Rock - Great with Essential Oils
Moss Agate - My Favorite and Great for Grounding
I also added the crystals from my last book.

But You Do You!

Sunstone

Magical Properties
Rest
Self-Healing
Humor
Cheerfulness/positivity
Self-confidence/self-esteem
Temperament
Self-love

Classification
Origin
Rarity

Draw or Paste your crystal

Crystal Pairs With
Don't Mix With
Cost
Got it from

Notes: Sacral Chakra
Libra and Pisces Signs

Identification
Color(s)
Transparency
Lustre
Crystal System
Chemical

I am confident in my unique gifts and share them with joy and generosity.

Selenite

Magical Properties
Resolution
Clarity
Enlightenment
Transformation
Clearingaway anger/negativity
Positivity
Past-Life regression
Psychic abilities
Calm & stress relief
Meditation
Healing
Cleanses/charges other crystals

Classification
Origin
Rarity

Crystal Pairs With
Don't Mix With Salt and water
Cost
Got it from

Notes: Delicate

Identification
Color(s)
Transparency
Lustre
Crystal System
Chemical

I am attuned to the energies of the moon and use its phases to enhance my life.

Clear Quartz

Magical Properties
Amplify spells/crystals
Clears away stagnant energy
Cleansing
Healing
Positive vibes
Programmable
Can substitute for any crystal

Classification
Origin
Rarity

Draw or Paste your crystal

Crystal Pairs With
Don't Mix With
Cost
Got it from

Notes: Crown Chakra
Leo Sign
Archangel Raziel

Identification
Color(s)
Transparency
Lustre
Crystal System
Chemical

I trust in the natural healing power of the earth and take care of my physical and spiritual health.

Lava Rock

Magical Properties
Vitality
Protection
Luck
Love
Calming

Classification
Origin
Rarity

Draw or Paste your crystal

Crystal Pairs With
Don't Mix With
Cost
Got it from
Notes: Lava beads are porous and can absorb essential oils

Identification
Color(s)
Transparency
Lustre
Crystal System
Chemical

I am open to receiving signs and messages from the universe.

Moss Agate

Magical Properties
Growing Love
New beginnings
Trust
Release old fears
New lease on life
Grounding
Drawing strength from nature
Connecting with Fairie
New business/prosperity
Luck

Classification
Origin
Rarity

Crystal Pairs With
Don't Mix With
Cost
Got it from

Notes:
Cancer and Virgo Signs

Identification
Color(s)
Transparency
Lustre
Crystal System
Chemical

I accept myself for who I am and create peace, power, and confidence of mind and of heart.

Black Obsidian

Magical Properties
Truth-enhancing
Deep soul healing
Protection
Relieves stress and tension
Absorbs negative energy
Gives clarity of emotions
Blocks psychic attacks
Removes negativity influences
Helps to expose flaws, weakness & blockages
Calming
Compassion
Strength
Prophesy
Helps with shadow self & brings them to the forefront to be acknolgeked
Breaks through mental barriers
Dissolves mental conditioning

Classification cooled molten lava
Origin
Rarity

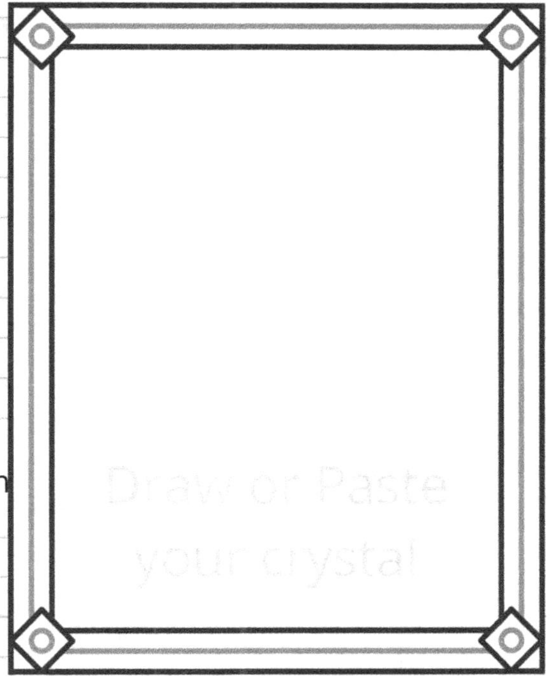

Crystal Pairs With

Don't Mix With water

Cost
Got it from

Identification
Color(s)
Transparency
Lustre
Crystal System
Chemical

Notes: Base chakra
Scorpio Sign

Put by the bed or under your pillow to draw out mental stress and tension.

I believe in myself, and trust my own wisdom.

Crystal Name

Magical Properties

Classification
Origin
Rarity

Draw or Paste your crystal

Crystal Pairs With
Don't Mix With
Cost
Got it from

Notes:

Identification
Color(s)
Transparency
Lustre
Crystal System
Chemical

I am connected to the spirits of the natural world and treat them with respect and gratitude.

Crystal Name

Magical Properties

Classification
Origin
Rarity

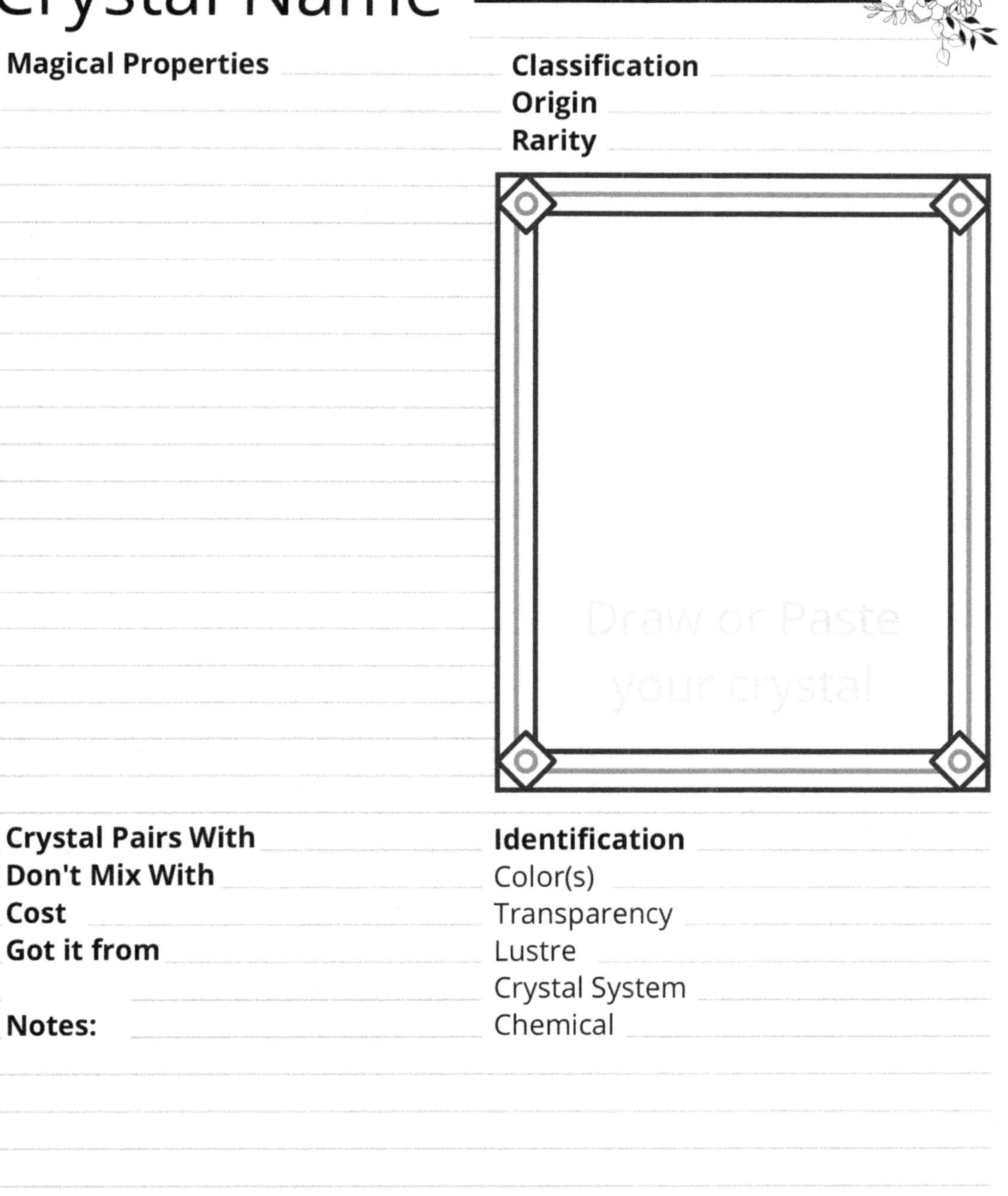

Crystal Pairs With
Don't Mix With
Cost
Got it from

Notes:

Identification
Color(s)
Transparency
Lustre
Crystal System
Chemical

I am a co-creator of my life and work with the universe to manifest my dreams.

Crystal Name

Magical Properties

Classification
Origin
Rarity

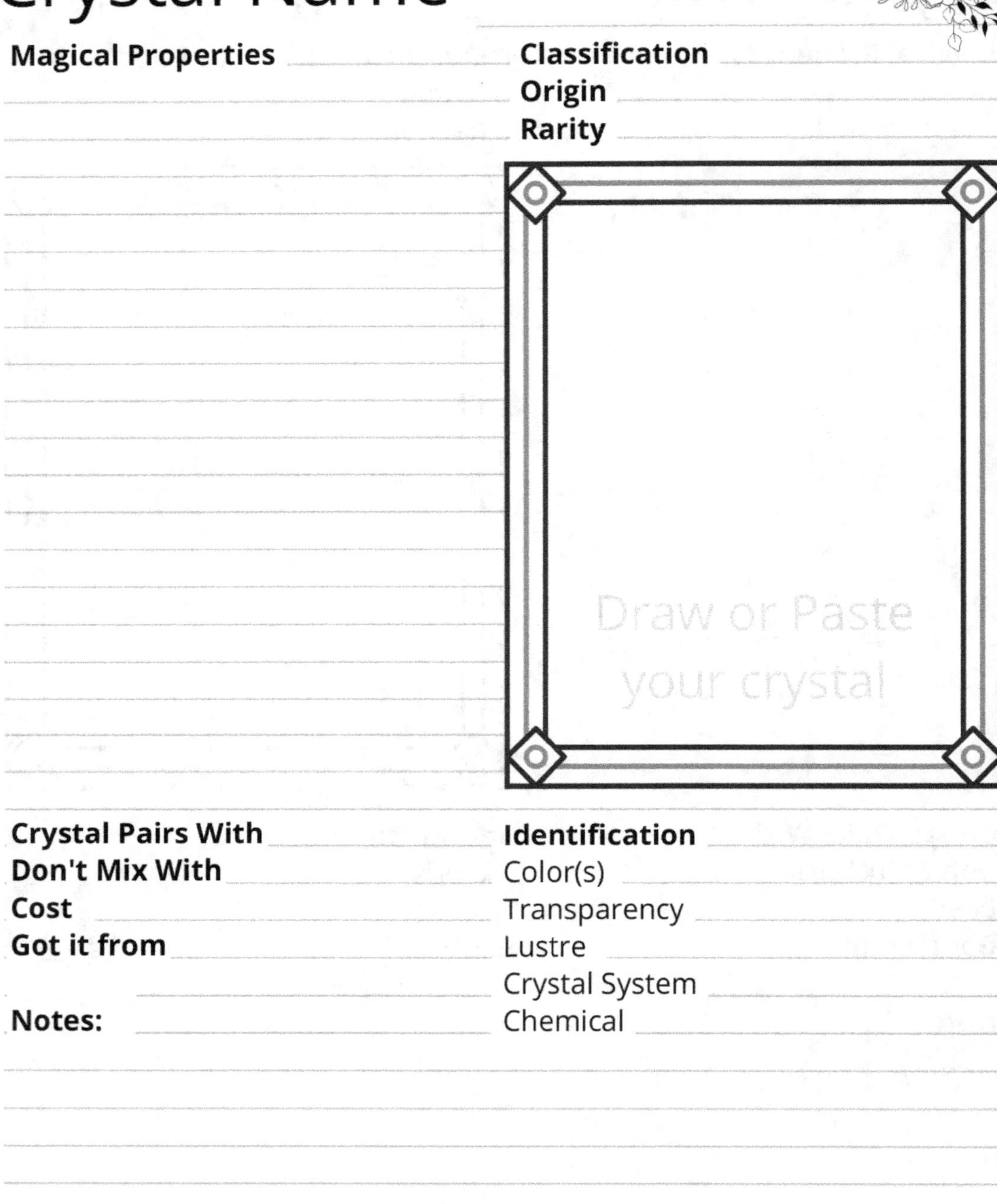

Crystal Pairs With
Don't Mix With
Cost
Got it from

Notes:

Identification
Color(s)
Transparency
Lustre
Crystal System
Chemical

I am a witch, and I embrace my power, my light, and my magic.

If you're looking for a way to add some beauty and tranquility to your home and are in the broom closet and need something that doesn't scream, "Look At Me, I Am A Witch," Then consider making crystal bowls. They're pretty to look at and can also be used for spells and other magical purposes.

Grab and Go Combos

Insight
rosemary, lemongrass, nutmeg, orange, aquamarine, howlite, or clear citrine.

Wisdom
parsley, thyme, chamomile, cumin, yellow quartz, and, lapis lazuli

Money
ginger, patchouly, dill, spearmint, gold, malachite, moss agate, and pearl

Peace
cumin, lavender, violet, marjoram, amazonite, blue lace agate, and silver

Relations
pansy, rose, valerian, moss agate, peridot, and sapphire

Love
vanilla, apple, clove, lavender, rose, amber, calcite, moonstone, and rose quartz

Banishing
clove, dragon's blood, garlic, hot pepper, obsidian, jet, and smoky quartz

Protection
angelica, frankincense, sandalwood, amber, carnelian, citrine, and petrified wood

Travel
dill, caraway, fennel mustard, malachite, moonstone, or tiger's eye

Communication
mint, turquoise, tiger's eye, and sodalite

Success
rosemary, saffron, bay, pyrite, clear quartz, and selenite

Courage
horseradish, basil, chives, nettle, pepper, tigers eye, carnelian, and pyrite

Happiness
cinnamon, mint, thyme, lavender, rose quartz, amethyst, citrine, and clear quartz

Health
cinnamon, coriander, eucalyptus, rosemary, sage, thyme, agate, amethyst, jade, and sunstone.

Binding
spiderwort, witch hazel, knotweed, agrimony, and jet

Grab and Go Crystals

Abundance crystals
citrine
clear quartz
amazonite
pyrite
adventurine
tiger's eye

Breaking Bad Habits crystals
amethyst
carnelian
garnet
hematite
lepidolite
citrine

Productivity crystals
tourmaline
green aventurine
pyrite
amazonite
citrine
smoky quartz

Mindfulness crystals
malachite
citrine
obsidian
turquoises
calcite
carnelian

Healing crystals
clear quartz
lapis lazuli
rose quartz
amethyst
aquamarine
garnet

Motivation crystals
pyrite
carnelian
amethyst
bumblebee
unakite
citrine

Friendship crystals
rose quartz
lapis lazuli
emerald
carnelian
blue lace agate
unakite

Happiness crystals
amazonite
amethyst
tourmaline
citrine
clear quartz
smoky quartz

Protection crystals
labradorite
amethyst
tourmaline
smoky quartz
obsidian
prehnite

Manifestation crystals
rose quartz
green jade
sodalite
citrine
selenite
amethyst

Lucky crystals
pyrite
green jade
tiger's eye
citrine
labradorite
carnelian

Work crystals
tourmaline
amethyst
rose quartz
pyrite
selenite
aventurine

Stress Relief crystals
lepidolite
amethyst
rose quarts
fluorite
sodalite
aquamarine

New Start crystals
aventurine
citrine
kyanite
rutile quartz
moonstone
labradorite

Grab and Go Crystals

New Home crystals
tourmaline
amethyst
rose quartz
clear quartz
sodalite
citrine

Anxiety crystals
moonstone
labradorite
rose quartz
amethyst
clear quartz
aquamarine

Love crystals
rhodonite
garnet
moonstone
sodalite
rose quartz
selenite

Letting Go crystals
Rutilated Quartz
Fire Quartz
smoky quartz
serpentine
black obsidian
rose quartz

Student crystals
amethyst
carnelian
fluorite
howlite
tiger's eye
clear quartz

Confidence crystals
citrine
carnelian
rose quartz
red jasper
orange calcite
tiger's eye

Relaxation crystals
amethyst
celestite
fluorite
tourmaline
angelite
howlite

Spirituality crystals
Fluorite
white howlite
labradorite
aura quartz
blue obsidian
amethyst

Creativity crystals
carnelian
amethyst
smoky quartz
clear quartz
citrine
tiger's eye

Trauma crystals
amazonite
lepidolite
fluorite
black line jasper
rose quartz
mangano calcite

Mental Clarity crystals
amethyst
hematite
apatite
sodalite
fluorite
citrine

Animal crystals
amethyst
smoky quartz
selenite
rose quartz
carnelian
agate

Crystals for breakups
rose quartz
malachite
pyrite
septarian
rhodonite
amethyst

Communication crystals
fluorite
kyanite
amazonite
sodalite
smokey quartz
lapis lazuli

Good Sleep crystals
amethyst
clear quartz
hematite
howlite
agate
moonstone

Grab and Go Crystals

Energy crystals
clear quartz
ruby
orange calcite
amethyst
carnelian
fuorite

Plant crystals
moonstone
tourmaline
aventurine
amethyst
clear quartz
malachite

Driving crystals
amethyst
rose quartz
tourmaline
malachite
carnelian
jasper

Crystals for breakups
rose quartz
malachite
pyrite
septarian
rhodonite
amethyst

Crystals for the bath
rose quartz
carnelian
tiger's eye
citrine
amethyst
clear quartz

Crystals for bedroom
celestite
rose quartz
labradorite
selenite
smoky quartz
howlite

I put them in bowls and up high so the wieners don't get into them. I usually add some salt and lavender, and rose quartz to all of them, but whatever feels right or even gives comfort. So you do you, Boo.

I pair selenite and rosemary for protection and cleansing

I pair rose quartz with (duh) roses for love and forgiveness.

I pair amethyst and chamomile for anxiety and stress relief

I pair garnet and pine for commitment and longevity

I pair black tourmaline and sage for dissolving negativity

I pair citrine with bay leaf for manifestation magic

I pair green adventure and basil for good fortune

I pair carnelian and cinnamon for sparking creativity

I pair moonstone and jasmine for harnessing confidence

Grab and Go Combo List

Crystal Energy

Each stone has a range of metaphysical properties that can be used for healing emotionally, physically, and spiritually. They can also be carried for protection or to bring luck, boost healing or psychic attunement, or balance emotions.

Hold the stone whose properties you want to pull out or force (project) from your life. (Negativity, confusion, being UNgrounded unbalanced emotions, anger, etc.) Right (Projection)

Sit quietly or meditate with these stones and focus on the energy flowing through you.

Creates a continuous flow of energy (a circuit)

Hold the stone whose properties you want to bring to your life. (Luck, self-love, grounding, balanced emotions, mental focus, etc.) Left (Receiving)

Ring Magic

The Pinky represents the element of Air.
It improves communication, expresses your sexuality, and increases your magnetism.

The Ring represents the element of Fire.
It activates and increases creativity, improves aesthetic awareness, and shows friendliness.

The Middle represents the element of Earth.
It reduces anxiety, helps you feel more emotionally stable, and increases the desire for self-development

The Pointer represents the element of Water.
It improves confidence, boosts self-esteem, and increases your feeling of authority.

The Thumb represents the element of Ether.
Increases will, increases your energy, and gives you comfort.

I Got a Jar of Dirt!

Types of dirt and their Magical Uses

Graveyard
Traditionally used in divination, cursing, love & protection spells
Avoid collecting from an unclean spirits grave for most workings
Leave an offering in exchange for the dirt
Try to collect from an ancestor's grave to ensure the energy you are collecting.

Churchyard
Traditionally used for many intentions and spells:
Healing
Prosperity
Purification
Protection
Mending Relationships
Justice workings

Crossroad
They are traditionally used in road-opening spells.
Used in journeying to the underworld, as it helps open the gate to the other realms
Used as offerings to guardians and gods of the crossroads:
Hecate, Hermes, Papa Legba, etc.

Backyard
Traditionally used in workings for the family, home, and property:
Purification
Protection
Peace
Collect from the 4 corners of the property if possible

Cemetery vs. Graveyard

What's a Cemetery?
A cemetery is a place where people are buried. They are not associated with a church, so they are often larger as they can spread out beyond land adjacent to a church. Both religious and non-religious people can be buried there.

The word cemetery dates back to the late 14th century. However, its roots can be traced back to the Old French word "cimetiere," derived from the Medieval Latin "cemeterium." Its literal translation is "a place set aside for the burial of the dead."

What's a Graveyard?
A graveyard, like a cemetery, is where people are buried after death. Graveyards are affiliated with a church and are typically located on church grounds. They tend to be smaller due to land limitations and, thus, are often choosier. Only members of their religion and sometimes only members of that specific Church can be buried in a graveyard.

The origin of the word graveyard is somewhat straightforward. It is, after all, a yard filled with graves. It is interesting to note, though, that the word "grave" is derived from a proto-Germanic word "graban," which means "to dig".231

People are buried in graveyards; in a cemetery, it is possible to bury an individual's ashes. When Christians talk about "holy ground," it is typically about a church building where God's presence is most keenly felt. While that may be true, one holy place that is often neglected is the local cemetery.

The Church has always treated the dead with the utmost respect, and the cemetery is where that belief is practiced. For example, when a new Catholic cemetery is created, the bishop (or sometimes a priest appointed by him) will come out to bless it and hallow the ground where the dead will be buried. The first action of the bishop is to walk around the entire cemetery, sprinkling holy water on the earth.

Know the Rules

There are mundane rules and occult rules for working in cemeteries. First, the mundane rules. These will usually be posted at the entrance, especially in newer and commercially maintained burial grounds.

Graveyard visiting hours are important to consider for any Witch. These hours are usually unposted and governed by state laws or local ordinances. Knowing these laws is important, as many cemeteries require you to leave at sundown. Violating these rules can result in a range of penalties, from being asked to leave to being arrested. So please be respectful of the dead and the grieving, and observe all rules and regulations.

The magickal rules can be quite complicated. As human beings, we don't have much knowledge about death, so we've had to make up many superstitions over the years. There are now many different beliefs surrounding graveyard visits.
Here are some cool ones:

Don't point at graves or photograph them. (This rule probably gets broken the most.)

Say "sorry" when stepping over a gravesite. (observed 100% of the time in Irish cemeteries and was taught to me as a child)

It is bad luck to wear anything new to a cemetery, especially shoes.

Don't whistle in a graveyard, or you tempt Death.

Leaving coins on a grave is a token of respect.

Don't yawn near a grave, or ghosts could get inside your body.

Smelling roses when there are none around is a sign that a benevolent spirit is nearby.

The person who takes something from a graveyard will return more than he took.

Working in cemeteries requires more than a little occult wisdom to master the art of magick. Each graveyard has its own unique energy, spirits, and customs – so it's hard to know what rules apply to every situation. But one universal truth remains: respect must be shown at all times - otherwise, your work will likely meet with resistance or, even worse...unpleasant consequences! Paying proper homage demonstrates reverence towards our dearly departed, allowing practitioners access to magical realms that would remain out of reach without due deference.

How to use water in your magic

Water is cleansing, quenching, and enchanting. It carries the vibrations of the ocean and the moon. You can make and use many different kinds of magical waters in your craft. Here's how to make moon water, sun water, rose water, and many more! We also give you tips on how to use magical waters and cast water magic spells.

The Water Element and Its Properties - Before we talk about specific magically-infused waters, let's talk about the power of the water element. Our planet is covered in 71% water. Our bodies are made up of at least 60% of water. So this should come as no surprise that water is crucial to our survival. Physically, we need it to function. But so do animals, plants, trees, and the earth overall. In addition to its physical qualities, the water element holds unique magical properties. Water represents our emotional side, our dreams, and our intuition. When used in magic and ritual, water is a purifier and brings many qualities to the table. Learn how to harness the energy of the water element and make some of these magical waters.

Catching Magical Water

Instructions - Fill the jar (or bowl or glass) with clean filtered spring water (and set it out. All you need to do is set the intention for the power with which you will infuse the water. If you need to say an incantation or charge the water with your hands, then, by all means, do so! Whatever you feel is okay and correct.

Optional: Put clean water-safe crystals into the water. Bottle and label it.
Use this recipe for any collection of water.

Types of Magical Water - Sun and Storm Water, Snow and Rose Water, Holy Water, War, Magical, and Dew Water

Magical Water Properties

Rain Water: Growth and rebirth spells, cleansing, scrying, altar water, and ritual baths.

Storm Water: Vitality, self-esteem, courage, mental strength, strengthening spells, and protection.

Dew Water: Healing, beauty, eyesight, love, fertility, working with the fae, and cleansing.

Snow Water: Unthaw a situation, transformation, balance, peace, consecrating, and endings.

Moon Water: Charging, blessing or cleanse, bath rituals, powering spells, healing magic, curses, and hexes.

Sun Water: Protection, healing, clairvoyance, happiness, fertility, and creativity.

River Water: Moving on, focusing energy, warding, breakthrough, power, and charging.

Sea Water: Cleansing, banishing, protection, emotional balance, healing rituals, and manifestation.

Spring Water: Growth, holy water, cleansing, abundance, potions, and beauty.

Lake Water: Peace, joy, contentment, relaxation, self-reflection, and self-discovery.

Well Water: Healing, wishes, intuition, manifestation, connection to otherworldly beings.

Swamp Water: Banishing, binding, hexing, cursing, and reversing.

Some recipes call for water, so why not clean, magical filtered water? For example, when putting water out for the sun or moon, use distilled water (distilled water is steam from boiling water that's been cooled and returned to its liquid state. Some people claim distilled water is the purest water you can drink.) or spring water. Then, use it in your recipes to make them more magical.

Spiritual Water Properties

Fast Luck
Fast luck, money luck, quick outcomes, and manifestation.

Love Water
Bring love, and resonate in love, harmony, and compassion.

7 African Powers
Draws strength from the 7 African Orishas.

Protection
Protect you, your space, your place, and your things.

Road Opener
Removes obstacles, new opportunities, and open pathway

Peruvian FL Water
Spiritual work, purification, rituals, and cleansing

Destroy Everything
Destroys all conditions, jinxes, and curses and removes all things that do not serve you

Attraction or Come To Me
Attract the things you want, need, or desire in your life

Tobacco Water
Spirits of nature, communication between worlds, and honor ancestors

Success & Prosperity
Success, and abundance, attract money and positivity.

Florida Water
Protection, spiritual cleansing, and positive vibes

Spiritual Oil Properties

Uncrossing Oil

Uncrossing oil is used to shake off jinxes, hexes, and plain old bad luck. Being "crossed" means feeling magickally out of sorts. Being down on your luck, off your game, hitting a wall, losing your mojo—everybody knows what that feels like. Uncrossing magick is sometimes necessary to get the good vibes flowing again. Most Uncrossing Oils contain garden plants with high spiritual vibrations and a reputation for cleansing. Common ingredients are Verbena, Hyssop (and its relative, Mint), Lavender, and Rose. Their aromas help break up stagnant energy patterns, impart a holy aura to places and people, and function as mood-lifters to get the magick back on track.

Van Van Oil

A traditional New Orleans Voodoo oil, Van Van is worn as a lucky all-purpose oil, protective ointment, and bayou Witch's signature fragrance. It's hard to describe, but once you've smelled it, you will recognize it anywhere. Says cat yronwode, "At one time, it is said, a person could not walk down a street in the Algiers district (of New Orleans) without smelling the scent of Van Van oil." Use it to anoint lucky charms and magickal tools. Dress candles. Cleanse and bless. Mix into floor washes and room sprays to banish negativity. Then, splash some into a cleansing bath to boost your mojo before any spell works.

Black Cat Oil

Black Cat Oil is another traditional New Orleans preparation. It is a lucky oil, particularly for Witches, tricksters, charmers, and loners—that is, people of a feline nature. European tradition says a black cat is unlucky, but in Afro-American folk magick, black cats are considered good luck and the wise man or woman's helper. Use Black Cat Oil as an anointing oil to boost witchy powers and slip away from bad luck. Invisibility, enthrallment, clairvoyance, charisma—all fall into Black Cat magick's domain. Work Black Cat Oil spells during the waning or dark moon.

Abramelin Oil

The oldest recipe on this list, Abramelin Oil, appears in the late medieval grimoire The Book of the Sacred Magic of Abramelin the Mage. The formula was later seized upon by members of the 19th-century Hermetic Order of the Golden Dawn. It appears in modern high magick traditions (notably Thelema) and has also trickled down into the altars of Pagan and folk-magick conjurors.

How to use Abramelin Oil: Consecrating altar tools, evoking or communing with not-nice spirits, anointing the body for Great Work-y high magick stuff. Abramelin Oil is highly stimulating and purifying. When applied to the brow or other chakras, it creates a warming sensation that enhances focus and energy flow for ritual.

Come To Me Oil
Come To Me Oil is a top choice for anointing love spell candles and figure candles. Choose one candle to represent yourself and another of your intended partner, dress them with oil and burn them together. Visualize your partner in your arms while reciting Psalm 23 or the erotic passages from the Song of Solomon (traditional), or any love poem that turns your crank

Road Opener Oils
Road Opener Oils are usually blended from scents that are fresh and clean. Solar essences like Orange and Lemon lend intense positive energy. Verbena or Sandalwood raises the spiritual vibration of the mix. Road Opener Oil belongs in any spell for a new beginning. Put it on job or loan applications. Anoint your shoes, car, and trade tools—whatever object will (literally or figuratively) move you to the next place in life.

Do As I Say Oil: Use Do As I Say Oil to gain the upper hand in a business or personal relationship. Anoint a ritual candle—red for power or lust, black for more nefarious magick. Use on a poppet or photo of your intended target. One of the slyest uses of Do As I Say Oil is to sneak it onto places you know the object of your spell will step or touch. If you transfer it to your target's hand with a handshake, it is said that they will be unable to break an agreement with you.

Four Thieves Oil: For a quick protection spell, draw a pentagram on your body with Four Thieves Oil. Mix into floor washes and baths. Place invisible sigils with the oil over windowsills and doorjambs. Anointing your doorknob with Four Thieves Oil is said to foil burglars and swindlers.

What's in Four Thieves Oil: A bouquet of aromatic herbs, including Cloves, Lemon, Cinnamon, Eucalyptus, and Rosemary. In addition, some recipes include Peppercorns, Garlic, and Chilis. Many of these ingredients have antimicrobial and infection-fighting properties, contributing to Four Thieves' reputation as a warding potion.

Types of Salt for Magic

Himalayan/Pink Salt ("purest salt on Earth" because of maturing for 250 million years)
Love, Removes negative blockages & curses, and cleansing
Hawaiian Black Salt (harvested from the evaporated water on Hawaiian Island Molokai)
Extra strength
Table Salt
Purifying, protecting, cleansing, and used in culinary recipes
Kosher Salt (blessed by a Jewish rabbi)
Draws out negativity or absorbs negativity
Black Salt (leftover ashes or scrapings from cast iron)
Banishing and protection
Alaea/Hawaiian Red Salt (From iron-rich volcanic clay)
Love, and sex, block negative energy, protect aggressively to defend an area that has been set with or encircled with it, and are used in culinary recipes (high in nutrients 80+)
Sel Gris Sea Salt
Blessing
Celtic Sea Salt
Protection and attracts financial abundance
Sea Salt (carries the power of the sea and water elements)
Purification and cleansing help balance emotions
Cyprus Black Salt (sea water dried in lav beds mixed with charcoal)
Evokes properties of the pyramids, energy from heaven, used in culinary recipes
Rock Salt
Return to sender, use to reflect negativity to sender
Fleur de Sel Salt (sea salt from France)
Gentler salt, fairies, and elementals
Gray Salt (developed in clay pools)
Used in liminal workings
Blue Salt (sea salt mixed with blue flowers)
Protection from the Evil eye, justice, and healing
That being said, you can make any color salt by mixing colored herbs with it.
Herb infused Salts (salt infused with edible herbs)
Choose an herb that aligns with your intentions
Epsom Salt
Use in the bath to reduce inflammation and muscle pain, and destress
Pickling Salt (purest form, no added agents)
Purification, preservation of love, prosperity, etc., and used in culinary recipes

Carrier Oils and Their Uses

A carrier oil is oil we use to dilute essential oils before applying them to our bodies. Essential oils are often too potent for direct application to the skin. Instead, the oils must be diluted by mixing with an agent that will be readily absorbable by the skin, and the oils listed below are perfect for combining with essential oils. The carrier oil must be good for the skin, absorbable, and not have an overpowering aroma.

Essential oils can be applied to just about any body area once diluted with a carrier oil. However, never apply essential oils on mucus membranes, open wounds, eyeballs, genitals, inside ears, or other sensitive areas.

Experiment with your carrier oils and see which ones you like best! My general rule is to use ½ teaspoon of carrier oil per 5-8 drops of essential oil. Mix it, rub it on, and you're good to go!

I have given a particular type of carrier oil in some of the recipes, but in most of them, I leave it up to you to decide which carrier oil works best for you and your situation.

Take the same precautions with carrier oils that you would with essential oils. Read the labels to determine if it is 100 percent pure or has been cut with cheaper oil. Note the expiration dates and the ingredients, and use your eyes to determine if the oil looks clear or cloudy. Always smell your carrier oil before adding essential oil to it. Carrier oils give a bitter aroma once they have turned rancid. Ensure your carrier oil is fresh and pure before mixing it with your precious essential oils.

Quick Reference
Types of Carrier Oils

Normal Skin
Hempseed, Coconut, Grapeseed, Sunflower, & Sweet Almond

Oily Skin
Grapeseed, Sweet Almond, Apricot, Jojoba, & Sunflower

Dry Skin
Avocado, Sweet Almond, Rosehips, Argan & Olive

Sensitive Skin
Jojoba, Sesame Seed, Sweet Almond, & Apricot

Mature Skin
Jojoba, Sesame Seed, Rosehips, Maracu, Almond, & Apricot

	10 ml Carrier oil	**20 ml Carrier oil**	**30 ml Carrier oil**	**60 ml Carrier oil**
0.5%	1 drop	3 drops	4 drops	8 drops
1%	3 drops	6 drops	9 drops	18 drops
2%	6 drops	12 drops	18 drops	36 drops
3%	9 drops	18 drops	27 drops	54 drops
4%	12 drops	25 drops	36 drops	72 drops
5%	15 drops	30 drops	45 drops	90 drops

30ml = 1oz = 2 tablespoons
60ml = 2oz = 4 tablespoons

Types of Carrier Oils

Sweet Almond Oil
This carrier oil is cheap and readily available, and It's loaded with vitamins, so it's good for your skin. Almond oil will last a year on the shelf. It has lots of protein and is excellent to use in massage oils.

Apricot Kernel Oil
This carrier oil is excellent for dry, aged skin (like mine). It works wonders as a moisturizing lotion and is used in antiaging products worldwide. In addition, it's loaded with vitamin A and is a good base for healing products.

Grape Seed Oil
This carrier oil is inexpensive, but It has a short shelf life. However, it has vitamins A and E, so it's perfect for your skin.

Jojoba Oil
This carrier oil is my favorite and is terrific for all skin types, and it's perfect for skin conditions. It will keep forever on the shelf and mixes beautifully with EOs. It's great for the hair, scalp, and skin.

Sesame Oil
This carrier oil works well for sensitive skin because it has protein, vitamins, and minerals, which are very good for the body and the skin.

These are the most common, but here are some that I didn't include last time:
Aloe vera, Apricot, Avocado, Borage, Calendula, Coconut, Evening Primrose, Hazelnut, Macadamia, Meadowfoam, Olive, Pumpkinseed, Rosehip, Safflower, Soybean, Sunflower, Walnut, and Wheat germ.

How Different Scents Influence Our Mood

When I smell certain scents, I know it brings back memories and can totally change my mood for the day.

Citrus: Promotes productivity and calmness
Orange: Reduces anxiety
Vanilla: Strong relaxation effect
Peppermint: Boosts physical energy and alertness
Cedar: Reduces tension
Lavender: Promotes relaxation and sleep
Jasmine: Improves sleep and reduces anxiety
Rosemary: Improves long-term memory & boosts mood
Grapefruit: Increases energy
Lemon and Jasmine: Improves cognitive performance
Cinnamon-vanilla: Improves creativity
Frankincense: Reduces anxiety and depression
Rosemary and Grapefruit: boost long-term memory & energy
Ylang-Ylang: Reduces stress and promotes calmness
Lemon: Reduces stress and improves mood
Geranium plant: Reduces stress
Bergamot: Reduces anxiety
Chamomile flowers: Promotes calmness and relaxation.
Valerian: Reduces anxiety & improves sleep.
Chocolate: Increases theta brain waves & Relaxation

Disposal of Ritual Offerings

The Power of Fire - Nearly any ritual offering can be disposed of by burning. Sometimes, burning an item can be tied into the working of the spell; if you're trying to get rid of something in your life permanently, burning is a great way to ensure it won't return.

Earth & Water - If your offering is an organic item, such as fruits, vegetables, tobacco, or other plant material, you may want to consider burying it. A garden is an excellent place to do this, particularly if you have a compost bin because the nutrients will go back into the soil as the offering biodegrades, continuing the life cycle. Disposal of organic items into a moving body of water, such as a river or the ocean, is also acceptable in many traditions. Make sure that you're not putting any non-organic materials in the water.

Sharing With Wildlife - As long as they haven't been tainted with anything toxic, you can feel free to scatter them outdoors for the local critters to snack on. They consume it, and the life cycle of the continues on."

Also, please don't discount the science of nature itself. Some offering items can be left out until they go away on their own. For instance, if you make an offering of consecrated water in a bowl, it will eventually evaporate. Likewise, if you do an outdoor ritual and offered herbs and flowers, those will blow away at some point and find their way to a new home.

What About Messy, Gross Things? - Sometimes, let's face it, we do work that involves something negative. In cases like this, you probably want to get the item as far away as possible. In cases like this, simply because of the nature of the ritual, you may want to go ahead and find a place such as a landfill, a port-a-john, or some other foul place to be rid of the items. Just ensure you're not putting anything into the ecosystem that will cause damage down the road.

Runes

The Germanic tribes of Northern Europe used runes for both religious and secular purposes. The earliest examples of runes phonetically representing language date back to the second century BCE. The development of the rune alphabet was spurred by increased trade activity with Mediterranean cultures that already had a fully developed alphabet.

Before, the runes were primarily used as a magical system of pictographs representing natural forces and objects. People believed that by invoking the appropriate rune, they could contact the corresponding force in nature.

There were several different runic alphabets throughout Northern Europe over the centuries, but the most common is the Germanic alphabet.

or Elder FUTHARK. This alphabet received its name from its first six letters- F, U, TH, A, R, and K. The system most widely used from 200 B.C.E. to the late eighth century was the 24-letter alphabet. This alphabet was divided into three groups of eight: Freya's Eight, Hagall's Eight, and Tir's Eight.

Fehu

Fehu, a rune that translates to "cattle," denotes abundance, wealth, security, and fertility. Having cattle or observing them prosper is considered an indicator of success and prosperity.

Keywords: abundance, good fortune, wealth, security, success

Notes:

Uruz

Uruz, a rune that translates to "wild ox," represents determination, courage, will, vitality, primal power, manifestation, and endurance. It symbolizes the strength and intensity of a bull.

Keywords: strength, willpower, endurance, determination, courage

Notes:

Thurisaz

Thurisaz is a complex symbol that has a few different translations depending on the source. In Old Norse, it translates to "giant," while in Old English, it means "thorn." In the context of divination, Thurisaz is often associated with intense change or danger. It is seen as a powerful, disruptive force that shakes things up, much like the lightning that Thor wields with his hammer, Mjolnir. The card symbolizes a transformative and potentially destructive power that can bring about change, but also challenges and obstacles. It also symbolize the need for strength and protection to overcome the challenges.

Keywords: disruption, change, destruction, obstacle clearer, wildness, lust, rage

Notes:

Ansuz

Ansuz is a rune that symbolizes the breath of Odin and can represent the concept of a god. In the Old Norse rune poem, it is translated as "estuary," which is where a body of water meets the ocean. This symbolizes the awakening that often precedes deep spiritual work and can help release stuck energy.

Keywords: door opener, expansion of consciousness, remover of blockages, cleansing

Notes:

Raidho

Raido represents the concept of a journey, both literally and spiritually. It can also be translated as "riding" or "wagon." Spiritually, it symbolizes the movement forward after experiencing a dark night of the soul or intense spiritual awakening. Practically, it represents the decision to take action and move forward on one's journey. It can also represent physical travel.

Keywords: movement, overcoming obstacles, forward momentum, travel

Notes:

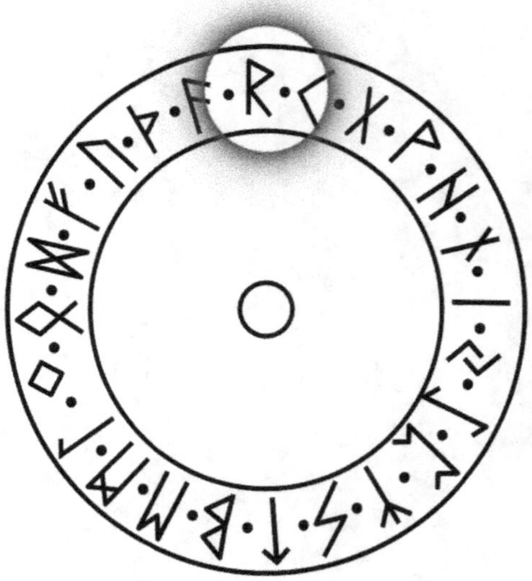

Kenaz

Kenaz represents the concept of a torch, which symbolizes illumination and manifestation. The rune represents the inner light or sense of purpose that drives one forward. It is associated with the idea of taking the first step to bring something into existence. Without this inner light, one may feel like they are fumbling through darkness.

Keywords: manifestation, will, divine spark, the light within, guidance, inner wisdom

Notes:

Gifu

Gifu represents the gift or exchange. It symbolizes the power of gratitude, which can lead to more generosity, and the energy that is created when gifts are exchanged. The rune is depicted as a crossroads, where two branches intersect, symbolizing the union that occurs when a gift is given from one to another. It serves as a reminder to be grateful and to recognize that every interaction involves an exchange of energy. When cast, it may also represent the need for balance in one's energy or spiritual life.

Keywords: giving, balance, union, energy or power exchange, crossroads, partnership

Notes:

Wunjo

Wunjo brings the concept of joy. It symbolizes the intense feeling of ecstasy and alignment that occurs when everything comes together and the world feels charged. It also represents moments of happiness, fulfillment, and prosperity.

Keywords: fulfillment, ecstasy, moment of spiritual enlightenment, flow state

Notes:

Hagall

Hagalaz represents the hail, symbolizing the destructive and transformative power of nature. The rune can also be associated with intense emotions such as wrath and can represent being tested. It is often associated with the "dark night of the soul" and can indicate that it is a time for shadow work or for pausing and contemplating things from a different viewpoint before continuing. As the first rune of the next series, it represents the descent into the underworld and the transformative power of facing our shadows.

Keywords: obstacles, challenges, delays, temporary delays, tests, dark night of the soul, spiritual descent

Notes:

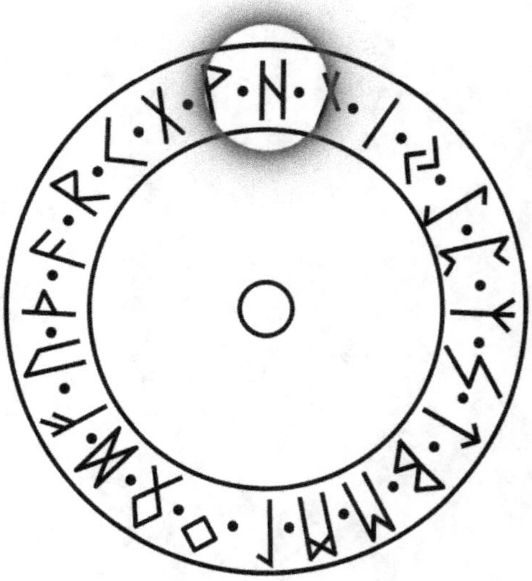

Nied

Nauthiz represents the concept of necessity and the struggle that comes with it. This rune symbolizes a time when you may be feeling unfulfilled, whether it be due to a lack of attention to your needs or because they are not being met. It serves as a reminder to take a deeper look within and assess what is missing in your life and what steps need to be taken to bring balance. It also represents your inner strength and determination to push through difficult times and to keep moving forward on your journey.

Keywords: yearning, lack, struggle, turmoil, persistence, determination, resilience
Notes:

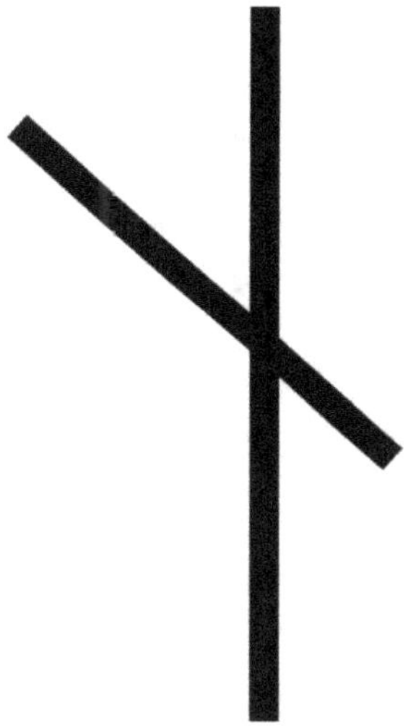

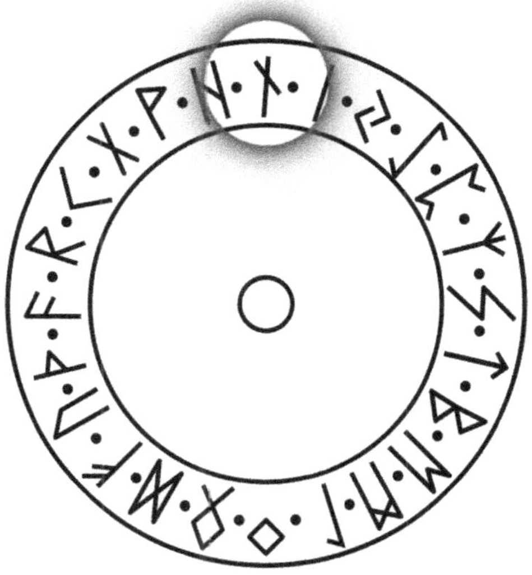

Isa

Isa symbolizes the concept of ice or being frozen. It represents a time when one feels unable to move forward, whether it be in a spiritual sense or in regard to a specific project, plan, or relationship. This rune serves as a reminder that things may have been put on hold and it is a time to go within and reflect. It could also indicate the need for setting boundaries, especially if negative energy has been overwhelming.

Keywords: Pause, waiting, delay, suspension

Notes:

Jera

Jera signifies the idea of reaping the rewards of one's labor. Unlike Isa, which represents being frozen, Jera symbolizes a time when one can savor the outcome of their efforts. This rune serves as a reminder that there is a natural flow to things, a cycle of growth and fruition.

Keywords: cycle, abundance, harvest, slow growth, extension, process

Notes:

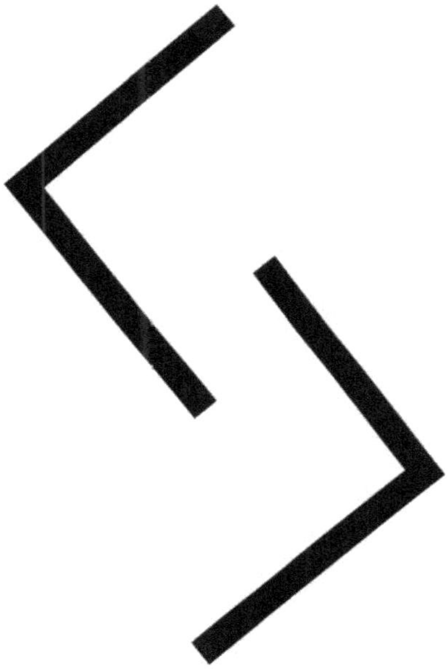

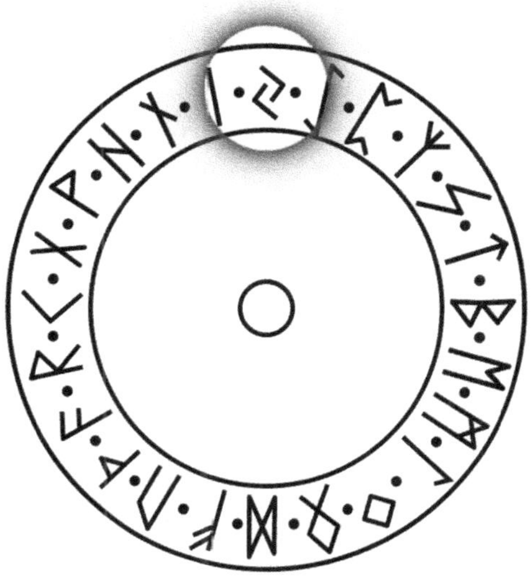

Eihwaz

Eihwaz is a rune that represents the ash or yew tree, but it also symbolizes Yggdrasil, the central sacred tree in Norse mythology. This tree is often associated with death, but it also represents the passing of old beliefs and the potential for healing and transformation that comes with gaining new knowledge.

Keywords: death, transformation, understanding, transition, life cycle

Notes:

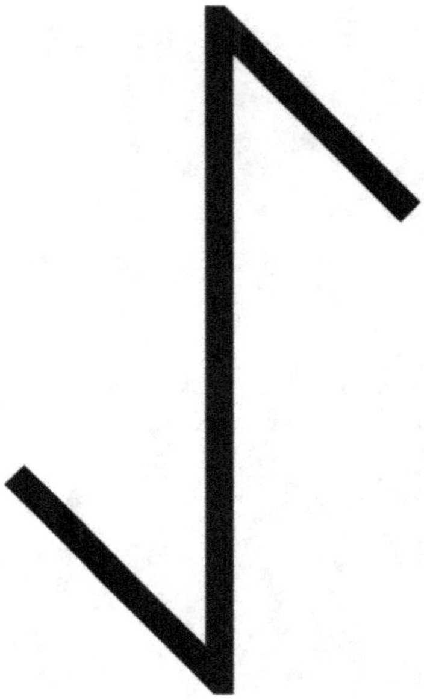

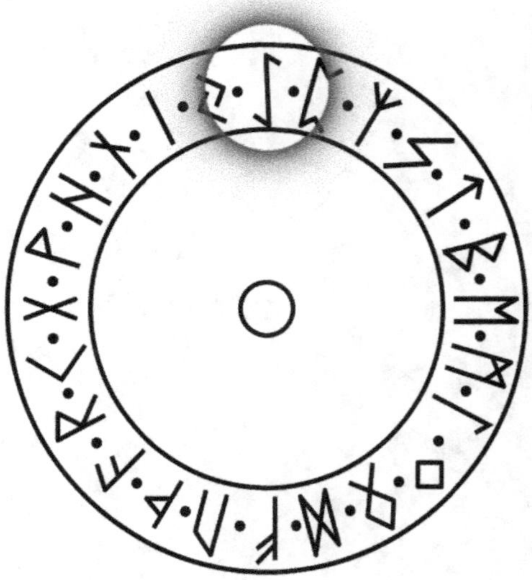

Perdhro

Perthro represents the concept of fortune. It suggests that when we have a clear understanding of our destiny, we have the power to shape it. This rune prompts us to reflect on whether we want to stay the course or make adjustments to alter the outcome. It encourages us to consider the insights revealed in our readings and think about ways in which we can actively work on manifesting our desired future.

Keywords: fortune, fate, chance, mystery, the occult, the unknown, the beyond, destiny

Notes:

Eolh

Eolh represents the concept of the elk, but in the context of protection. This rune serves as a reminder to be assertive and to stand your ground when faced with challenges. It may also indicate that it's a time to call on the gods for extra guidance and support.

Keywords: defense, protection, grounding, strength

Notes:

Sigel

Sigel represents the life-giving energy of the sun and the illumination it brings. It symbolizes the healing and restorative power of light, particularly for those who have been going through a difficult period of self-discovery. This rune serves as a reminder that, like the sun, there is always hope for growth and renewal, and to move forward towards one's destiny.

Keywords: awakening, exuberance, healing energy, victory, power

Notes:

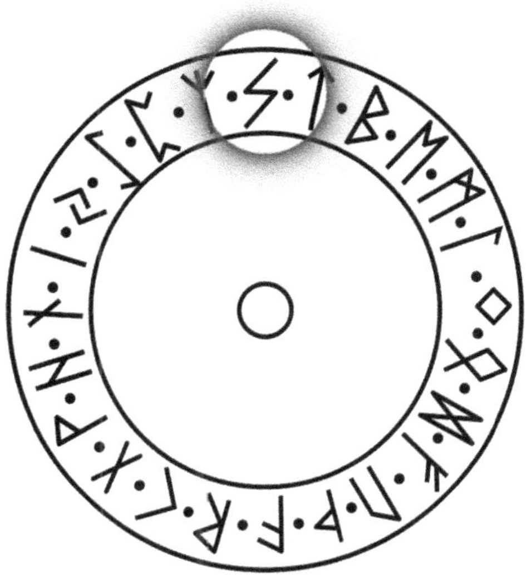

Tir

Tyr represents the powerful god of warriors, known for his fierce determination, unwavering sense of righteousness, and unshakable discipline. When cast, the rune symbolizes the courage and self-mastery needed to overcome obstacles, stay true to one's values and remain undeterred by the ebbs and flows of emotions. It serves as a reminder to reconnect with one's inner strength and purpose, and to step up as a leader of one's own life.

Keywords: determination, justice, self-mastery, discipline, integrity, leadership

Notes:

Beorc

Beorc represents the birch tree and new beginnings. This rune symbolizes a gentle and organic process of rebirth or renewal. It suggests that healing growth or change is imminent or necessary and indicates the power of conscious manifestation. This rune serves as a reminder that small, steady steps toward growth and change can lead to meaningful progress and transformation.

Keywords: healing, manifestation, rebirth, new beginnings, growth, renewal, nurturing

Notes:

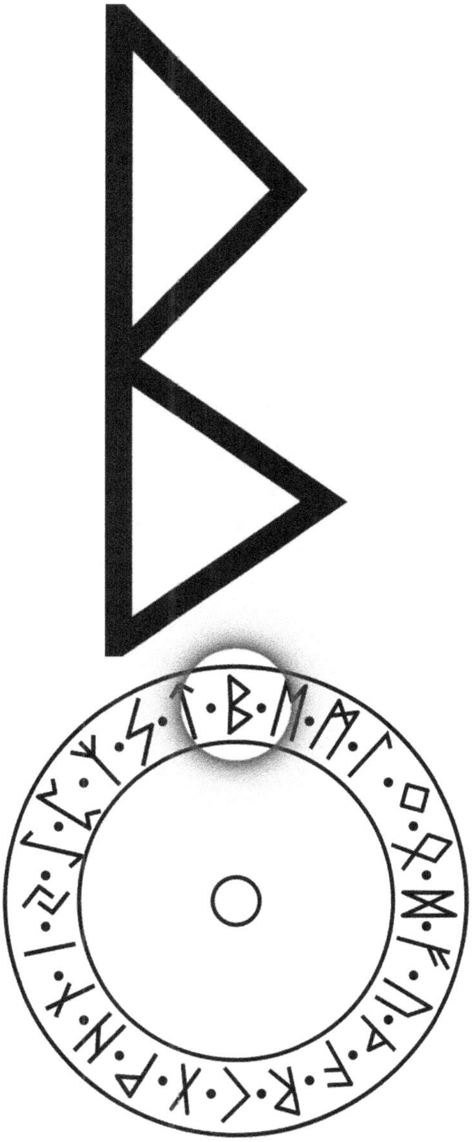

Ehwaz

Ehwaz represents the noble and powerful horse, known for its ability to facilitate communication and convey messages, as well as its capability to guide one through different worlds or states of being. This rune symbolizes the harmony and trust that exists between two entities, be it a horse and its rider, or two people in a partnership. It serves as a reminder of the importance of trust and partnership in making steady progress and reaching one's destination.

Keywords: partnership, connection, movement, harmony, trust, loyalty, progress

Notes:

Mannaz

Mannaz represents the concept of humanity and the role we play within our social communities. This rune symbolizes the importance of connection and the impact it has on our well-being. If you've been feeling isolated, this rune may indicate the need for more social interaction. It also represents the ideal partnership, one that is built on mutual respect, healthy boundaries, and a balance of giving and receiving. Mannaz serves as a reminder to tend to both ourselves and others in order to foster strong, fulfilling relationships.

Keywords: balanced partnership, healthy boundaries, cooperation, friendship, community

Notes:

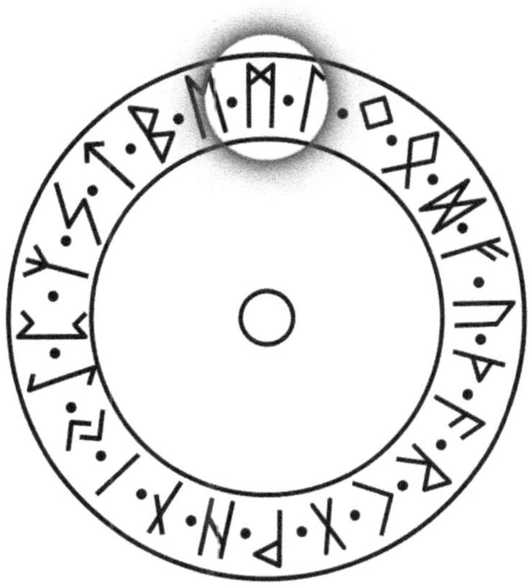

Lagaz

Laguz represents the raw and untamed energy of water. It symbolizes the unstoppable force of a waterfall or the ocean, and its ability to shape the world around it. This rune serves as a reminder of the power of persistence and flow, even the toughest of obstacles can be worn down by the constant flow of energy. It encourages us to align with the energies around us in order to manifest our desires and goals.

Keywords: harnessing energy, power, movement, potentiality, manifestation, flow, desire

Notes:

Ing

Inguz represents the god Ing and symbolizes the abundance of fertility, sexuality, and intensity. This rune also represents the threshold of home, a reminder of where we come from and where we belong. It serves as a gentle reminder that emotional and spiritual healing is ongoing process, and that it's important to take care of ourselves. It may also indicate that new beginnings are on the horizon, and that a seed of potential is being nurtured before it can bloom.

Keywords: fertility, sexuality, harmony, emotional healing, balance, seed, potential

Notes:

Daeg

Daeg represents the emergence of a new day, symbolizing the end of one cycle and the start of another. It is a reminder of the constant shifts and changes that occur in life and the spiritual growth and transformation that come with them. This rune serves as a call to embrace new opportunities and to be open to the unknown as we step into a new day.

Keywords: change, illumination, awareness, transformation

Notes:

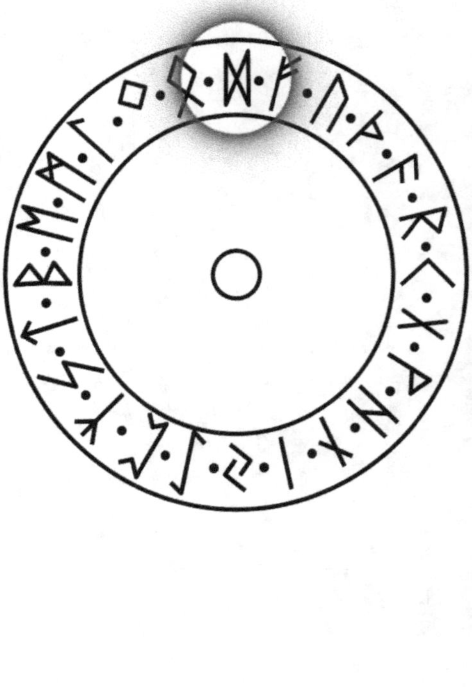

Self-Reflections

What parts of your daily life need to change? How will you go about making the changes needed?

Self-Reflections

What things do you need to make more time for?

Self-Reflections

What affirmations can you use to help you get through the day? What are some you could you to help you get through the bad days?

Self-Reflections

What are some new things that you want to try?

Self-Reflections

Today is the day to do your happy dance. What are you most proud of that you have accomplished so far this year.

Self-Reflections

What are some goals you want to work toward?

Some Witchy Self-Care

Create a witchy self-care routine that fits you.

If you have just a few moments at the beginning of the day, make the most of it with some self-care.

Even if your self-care consists of a beverage in the morning, you can expand from there.

Try meditation, and if that doesn't work for you, try non-traditional meditation.

Do spellwork around the phases of the moon.

Break out those cards, whether tarot or oracle and do a pull/draw each morning or evening just to get those manifestation images in your mind.

Like runes better? Ok, then break them out, whether Elder, Young Futhark, or Anglo-Saxon, and do a casting each morning or evening just to get those manifestation images in your mind.

Do a grab-and-go combo of crystals and herbs to help you navigate the day ahead. Check in with your trusted horoscope app to get a heads up for each day, if nothing else, to find what is in retrograde.

We all accumulate "STUFF," So we must regularly cleanse ourselves. Whether it's a quick smoke cleanse, egg cleanse ritual, bath, or shower purification. It is whatever works for you.

Add some of your favorite essential oils in a roll-on to have a pick-me-up throughout the day.

End your day with gratitude that you freaking rocked the day. Brain dump into your journal, and sleep well.

And don't let it get you down that you miss a step or even a day of your plan. Having just gotten out of bed and faced the day is a huge accomplishment.

Remember You Do You!

Index

www.ingramcontent.com/pod-product-compliance
Lightning Source LLC
Chambersburg PA
CBHW081208130726
47997CB00009B/2592

* 9 7 9 8 9 8 7 5 5 9 1 3 0 *